Hospitality, Tourism and Marketing Studies

nova science publishers
www.novapublishers.com

Hospitality, Tourism and Marketing Studies

Sustainability in Tourism: Understanding Sustainable Solutions for the Tourism Industry
Kannapa Pongponrat, PhD (Editor)
2022. ISBN: 978-1-68507-818-8 (Softcover)
2022. ISBN: 979-8-88697-023-4 (eBook)

Tourism Safety and Security Just After COVID-19
Maximiliano E. Korstanje (Editor)
2022. ISBN: 978-1-68507-738-9 (Softcover)
2022. ISBN: 978-1-68507-878-2 (eBook)

The Anthropology of Tourism Security
Maximiliano E. Korstanje (Editor)
2019. ISBN: 978-1-53616-134-2 (Hardcover)
2019. ISBN: 978-1-53616-135-9 (eBook)

Modeling and New Trends in Tourism: A Contribution to Social and Economic Development
Kostas Rontos (Editor)
José António Filipe (Editor)
Paris Tsartas (Editor)
2017. ISBN: 978-1-63485-920-2 (Hardcover)
2017. ISBN: 978-1-63485-943-1 (eBook)

More information about this series can be found at https://novapublishers.com/product-category/series/hospitality-tourism-and-marketing-studies/

Maximiliano E. Korstanje
Vanessa GB Gowreesunkar
and Shem Wambugu Maingi
Editors

Tourism in Crisis

nova
science publishers
www.novapublishers.com

https://doi.org/10.52305/JQWY2999

Library of Congress Cataloging-in-Publication Data

ISBN: 979-8-88697-643-4

Published by Nova Science Publishers, Inc. † New York

Contents

Introduction

Tourism in Crisis: New Problems, New Paradigms

Maximiliano E. Korstanje*
University of Palermo, Argentina

Introduction

Over recent years, the industry of tourism comes across different global [major] risks. These risks included terrorist attacks, natural disasters resulting from the acceleration of climate change as well as political instability, economic downturn, and the recent COVID-19 pandemic [only to name a few]. To put the same bluntly, the turn of the twentieth century witnessed a radical transformation in tourist demand and travel behavior worldwide (Korstanje & George 2021). Borrowed from psychology, risk perception theory shed originally the light on the first applied works oriented to describe how tourist demands evolve to these global risks. Of course, although risk perception theory has more than four decades in the fields of psychology and sociology, the attacks perpetrated by Al-Qaeda in 2001 paved the way for the rise of different studies mainly based on how tourists perceive risks and dangers (Fuchs & Reichel 2006; Yang & Nair, 2014). To some extent, the goals of these studies were twofold. On one hand, they have systematically striven for implementing different instruments and protocols to make destinations safer. Through the inference of algorithms and statistical methods, these publications contributed to the decision-making process for making safer destinations. On another, risk perception theory played a leading role in describing [if not measuring] the evolution of the international demand to some disrupting events. In so doing, these studies were based on large samples and questionnaires applicated to tourists in the most important travel hubs, airports, and stations (Floyd & Pennington Gray, 2004). Having said this, the risk perception theory started from the premise that risks are often perceived and internalized according to manifest variation by age, ethnicity,

* Corresponding Author's Email: mkorst@palermo.edu.

culture, ideology, and of course genre (Reisinger & Mavondo, 2006; Rather 2021). Knowing further how these risks are construed and lived is an efficient manner to placate their potential effects (Korstanje, Seraphin & Maigni, 2021). At a closer look, this corpus of studies emphasized quantitative methods while relegating the qualitative ones to a marginal position. It is not otiose to mention that tourism safety and security and risk management occupied a central position in the published content of top-tiered journals from 2001 to 2012 (Qian et al. 2019; Wang et al. 2019).

Somehow, the burgeoning growth of tourism made it more difficult to mitigate the consequences of global risks. Problems like terrorism or climate change have been simply aggravated in the threshold of time. New more radicalized cells perpetrated new attacks in France, Spain, Belgium, the UK, and the US. At the same time, governments failed to coordinate efforts toward a more sustainable agenda for the next decades. The precautionary doctrine which is the cornerstone of the risk perception theory as a leading paradigm sets the pace for new understandings and academic positions. The concept of precaution was plausibly replaced by adaptation. Post-disaster or post-conflict tourism and crisis tourism evolved as leading paradigms since 2012 to date. Likewise, scholars acknowledged overtly the urgency to contemplate the notion of crisis as a necessary component of the tourist system (Valeri 2022; Korstanje, Seraphin & Maigni, 2022). In sharp contrast with risk perception theory, post-disaster research focuses not only on the immediacy of the disaster but also on the need of co-existing with a potential crisis (Isaac, Cakmak & Butler 2019). It Is important to mention the concept of crisis never means the end of tourism consumption, but the opportunity for a new rebirth. The survival of a tourist destination depends on how efficiently crises are ultimately managed (Ritchie & Jiang 2019). What is more important to discuss, the COVID-19 pandemic grounded the international tourism industry into an unparalleled halt but paradoxically hid some other terminal crises as the humanitarian disaster of migration, the ecocide, as well as the material asymmetries between the Global South and North (Tzanelli 2021; Bianchi 2021). As Rodanthi Tzanelli (2021) eloquently observes, the crisis of mobilities elicited by the COVID-19 pandemic evinces two important things. At a closer look, the concept of virocene not only speaks to us of the circulation of different viruses which confront mankind but also marks the hegemony of bio-discourse. The spirit of globalization and grand mobilities that historically characterized capitalism has gone. COVID-19, instead, inaugurates a climate of low mobility but higher uncertainty that crystalizes in a political crisis. In this respect, lay citizens manifest their hostilities against authorities and foreigners. In a post-covid-19 world, the figure of the "Other" has been redrawn. For the sake of clarity, this moot point will be re-addressed in the end of this piece.

The present editorial project, which is drawn by book chapters authored by well-known experts who are global scholars in their fields, put the concept of the tourism crisis into the foreground. As debated, crises [as social construes] have been somehow overlooked from the academic discussion (Gale 2008). As their main object of study, tourism research ignored the important role played by crises in the configuration of the tourist system. The two World wars, not only accelerated a radical revolution in the transport system but also cemented a new worldmaking process [citing Hollinshead 2009a; 2009b; 2007].

As the previous backdrop is given, the first chapter, which is authored by Cyril Peter & Lim Kuang Long, discusses critically the place of safety in individual and collective travel plans. Having said this, the chapter looks to interrogate furtherly to what extent guests are willing to pay further for safer rooms. With echoes of the earlier terrorist attack in Christchurch, New Zealand [2015], authors hold the thesis that safety and security have been situated as new perceived facilities that often make more expensive tourist products. At a closer look, the specialized literature suggests that safety and security are ranked as more desirable when they are out from home. Under some conditions, foreign tourists not only are vulnerable to the locals` hostility but when tourists are vulnerated the social contract is breached. The tourism industry has expanded successfully and evolved according to a much deep social contract between hosts and guests. While terrorist groups look to harm tourists to destroy this social contract, no less true seems to be that hotels are public spaces with open entrances and exist. Terrorism is mainly motivated to affect the credibility of local governments stressing their incapacity to protect foreign tourists. In this way, terrorism accelerates a political crisis affecting seriously international destinations but paradoxically [at the same time] it builds the pathways for new products associated with safety and security. To put this simply, a safer New Zealand is globally preferred and ranked as a hallmark in the marketing campaign. Hence, it is not simply to say that marketing campaigns, terror, and engagement are inseparably entwined.

In the second chapter, Maximiliano Korstanje makes mentions the long-lasting effects of COVID-19 not only in the tourism industry but also in travel behavior. The COVID-19 pandemic, doubtless, opened the doors to an unparalleled crisis for the industry as well as for global trade. Governments imposed several restrictive measures to stop the virus contagion. This leads us to consider that tourism was not only the main carrier but also the main victim of COVID-19. In consonance with this, Governments entered into a crisis of sense where shared coordination and protocols simply fell short. While each country adopted different measures and steps to restrict public circulation, a new process of re-feudalization emerged. Global capitalism, as well as the international tourism industry, has set the pace for unseen geopolitical tensions, heavy travel bans, and even a sentiment of hostility against Asian [foreign] tourists. The question of whether J. Urry (1992) contemplated the tourist gaze as a magnificent figure of globalization, sets the pace to a new [dark] world where tourists became undesired guests. To what extent COVID-19 ignites a state of crisis in the industry or simply evinces the end of an epoch seems to be one of the aspects this book chapter unravels. Any state of crisis puts new challenges but at the same time new opportunities for evolution.

The risk perception theory has gained notable traction in recent years. The number of credited publications has exponentially grown. Anyway, less attention was paid to the role played by travel insurance as a key factor that predicts the levels of anxiety in travelers. The third chapter which is authored by Varghese, Sandhya & Thomas explores travel insurance as a fertile method to study risk perception in the context of tourism and hospitality. Having said this, travel insurance signals any type of full or partial coverage for travel which includes medical expenses, as well as any hurts incurred during the travel. In some nations, travelers are compelled to buy travel insurance as a precondition for migratory authorities. In other countries, travel expenses [which are based on expensive costs] are unfree and should be absorbed by tourists. The authors distinguish two types of profiles in travel insurance consumption. Those tourists who developed a high tolerance for uncertainty and those tourists who are prone to buy travel insurance when they travel abroad. Ultimately, they enumerate a list of interesting ethical dilemmas revolving around travel insurance as well as business travel.

In the fourth chapter, Keziah Odemba & Maingi Shem W. shed light on the necessary steps and protocols to mitigate the negative consequences of the COVID-19 pandemic in the Eastern Africa Region. This region not only has been devastated but also faces serious challenges in coping with the post-COVID-19 pandemic context. With the basis of the theory of resiliency and preparedness, the authors eloquently explain that there are several obstacles to planning strategies before disasters. The concept of crisis escapes any type of planning. The authors review systematically a set of different documents and studies that focus on tourism policy preparedness as well as the importance of post-pandemic practices and policies. The book chapter enumerates and carefully reviews a set of interesting and useful recommendations to be seriously taken by policymakers in the next decades.

As the previous argument is given, dark tourism occupies a central place as an instrument towards economic revitalization just after a disaster takes a hit. In consonance with the earlier chapter, Korstanje argues that the globalization of risks not only is placing the industry in jeopardy but also in creating new morbid forms of consumption where disaster becomes the main commodity to exchange. In this vein, if the precautionary logic which punctuated that studies should locate and eradicate risks failed to give responses to the new challenges, no less true seems to be the notion of adaptancy has played a leading role in the new tourism research. Like dark tourism or post-disaster tourism, new emerging paradigms emphasize the importance of adaptancy and preparedness to mitigate the negative effects of disasters. This is exactly the lesson left by COVID-19 or the attacks on the World Trade Center. The concept of crisis is very hard to grasp while escaping human control. This book chapter lays the foundations towards a new understanding of Thana-capitalism, which signals a new stage of capitalism where the "Other`s pain" is the main commodity to consume.

In the sixth chapter, Thiago Duarte Pimentel, Elias Mediotte, Paulo Rodrigues Cerqueira, Marcela B. Costa de Olivera, Mariana Pereira Chaves Pimentel and Stella Freesz examine the negative aftermaths of COVID-19 in the tourism industry in Juiz de Fora, Brazil. The chapter is originally orchestrated within the organizational ecology paradigm. The chapter aims to study how firms and subsectors not only move in a context of crisis but also how they ultimately survive. In this vein, the concept of adaptation plays a leading role in the future of the industry. The main thesis here is that firms and sectors are pressed to mutate to new forms because of external changes (threats) like COVID-19. In so doing, firms should turn their attention to the environmental factor.

The seventh chapter, which is authored by Maximiliano E. Korstanje, discusses critically to what extent the current tourism research enters a state of crisis as never before. Today`s scholars have enthusiastically applauded the introduction of metrics and the culture of publishing or perishing as a valuable option to enhance tourism research. From this perspective, the culture of metrics contributes directly to discipline maturation. Of course, some critical voices have alerted on the methodological limitations of the metrics culture as well as the problems associated with higher tourism education. Needless to say, in this direction the present book chapter goes. The recent over-valuation of the metric culture not only is wreaking havoc in professional fieldwork but also is leading the discipline into an unparalleled crisis.

After further examination, a correct definition of crisis is very hard to accomplish. This happens simply because there is no lineal definition of what a crisis means or what is more important its real impact on society. To some extent, the question of crisis seems to be incompatible with well-being and sustainable tourism. This point is widely discussed in the eight chapter, which is authored by K. P Anju, V. T Bindu & Babu George. Responsible tourism should be seen as a valid strategy towards safer and most resilient destinations. Having said this, one of the benefits of responsible tourism is associated with the control of crises. It is important not to lose sight of the fact that tourism growth often escapes to the nation-states` control. Unless dully regulated by other stakeholders or organizations, tourism accelerates a countless number of crises. At the time the precautionary doctrine failed to make safer destinations, the concept of responsible tourism and well-being tourism occupied a central position in the debate. The chapter is oriented to address two important questions: what are the methods to promote RT through wellness tourism practices? And how are responsible tourism practices situated at wellness centers minimizing tourism crises? Here authors open the doors towards a new type of sustainable practices finely organized in Ayuverdic therapies. Through well-being tourism, the involved stakeholders engage directly with a shared common good which avoids future disasters.

The question of responsibility straddles the classic application of environmentalism or sustainability. Being accountable or responsible draws the lines between rationality and the ability to make an individual decision. To put the same simply, responsibility plays a crucial role in indicating who are autonomous agents and those who are not. One of the young [promising] researchers in the field of special interest tourism, Bintang Handayani argues convincingly that even if the specialized literature in special tourism has advanced a lot in these years, little information is found on pets on vacation. To some extent, this happens because tourists are rational agents who are legally encouraged to visit different places, but the same does not apply to pets. However, the inclusion of pets in holidays enhances the personal quality of life. In this vein, knowledge production on pet vacation is not only needed but an urgent step to imagine the figure of the non-human tourist. Over the years, tourism was legally reserved for humans while non-humans have been systematically debarred from any leisure practice. During the COVID-19 pandemic, many families decided to travel with their pets for protection or an as a form of relational engagement. This triggers a hot-debate revolving around the new travel behavior in a troubled world while laying the foundations towards a much deep reconfiguration that transcends the classic definitions of tourism. The book chapter, which is based on Munar`s works, considers innovative epistemic discussions on pet tourism and social responsibility amid an unparalleled crisis for the tourism industry.

Last but not least, there is an interesting debate given in the core of English-speaking countries regarding the center-periphery dependency just after the COVID. In her new trailblazing book titled Cultural immobilities and the virocene: mutating the crisis, Rodanthi Tzanelli (2021) argues convincingly that there is a sharp inconsistency between the state of crisis accelerated by the COVID-19 pandemic, and the real challenges posed by mankind in the years to come. Beyond the promises of the de-growth tourism and sustainability paradigms, the post-COVID-19 world is mainly characterized by geopolitical tensions, frictions, and much deep sentiment of hostility against foreigners. Not only the effects on the tourism industry have been devastating [if not irreversible in some sectors] but also enacted a type of new biopolitical discipline based on the medical discourse. Having said this, the pandemic refers to a plague that often escapes to the control of nation-states. However, a closer insight suggests that this emergent state of crisis is culturally enrooted in a set of new emerging crises such as illegal migration, ethnic violence or racism, ecological pollution or the problems of states to reverse climate change, massive population and overcrowding, without mentioning human trafficking and enslavement. While over-exaggerating the COVID-19 effects, we neglect [if not passively accept] the other most important emergencies. It is not difficult to resist the impression that that in a climate of high uncertainty and unpredictability medical reasoning is never questioned. What is more important, before the crisis the Anglo-World seems to evoke a colonial archive of the virocene. The question of whether the virocene is understood as a new epoch where viruses mold human action on the earth, no less true is that some long-dormant discourses [originally coined in the colonial period separating The European culture from the periphery] have ultimately surfaced. As Tzanelli put it, the sense of immobility imposed by governments derives into a climate of recrimination directed against the local governments and foreigners. To some extent, crises impair human relations. At the same time, the Global North has developed a sentiment of recrimination against Asia [above all China] and the rest of the periphery. Tzanelli`s book is very helpful to expand the current understanding of the effects of pandemics on the Western social imaginary. As discussed, the central nations [first of all the US and the UK] are engulfed in a narrative of separatism where the "Other", the stranger is now "an undesired guest". Foreign tourists [above all Asian tourists] as seen as silent carriers of a lethal virus. For that reason, they should be closely scrutinized and quarantined. Some critical voices have alerted on the hospitality crisis in the Anglo-World (Korstanje 2017; Korstanje & George 2021a; 2021b; Korstanje & Seraphin 2022; Selwyn, 2019). The question of blame and blameworthy have been widely studied by philosophy. By blaming the "Other" the normal social conditions or local rules, which have been breached, are restored. This, so to speak, suggests that blaming "Others" entails common shared values and norms that have been ultimately vulnerated. It is safe to say that blame-worthy is one of the glues of social cohesion. Anyway, what does happen when the stranger should be blamed?

To wit, George Sher (2013) goes not to answer this question acknowledging that the relational paradigm has no few problems to resolve the philosophical quandary revolving around the blame. The victim`s vulnerability echoes the intervention of the state, as a Leviathan, which punishes the wrong-doer. Put things in these terms, whenever the state takes direct action the victim has not the status of victim any longer. In consonance with this, Jacques Derrida calls the attention on the law of hospitality as the preconditions towards hostility. As he describes, at the time the stranger violates the local law, he is isolated and trialed by the state. The borders of hospitality collide with hostility, which sparks at the moment the law is breached. Given the problem, as Derrida understands, under some conditions strangers can be very well vulnerated and persecuted [as parasites in his words] when hospitality is negated. After all, hospitality can be given only when two questions are successfully answered: who are you and what do you want?

Not surprisingly, the COVID-19 pandemic not only woke up the Western hemisphere from the slumber it was, but also paved the ways for the emergence of countless separatist and racists discourses finely-ingrained to undermine the "stranger". It is important to remind that the figure of "neglected Other" has opened an unparalleled state of fear that invariably led the Western nations into a deep crisis (Korstanje 2017). Given this context, the present book is plausibly formed by global and well-versed authors who anyway come from peripheral nations. Their stances confront directly with the hegemonic discourse monopolized by the Global North. Part of the material published here has no place in the leading journals or the main narratives formed in the core of the Anglo-centrism. To some extent, this editorial project situates as a multicultural and multidisciplinary approach to understand the crisis the industry is facing today while laying new perspectives to understand the phenomenon. Humbly, this book appears to be an initial contribution to rethink tourism in a post COVID-19 world. Hence, we [the editors and invited authors] not only limit our analysis to the effects of the pandemic, but also we discuss other profound crises in the tourism industries which remain unlooked in the specialized literature. This begs some pungent questions: is the crisis of tourism the crisis of global capitalism? Or put more simply, the rise of a new re-feudalization process?

References

Bianchi, R. V. (2021). *Tourism, COVID-19 and crisis: The case for a radical turn. In Socialising Tourism* (pp. 93-108). Higgins-Desbiolles, F, Doering A & Chew B. (eds) Abingdon, Routledge.

Derrida J (2000) *Of Hospitality*. Stanford, Stanford University Press.

Floyd, M. F., & Pennington-Gray, L. (2004). Profiling risk perceptions of tourists. *Annals of Tourism Research*, 31(4), 1051-1054.

Fuchs, G., & Reichel, A. (2006). Tourist destination risk perception: The case of Israel. *Journal of Hospitality & Leisure Marketing*, 14(2), 83-108.

Gale, T. (2008). The end of tourism, or endings in tourism. *Tourism and mobilities: Local-global connections*, 1-14.

Hollinshead, K. (2009a). The "worldmaking" prodigy of tourism: The reach and power of tourism in the dynamics of change and transformation. *Tourism Analysis*, 14(1), 139-152.

Hollinshead, K. (2009b). 'Tourism state' cultural production: the re-making of Nova Scotia. *Tourism Geographies*, 11(4), 526-545.

Hollinshead, K. (2007). 'Worldmaking'and the transformation of place and culture: The enlargement of Meethan's analysis of tourism and global change. In *The critical turn in tourism studies* (pp. 187-216). Abingdon, Routledge.

Isaac, R. K., Çakmak, E., & Butler, R. (Eds.). (2019). *Tourism and hospitality in conflict-ridden destinations*. Abingdon, Routledge.

Korstanje M. E (2017). *Terrorism, tourism and the end of hospitality in the West*. Basingstoke, Palgrave Macmillan.

Korstanje, M. E., & George, B. (2021a). *Mobility and globalization in the aftermath of COVID-19: Emerging new geographies in a locked world*. Basingstoke, UK: Palgrave Macmillan.

Korstanje, M. E., & George, B. P. (2021b). *COVID-19 and the End of Hospitality: At Least as We Know It in the West. In Socio-Economic Effects and Recovery Efforts for the Rental Industry: Post-COVID-19 Strategies* (pp. 148-164). Hershey, IGI Global.

Korstanje, M. E., & Seraphin, H. (2022). *A Problem Called Alterity: The Position of the 'Other'in HBO Saga Westworld. In Tourism Through Troubled Times* (pp. 7-20). Korstanje M. Seraphin H & Maingi S. W (eds). Bingley, Emerald Publishing Limited.

Korstanje, M. E., Seraphin, H., & Maingi, S. W. (Eds.). (2022). *Tourism Through Troubled Times: Challenges and Opportunities of the Tourism Industry in 21st Century*. Bingley, Emerald Group.

Qian, J., Law, R., Wei, J., & Wu, Y. (2019). Trends in global tourism studies: A content analysis of the publications in tourism management. *Journal of Quality Assurance in Hospitality & Tourism*, 20(6), 753-768.

Rather, R. A. (2021). Monitoring the impacts of tourism-based social media, risk perception and fear on tourist's attitude and revisiting behaviour in the wake of COVID-19 pandemic. *Current Issues in Tourism*, 24(23), 3275-3283.

Reisinger, Y., & Mavondo, F. (2006). Cultural differences in travel risk perception. *Journal of Travel & Tourism Marketing*, 20(1), 13-31.

Selwyn, T. (2019) "Hostility and hospitality: connecting Brexit, Grenfell, Windrush". In *Experiencing Hospitality*. B Rowson & C Lashley (eds) (51-72), Hauppauge, Nova Science Publishers.

Tzanelli, R. (2021). *Cultural (Im) Mobilities and the Virocene: Mutating the Crisis*. Cheltenham, Edward Elgar Publishing.

Sher, G. (2013). Wrongdoing and relationships: The problem of the stranger. *Blame: its nature and norms*, Coates J & Tognazzini N (eds). (49-65) Oxford, Oxford University Press.

Urry, J. (1992). The tourist gaze "revisited". *American Behavioral Scientist*, 36(2), 172-186.

Valeri, M. (Ed.). (2022). *Tourism Risk: Crisis and Recovery Management*. Bingley, Emerald Group Publishing.

Wang, J., Liu-Lastres, B., Ritchie, B. W., & Pan, D. Z. (2019). Risk reduction and adventure tourism safety: An extension of the risk perception attitude framework (RPAF). *Tourism Management*, 74, 247-257.

Yang, C. L., & Nair, V. (2014). Risk perception study in tourism: Are we really measuring perceived risk?. *Procedia-Social and Behavioral Sciences*, 144, 322-327.

Chapter 1

Is Safety an Important Consideration When Making Travel Plans? An Interpretive Study of Guests' Perceptions

Cyril Peter[1,*]
and Lim Kuang Long[2,†]
[1]School of Innovation, Design and Technology, Wellington Institute of Technology, Wellington, New Zealand
[2]Department of Social Science and Hospitality, Tunku Abdul Rahman University College, Jalan Kolej, Taman Bandar Baru, Kampar, Perak, Malaysia

Abstract

This research was conducted to understand guests' perceptions of security in New Zealand. Before COVID-19 lockdowns and closed borders (2019), international tourism expenditure accounted for $17.5 billion (Tourism Industry Aotearoa, 2021). In comparison, revenue from the dairy industry in 2019 was $18.11 billion (Hinton, 2022). Tourism is important to New Zealand and only second in earning potential to dairy. It makes a valuable contribution to the New Zealand economy. Hence, the reason for this research. The assumption from the onset was that to preserve and protect the tourism industry, security had an important part to play, especially with terrorism shifting its interest to softer targets. However, the specific needs want and expectations of tourists and hotel guests in New Zealand were not clear. Using interpretivism and semi-structured interviews, this study focused on hotel guests and their security expectations. A total of 10 guests participated in this study and they were each asked 10 questions. However, the responses to only eight

* Corresponding Author's Email: cyril.peter@weltec.ac.nz.
† Author's Email: limkl@tarc.edu.my.

In: Tourism in Crisis
Editors: M.E. Korstanje, V. GB Gowreesunkar and S.W. Maingi
ISBN: 979-8-88697-643-4

of those questions have been analysed and presented in this article. The findings confirmed that security was a concern for guests when they made travel plans. It also found that most guests considered New Zealand to be safe.

A significant finding from this study was that guests were willing to pay extra for better-quality of security protocols. Well-travelled guests were able to compare the difference between New Zealand hotel security and that of other hotels around the world.

Keywords: safety, security, tourism consumption, New Zealand, well-travelled guest

Introduction

This exploratory study was conducted in New Zealand as part of a PhD thesis. This research intends to understand guests' perceptions of New Zealand's hospitality security. In an era where terrorism is a major concern, is it common practice to emphasise safety and security? How does it affect planned travel behaviour? What are some of the guests' expectations around security? Will guests be willing to pay a higher room rate for a better level of security?

The data for this study was collected in 2018. Before 2019, New Zealand hadn't experienced any major terrorist events. So, the data in some ways perhaps demonstrates the attitudes earlier than the March 15th, 2019, Christchurch attacks. On Friday 3rd September 2021, another terrorist attack occurred in New Zealand. A Sri Lankan-born terrorist attacked and stabbed several shoppers at a supermarket in Auckland. While New Zealand has been largely terrorism-free for a long time before 2019, the events since 2019 have certainly changed the security landscape quite a bit. This research was designed to draw on the perception of the hotel guests; trying to understand their expectations, wants and needs, and what the hospitality industry is doing to meet those needs. This article is purely from the perspective of the guests.

In this study, hotels referred to are generally variations of paid commercial accommodation where they have guest rooms, restaurants, and other services. Some hotels will have gyms, swimming pools, nightclubs, banquet rooms and other facilities. What this definition of hotels does not include are Airbnb, small motels, caravan parks, backpackers etc. The reason for this is that it is not reasonable to expect an Airbnb (for instance) to have security guards or other security features. Also, the guests referred to in this study are guests who stay in paid accommodation, not the likes of caravan parks and backpackers.

Literature Review

Concept of Safety and Security

Security as an attribute has been ranked very high when compared to other attributes of a hotel. It scored 4.8 out of 5 with 5 being *a 'relevant attribute'* Marić, Marinković, Marić, & Dimitrovski (2016). Safety and security broadly refer to a desire to be harm free. Blokland & Reniers (2020), provide an in-depth study of what each word means and they also discuss risk as a part of the discussion around the definition of safety and security. In everyday use, safety and security are used interchangeably. Wanting to be safe & secure, in the context of this study, it can be said that guests want to avoid harm, and disruptions to their travel plans and they largely want to avoid threats and the associated stress (Anichiti, Dragolea, Hars, Haller, & Butnaru, 2021). Safety and security become more important when people are away from their normal habitat, their home, and all that is familiar to them. While travelling overseas, they could be in an unfamiliar environment, or they may not be fluent in the local language and dialects. Despite this, there is a reasonable expectation to be safe and secure. Who bears the responsibility to keep guests safe and secure? Is it a case of *caveat emptor*? Is it the guest's responsibility to do due diligence or can they reasonably expect the hotel to ensure their safety?

It is not just about being harmed; it is about identifying and mitigating the risk. Studies have shown that females tend to be more risk-averse, they tend to be more careful. Males, on the other hand, tend to ignore risks or pay less attention to risks. This is known as the *white male effect* (Sansani, 2018). This would explain the risk-taking activities sportsmen tend to partake in.

Travel Behaviour

Planning a holiday or even a work-related trip takes a lot of effort. With work-related travel, the destination often has already been decided. It's just the logistics of the trip that needs to be worked out. With a family holiday or even a holiday for one, the planning must include destination choice, budget, routes, and requirements of all the travellers amongst other considerations. It's not easy to organise holidays especially if it is for a group of people. It is much easier when the planning is just for yourself. You know what you want from your holiday.

Security and safety considerations limit options and make planning slightly more difficult. Which destination is safer? Which hotel will be more secure? Where can we travel unimpeded? People don't want their holiday plans disrupted. Even if they are not personally hurt or injured, travel and movement, in general, might be disrupted. So, the tendency is to find stable destinations for their holidays. Opinions of family and friends, news stories, travel advisories etc may impact travel planning (Kapuscinski & Richards, 2016; Buigut, Braendle, & Sajeewani, 2017).

Tourists tend to change their travel plans once news about a particular destination is released e.g., terrorist attack. Hajibaba, Boztug, & Dolnicar (2016) have concluded a study to explore how hotels can avoid cancellations. Their findings show that a change of accommodation and if coupled with a room upgrade could work. Another finding that could help to avoid cancellations is if tourists/guests are provided with more up-to-date information about the situation. Guests want to know whether it's safe for them to travel.

Hotel Security

There is a realistic expectation that hotels are safe for guests to stay in. In accepting a reservation, the hotel enters into a contract to protect, service and take care of their guests. This a serious obligation and one that hotels should undertake, secure in their minds that they have done their utmost to keep their guests safe. Efendi (2020) and Nwokorie & Igbojekwe (2019) both discuss safety and security and the issues hotels face but from different perspectives. The bottom line is that security is important and that there is a reasonable expectation that hotels will ensure that their guests are safe. Hotels are generally very public spaces, with several entrances and exits. It is extremely difficult to secure all points of entry and exits. Hotels, by their very nature, are expected to be porous, with very few restrictions. The reason for this is to emit a welcoming and inviting feeling. If there are too many restrictions, guests will not feel comfortable.

Hospitality Terrorism

The relationship between hospitality, tourism and terrorism has been around for a long time. Now, with the increased difficulty for terrorists to penetrate or attack military and government properties, soft targets, such as hotels have become the preferred targets. Terrorists want to utilise their limited resources effectively and efficiently. So, they make every attack count. They want to ensure that they get the best return for their effort. Zeman (2020) describes soft targets as places that have a high chance of being attacked but they don't possess the means to protect themselves. Hotels along with restaurants, shopping malls and schools, will fall in this category.

Bac, Bugnar, & Mester (2015) describe the effects of a terrorist attack as being temporary. What they mean is that the destination will not suffer long term. However, it must be noted that not all destinations are built the same, nor are they all similarly resilient. Some may fall over after just one, single attack. They present Northern Ireland and Turkeys as examples of destinations that have bounced back after countless attacks. Gurtner (2016) also states, using the example of Bali, that returning to normalcy is possible, but it is fraught with difficulties and challenges. Even today, Bali is vulnerable because the threat is still alive. Seabra, Reis, & Abrantes (2020) state that destinations that are geographically close to existing terrorism targets are also affected. So, the threat is not just to that particular destination or country. The surrounding areas will also be negatively affected.

Paraskevas (2013) understanding the close relationship between hospitality and terrorism devised a six-step strategy to prevent or disrupt any terrorist attempts on hospitality properties. If properties can break up one of the six steps, they would have effectively prevented a terrorist attack. Hotels must be watchful and try and avert terrorist attacks. They must find ways to implement deterrents into their properties.

Risk and Insurance

Morakabati & Kapuscinski (2016) discuss risk and how reactions to threats depend on the personality of the individual. Not everyone reacts in the same manner. The article also goes on to explain how the cycle perpetuates. If tourists are fearful, they will avoid specific destinations. This in turn affects tourism in that area and that reduces employment opportunities. Some destinations are very dependent on tourism. So when tourism ceases, there is mass unemployment and hardship, and this now becomes the breeding ground for terrorists. Terrorist groups find recruits in these affected areas.

Insurance will not prevent any incident or accident from occurring. It is merely a tool used to help after an event occurs. It can compensate when you need to change flights, travel itinerary and even in cases where medical assistance or evacuation is required. It is also useful when someone dies, and the body needs to be repatriated to their home country. But it does nothing before the event, aside from providing some comfort knowing that should one have to alter their travel plans due to terrorism, they will be compensated. This does not alter the fact that insurance is useful, and tourists should always be insured when travelling.

Fanelli (2016) describes and discusses in detail a myriad of claims by victims, their families, and guests against hotels. These are cases involving acts of terror. Hotels must defend against these lawsuits which can be costly and damaging to their brand.

Risk profiles differ according to the destination, property, event, time of year etc. Travelling in a pandemic for instance will be harder to insure. Similarly, travelling to a known warzone will also be difficult to insure.

From the perspective of the hotel property, they too will find it difficult to insure against terrorist acts, if they do not have basic security. Hotels are eventually liable to provide safety and protect their guests. To provide this protection, hotels will need to be insured. But insurance companies may steer clear of protecting against terrorist acts because of the many unknowns involved. Hotels need to be able to show that they have provided reasonable care and security for their guests and that they could not have known about the possibility of an attack. This means that they could not foresee a specific danger or attack. Even if a court rules in favour of the hotel property, any drawn-out lengthy court process will be expensive for hotels.

Paying Extra for Security

The idea of paying extra for security, even though it should already be a part of the package, is because tourists are now more security conscious. The general idea is to avoid terrorist or criminal acts at all costs. So, guests tend to lean towards a more expensive property due to the implied additional security. Mekinc and Cvikl (2013), discuss the importance of recognising safety breaches, especially the type of breach. Breaches that are deemed to be beyond the control of the hotel are less likely to be of concern to tourists and guests. Guests are more concerned about situations where hotels could take reasonable actions to prevent breaches.

A study conducted by Kim, Brewer and Bernhard (2008), about guests' understanding of biometrics, concluded that guests are security conscious and support the use of such technology to keep them safe. Such high technology comes with a big price tag attached. Yet, it appears that guests are willing to pay that extra for security. Will hotels invest?

Another piece of evidence that guests are prepared to pay extra for security comes from a study conducted by Hilliard and Balogu (2008). This study covers guests as well as conference organisers and their expectations around security. The conclusion is that guests and other users of hotels expect to be safe and secure. There is perhaps a need for safety and security certification so that consumers can be assured that the property has been checked and certified. Kekovic and Markovic (2009) have extended the concept in that they have concluded that hotels that have a security certification or security rating, can use it as a competitive advantage. They will rank higher when compared with hotels that are not certified.

Methodology

This exploratory, qualitative research used interpretivism extensively. In total ten hotel guests were interviewed using the semi-structured interview method, and they were asked a total of ten questions each. That makes it 100 responses in total to analyse and discuss. The main reason for using the semi-structured interview method is because, especially with sensitive topics such as security and terrorism, they elicit better, richer responses. People are more likely to respond to questions about security and terrorism only if they feel safe discussing them. Adeloye, Carr, & Insch (2020), Cohen-Louck (2019), Cornejo, Rubilar, & Zapata-Sepulveda (2019), Fenge, Oakley, Taylor, & Beer (2019) have all employed qualitative research methods in research including sensitive issues such as war, terrorism, health, drugs, violence etc. A survey will not do the job effectively. With semi-structured interviews, the researcher can follow new lines of questioning if they discover something interesting or significant during the interview. They start with a list of questions that Bryman (2016) refers to as interview guides. It is a very flexible method. The only concern is the bias of the interviewer or researcher themselves. They need to know their own biases and be mindful of them and not allow their biases to interfere with the research itself. One of the biggest challenges with this group of participants was their English. They could not articulate properly what they wanted to say. So, the discussions were very limited. There were a lot of hand gestures to make up for the lack of English. Some participants relied on their electronic dictionaries or discussed with friends before providing answers.

Findings, Analysis, and Discussion

While a total of ten questions were asked of the ten guest participants of this study, only eight of those questions will be addressed here. They are the ones that will help us understand the importance placed on safety and security when travelling.

Q1 - What kind of security arrangements have you encountered in your stay at various accommodation properties around the world e.g., x-ray machines, luggage checks and explosives detecting dogs? Where have you encountered this? How did you feel about this level of security? Did you feel safer or more concerned?

G1 - No. We were only staying at a bed & breakfast [motel type accommodation]. They all just mainly have gates and locked doors.
G2 - No. No actually [nothing special].
G3 - Not really. Maybe only luggage checks.
G4 - No [no special checks]
G5 - No. I haven't seen those [x-ray machines, luggage check etc]
G6 - The only thing is like lockers, to lock our [valuables]. Nothing special to be honest
G7 - Not really about luggage and stuff. About earthquake. Security - no I didn't pay attention to that. In New Zealand - not really. It looks pretty safe country, to be honest.
G8 - No. There's not been much security at all. No bomb dogs. No one's checking my luggage. Nothing out of the ordinary.
G9 - I've worked a bit offshore so there have been several x-ray machines. I've stayed in Iraq so you would expect some sort of level of security. And Middle East, Qatar. It's only in the Middle East that I've had x-ray machines. No [New Zealand]. Nowhere that comes to mind [security in Asia].
G10 - We have a card that we use to lock the door. No [x-ray machines or luggage checks]. It's just a normal hotel.

Question one was designed to ascertain what security features guests had encountered in their travels and what they thought of that experience. Security features such as luggage x-ray machines, vehicle undercarriage checks, and explosive-detecting dogs are popular in some parts of the world but not all. They are generally not part of the security protocol in New Zealand. So, it wasn't surprising that they had not experienced any of the security features discussed while travelling through New Zealand. Some participants were perplexed and puzzled by the question. Feickert, Verma, Plaschka and Dev (2006), through their study, have concluded that some segments of the population would appreciate more security features.

The only discussion around security they have had with hotels was around the use of key cards, and public access to guest room floors. They appeared to be more concerned about criminal activities as opposed to terrorism. They also appeared to think the higher the quality of the hotel itself, the better the security protocols. This was concerning because providing good, effective security should not be dependent on the quality of the hotel.

Q2 - Were you informed about security by the property at any time before or during your stay?

This question was to find out what, if any, information was provided about the property's security protocols. This would give an idea of the emphasis on security or whether security wasn't an important feature.

G1 - Yes [was briefed about security].
G2 - Yea [briefed about key cards]. When we checked in, they tell us that.
G3 - No. Not really.
G4 - Yes
G5 - Yes. They tell us that they have security outside, both doors and that the rooms and hallways are checked.
G6 - No.
G7 - Yes, of course. They are pretty clear about it [security provisions].
G8 - No. There was nothing [they weren't informed].
G9 - With regards to safety aspects regarding earthquakes, but nothing else.
G10 - We were just pointed to the room, and that's it

50% of the participants stated that security information wasn't provided, nor did they ask. They did not feel the need to. There was some mention of natural disasters and earthquakes but nothing specific to security. The other 50% had some interaction around security but they seemed to focus on the key card and Closed-Circuit Television cameras (CCTV).

Q3 -Do you consider personal security and safety when making travel plans?

This question tries to understand individual tourists' decision-making process when it comes to travel plans. Is security important when making travel plans?

G1 - Yes
G2 - It's very important to us. Ya, it's important.
G3 - Ya. It's very important.
G4 - I think so [important]
G5 - No.
G6 - Yea, sometimes
G7 - Yea, of course [laughs].
G8 - No, I never think about it at all [laughs].
G9 - Yes, I do because of some of the places I go.
G10 - It's like life risks. No, we never consider things like that. I reckon this country is safe enough. We always consider our belongings, not being stolen and things like that.

70% claimed that security was an important factor when making travel plans but they were not able to elaborate. For instance, did they specifically choose better quality, more expensive hotels to ensure better security? The balance of 30% did not make security a deciding factor. G10 seems to imply that risks are a part of life. However, they also stated that New Zealand was safe and so security wasn't a consideration. Brossman (2016) stresses the importance of security in his book about travel risk and findings from this study generally tend to agree with that sentiment. Henderson (2016) also expresses the same sentiments in that people need to always feel secure, even when they are out and about in commercial spaces. The relevance of Maslow's theory around security is very clear (Abulof, 2017).

Q4 - What do you do to mitigate security risks while travelling? e.g., avoid particular destinations or activities.

This question was about understanding how guests mitigated travel risks. Did they have specific strategies that they employed?

G1 - I avoid particular countries.
G2 - Ya, if I travel alone, I won't go out at night.
G3 - Try not to go out at night. Only stay in big cities.
G4 - I don't go outside at night.
G5 - I would avoid destinations and certain activities if I know that it was life-threatening. Or if people [say] that's dangerous. There's usually more than one person with me.
G6 - Probably [not go out at night].
G8 - We might avoid small alleyways at night. Probably stay in the central part.
G9 - Usually common sense stuff. As you would in your home cities. Stick to well-lit streets. Take care when you are carrying things of obvious value. Be aware of your surroundings.
G10 - Yes. Pretty much. That's true. Sometimes if we are informed or if we get information about whether they are not safe, we will just choose whether to go out.

A few participants said it is as easy as simply avoiding some countries that they deemed unsafe. They took their advice from the experiences of others such as friends, family, and even social media. This is not necessarily good because the advice they are receiving may not be accurate and is often biased. Some claim that they will not go out at night when they are travelling because, for some reason, night-time is when it is unsafe. Also, one participant claimed that keeping yourself safe, was basic common sense. That again is not necessarily true. They suggest that people should follow whatever they did in their home country to keep safe. However, it must be noted that when you are travelling, you are in an unfamiliar environment, you may not be familiar with the language, and you will also not have your support network around you in case of an emergency. So how you behave when you are travelling will be drastically different to how you live your life in your home country.

Q5 - Are there any particular countries/regions that you would not visit and why?

Here the purpose was to understand whether participants avoided specific countries, whether New Zealand was one of those countries and how they came to decide which countries to avoid.

G1 - Probably some in the Middle East that I would not visit.
G2 - Maybe India. Just some news that makes me a little bit nervous when I will go to travel.
G3 - No. Not really. Maybe in another country, I take a group. So that I am not alone.
G4 - Africa
G6 - Papua New Guinea. I would love to go but I heard that it's really dangerous for a tourist.
G7 - Iran, Iraq, Syria - not fun at all.
G8 - I would avoid North Korea and stuff like that. I would avoid all advertised 3rd world countries.
G9 - No. I tend to go everywhere. They won't send us to Iraq at the moment, or Afghanistan.
G10 - That's hard to say but I think probably like the country where they have war, terrorism [avoid].

Their answers seem to imply that they considered New Zealand safe since it did not make it into the list of countries to avoid. However, the list does not appear to be fair. They seemed to have taken negative stories from the media and made decisions based on that. The list did not include the United States of America, the United Kingdom and France. They seemed to have omitted western countries. These countries and many others have experienced terrorism firsthand. Yet they did not make the list. So, at the very least, the list is biased and not well thought through.

Q6 - Do you think that accommodation security is important and why? Would you choose a particular property because of its high level of security? Do you think security will be rated highly like cost and location? Security, Cost, Location – Prioritise them (1 most important – 3 least important)

Evaluating the importance of security and gaining respondents' perspectives on it is the main crux of this study. The question is not just whether security was important, but also how important is it. That is where the ranking exercise comes in. 100% of the respondents, stated that security was important to them. They understood that the study was specifically about security while travelling. Security in our home country is different to security while travelling. If there is a terrorist incident in our home country, we are in an environment that we are familiar with and we will have our support networks around us.

G1 - Yes. Just a personal safety.
G2 - Ya, it's really important.
G3 - Yes.
G4 - Yes, it's important.
G5 - Yes, because it's like really important.
G6 - Yea. I think so. Depending on how high or low the normal [security standard] standard of a hotel are [stay in accommodation with extra security]. I've never asked or looked for it. I cannot say whether it's worth it for me to pay extra.
G7 - Yes
G8 - Yes, it is.
G9 - I think so. In Australia, we are very complacent. I am sure New Zealand might be the same. Until there has been an incident and then everything will escalate.
G10 - Yes, of course. Definitely

While all the respondents consider security to be important, the degree of importance varied when we compared security with cost and location. Marić, Marinković, Marić, & Dimitrovski (2016) and Blokland & Reniers (2020) both demonstrate through their research that security is important and that tourists/guests want to avoid harm and disruptions at all costs. From the ranking exercise (Table 1), 40% of the respondents put security in the 1st position, meaning that security would be their most important criterion when making travel decisions. Another 30% placed security in 2nd position, meaning that either cost or location was more important to them. With regards to location, travellers tend to stay close to their activities or planned reasons for travel. This means if one was travelling for medical reasons, they would stay close to the hospital or if they were visiting to attend a concert or a conference, they would tend to find a hotel close to the venue. Cost and budgetary constraints will also dictate where one stayed, or the quality of the hotel selected. So, with 70% of the respondents placing security in either 1st or 2nd

position, makes security an important consideration for travellers. So, hotels should be aware of this and work their best to make their property safe.

Table 1. Security ranking

Security	
1st choice	40%
2nd choice	30%
3rd choice	30%
Total	100%

Q7 - How do you rate accommodation security in New Zealand? Why is this so?

The seventh question looks to understand how guests rank New Zealand's hotel security. This is a key question to this study. The very essence of this study is to ascertain the perception of security in New Zealand. What do guests think about security and why? The ranking ranged between high, medium, and low. It is expected that guests will base their ranking on their knowledge and experiences. They should be able to explain to justify their responses.

High

G1 - Very high. Everything has been wonderful.
G2 - It's quite good.
G3 - It's perfect, I think.
G4 - High [standard].
G5 - 9 [out of 10]
G6 - I have just been to Huka Lodge which has a pretty high standard. They were all pretty good. And now I start going to other places, where I realise there is no [security] - a bit dodgy. But I think you can still keep your things safe.
G9 - I think it's very good but I am not aware that there are any concerns or alerts or anything like that. There are security cameras everywhere. It's very subtle.
G10 - It's very good

The vast majority (80%) of the respondents in this study categorically stated that they considered the security to be high. Most of them arrived at this conclusion based on their own experiences, knowledge, and observations. To many, New Zealand feels safe and looks like a safe destination. Up until March 2019, New Zealand had not experienced any serious terrorist incidents that were noteworthy. So, the feeling is that New Zealand was generally terrorism free. Guests generally go about enjoying their country and their stay is relatively unimpeded. Generally, nobody bothers them. This gives a sense of security. Respondents used the words "wonderful," "perfect" and "good" to describe their time in New Zealand. When discussing Huka Lodge, Taupo (a luxury resort), G6 felt the security standard was very high. When staying at a smaller, lower standard, cheaper properties around the country, G6 said they were a little more concerned, but not so concerned that they decided to pack up and leave. G9 observed that there are a lot of security cameras within properties and all over the country. This again must provide some sort of sense of security. However, it must be noted here that when security cameras are unmanned, the recorded footage is only used after an event occurs. This means that when a complaint about criminal activity is made, the authorities can go back to a specific date and time and download the required evidence. This does not help anyone that is in danger and requires immediate help. Security cameras can be a deterrent in some cases. However, criminals and terrorists will make the extra effort to avoid these cameras where possible. But a suicide bomber, for instance, doesn't worry about being recognised. They have no intention of coming out alive from a mission. In many ways, it is an unfair fight. Terrorists do not seem to care about dying as a result of the mission, whereas counter-terrorism forces have to think about how to deal with the situation without any loss of lives.

Medium

The balance 20% ranked their security experience in New Zealand as a medium. They felt it was just right and quite average.

G7 - It's nice. For me, it's a pretty peaceful place.

G8 - The ones we are staying at. They are very average. The first place we stayed in Auckland, was dodgy. They would leave your luggage wherever and it wouldn't matter. They didn't give us tags. It was very dodgy.

20% of the respondents described the security as being medium. This means that no one considered the security as bad or low. So, it is good that 100% thought the security was either high or medium. G8 made a very useful and important observation. This was regarding left luggage. G8 claimed that luggage can be seen left around with nobody taking any action.

This is very risky. All luggage must be accounted for. It is common for guests who are on a long visit in a country and planning to return to the same property later, to request to have their luggage stored by the property till their return. These are commonly known in the industry as 'left luggage.' Left luggage must be properly identified and tagged and stored in a separate area, a luggage storeroom. This luggage storeroom should ideally be checked regularly to make sure only properly tagged items are stored. Some hotels in Asia tend to use explosive detection dogs (EDD) to patrol the storeroom several times each day. The dogs will be checking to make sure that the left luggage does not contain any explosives.

In 1984, an incendiary device, which was meant for the then Prime Minister Margaret Thatcher, was planted in the Brighton Hotel. It was planted more than three weeks ahead of schedule utilising a long delay timer. When the bomb, planted by the Irish Republican Army (IRA), eventually exploded, it missed its intended target, instead killing five others and injuring a few dozen more. According to Carroll (2021), time-delay bombs are quite commonly used. Unfortunately, nobody found or noticed the bomb for more than three weeks.

Q8 - Do you think that it is the responsibility of the property to protect you? Why? Would you be willing to pay a higher room rate if a particular hotel had extra security?

This question also ended up forming a very important part of this study which was to find out from guests who they believed should be responsible for security. Specifically, did they think the hotel was solely responsible to look after them and provide all security measures? Also, the study hoped to find out whether guests valued security and whether they would consider paying a higher room rate for better protection.

100% of the respondents stated that they believed that the hotel should be responsible to look after them. It is logical in some ways in that the hotel knows its own property best and the hotel will know its client base and the type of security required. For instance, a business-class hotel will need different security protocols for a resort. G2 said that the hotel will be the first place they would turn to in the event they needed help. So, in a way, it makes sense that the hotel took care of the security arrangements. G9, while agreeing that the hotel should provide security and keep everyone safe, they felt that guests also should bear some responsibility. They should be careful and minimise risk.

G1 - Yes

G2 - Ya, of course. If I have some problem, they need to help me. If I can handle it, I will pay [pay extra for more secure accommodation]

G3 - Yea. Yea, maybe [pay extra for more secure accommodation].

G4 - Yes, I think so. I choose a more expensive hotel [extra security]

G5 - Yes. It depends on what the security is doing. Okay [will pay for extra security]

G6 - If there are any safety issues, definitely

G7 - Of course, it's their [responsibility]. Yes [will pay for accommodation with extra security].

G8 - To an extent. You get what you pay for. Depends on which country I am staying in [pay more for extra accommodation security]. I guess New Zealand - No [won't want extra security].

G9 - A bit of both. If you are paying to stay somewhere, there should be an implied sense of security, keeping your belongings safe and keeping yourself safe. But it's not entirely on the hotel. Yea [pay more for extra security].

G10 - I think so. That's true. Do you mean to protect me from a terrorist attack? Terrorism - maybe they don't consider that enough, but for fire and from stealing - ya. They can protect me from disasters. It will depend on the country where you live [pay more for extra security at accommodation]. If there [New Zealand], you probably won't pay that extra.

With regards to paying extra for a better-class hotel with better security arrangements, 70% said that they would be willing to pay extra if it's affordable. As Table 2 shows, this finding agrees with the literature where Kim, Brewer and Bernhard (2008), explain that guests expect better security and are willing to pay for it. However, the balance 30% feel refused possibly because they believe that the hotel should bear that cost. They expect good security anyway. Also, 30% claimed that since New Zealand is a safe destination, they don't expect any problems or safety issues. Hence, the refusal to pay anything extra.

Themes

A few important themes came from these interviews, including a few that are significant and worth exploring further. In general, 100% of the respondents took security seriously and they all stated that security was important. Chan and Lam (2013) also express the importance of security and their study shows that guests want and, in some cases, demand certain security features. They claim that managers need to fully understand the sentiments and security requirements of their guests. Ritter (2020), describing the settlement of the Mandalay Bay Resort shooting case, stated that the parent company and their insurers paid about USD 800 million to the victim's families. The shooter was able to accumulate more than a dozen rifles and other weapons including about 1000 bullets. With these, he succeeded in killing 60 people and injured many more. How were these weapons brought into the hotel without anyone noticing or suspecting anything? Compensations and settlements as described in Ritter (2020) will become commonplace unless hotels take security seriously.

Table 2. Themes – Guests

	Code	Theme
GUEST	GT^{1}	Security is important
	GT^{2}	New Zealand is safe
	GT^{3}	Hotels responsible for guest's safety
	GT^{4}	No x-ray machines, bomb dogs
	GT^{5}	Insufficient security briefing
	GT^{6}	Security conscious
	GT^{7}	No need to ask about security
	GT^{8}	Security rating (High/Med)
	GT^{9}	Stay indoors/ No night outings
	GT^{10}	Avoid selected countries
	GT^{11}	Pay extra for security

With regards to making travel plans and decisions, 70% said that they made decisions with safety and security in mind. That would mean that they were security conscious even while travelling. Travelling often meant people were in unfamiliar territories and in some cases where even the language was unfamiliar. Respondents gave the impression that to them New Zealand was a safe destination and so they must have been wondering about the need for this study. This data was largely collected in 2018, before the March 2019 Christchurch terrorist attack.

Respondents were also generally in agreement when it came to who should be responsible for the provision of security. They agreed that the hotel should ensure their safety. Anichiti, Dragolea, Hars, Haller, & Butnaru (2021) concluded from their research that hotels should consider providing a sufficient level of security and this agrees with the findings of this particular study. There wasn't any discussion or mention of local government or central government responsibility. The host hotels should take care of them. Aside from just one respondent, all other guests had never encountered x-ray machines, luggage checks or explosive detection dogs (EDD) during their travels. They might have seen them in some airports, but not in their accommodation. Security features such as encountered x-ray machines, luggage checks or explosive detection dogs are a common sight in Asia. In larger properties, cars are not even allowed near the hotel until they have been checked properly. This can include checking the boot (storage compartment), bonnet (engine compartment) and undercarriage of vehicles. Often explosive detection dogs are used to check the vehicles as well.

About 50% of respondents weren't given any security briefing nor were they expecting and by the sounds of things since they deemed New Zealand to be safe. They weren't told what to do in an emergency. Most (90%) didn't have any security-related questions either. Their key cards were issued, and they were shown where the elevators were.

If they felt unsafe in any destination, they said that they would opt not to go out of the hotel at night. Somehow, they believed that the threat was only outside the hotel. They did not think that the threat could come to the hotel or already be inside the hotel. In their minds, the threat is external to the hotel or the hotel would have taken steps to ensure the premises are safe. In reality, this may not always be the case. They also claimed that they would avoid selected countries due to security reasons.

100% of respondents said that security was important but only 70% of them said that they would pay extra for security. It seems that the remaining 30% said that New Zealand was already safe and there was no need for additional security. Considering the 70% that were willing to pay a higher room rate, it can be concluded that there is a large segment within the tourism population that want safer properties, and this means that hotels can use this as a point of difference to market their properties. It is a clear competitive advantage. Paying extra for security is consistent with the literature and it is a significant finding.

Limitations and Opportunities for Further Research

While this is only an exploratory study, the sample size limits the ability to generalise the findings or make any business decisions based on them. However, given the findings and the recent terrorist events in New Zealand, it warrants a bigger, more in-depth study. The new research could also ascertain how much guests extra will guests be willing to pay for better security. This will help the hotel make investment decisions.

Conclusion

It can be concluded from this study that security is important and when travelling, guests place a huge emphasis on security and a large majority would pay extra for a safer stay. The willingness to pay extra is significant and hotels need to factor this into their thinking. So, it is safe to conclude that because of its importance, hotels can use security to differentiate themselves from the competition.

The two recent terrorist attacks (March 2019 and September 2021) would impact on any post-2019 research on New Zealand's hospitality security. It is possible, while New Zealand will still be classed as a safe destination, tourists would be more wary and careful when making travel plans. It is recommended that a more in-depth study be conducted.

References

Abulof, U. (2017). Introduction: Why we need Maslow in the twenty-first century. *Society. 54(6)*, 508-509.

Adeloye, D., Carr, N., & Insch, A. (2020). Conducting qualitative interviews on sensitive topics in sensitive places: the case of terrorism and tourism in Nigeria. *Tourism Recreation Research. 45(1),*, 69-79.

Anichiti, A., Dragolea, L. L., Hars, G.D. T., Haller, A. P., & Butnaru, G. I. (2021). Aspects Regarding Safety and Security in Hotels: Romanian Experience. *Information. 12(44)*, 1-23. https://doi.org/10.3390/info12010044.

Bac, D. P. (2015). Terrorism and its impact on the Tourism Industry. *Revista Română de Geografie Politică, 17(1),* 5-11.

Blokland, P. J., & Reniers, G. (2020). The Concepts of Risk, Safety, and Security: A Fundamental Exploration and Understanding of Similarities and Differences. In C.

Bieder, & G. K. Pettersen, *The Coupling of Safety and Security.* (pp. 9-16. https://doi.org/10.1007/978-3-030-47229-0_2). Springer, Cham.

Brossman, C. (2016). *Building a travel risk management program: Traveler safety and duty of care for any organisation.* Oxford: Elsevier.

Bryman, A. (2016). *Social Research Methods.* Oxford: Oxford University Press.

Buigut, S., Braendle, U., & Sajeewani, D. (2017). Steven Buigut, Udo Braendle and Disna Sajeewani. *Asia Pacific Journal of Tourism Research, 22(10)*, 991-1004. https://doi.org/10.1080/10941665.2017.1359193.

Carroll, R. (2021, March 15). *IRA Brighton bomber 'scouted Labour conference seven years earlier.'* Retrieved from The Guardian: https://www.theguardian.com/uk-news/2021/mar/15/ira-brighton-bomber-patrick-magee-scouted-labour-conference-seven-years-earlier.

Chan, E. S., & Lam, D. (2013). Hotel safety and security systems: Bridging the gap between managers and guests. *International Journal of Hospitality Management. 32*, 202-216.

Cohen-Louck, K. (2019). Perception of the Threat of Terrorism. *Journal of Interpersonal Violence. 34(5),*, 887-911.

Cornejo, M., Rubilar, G., & Zapata-Sepulveda, P. (2019). Researching Sensitive Topics in Sensitive Zones: Exploring Silences, "The Normal," and Tolerance in Chile. *International Journal of Qualitative Methods. 18,*, 1-11.

Efendi, M. (2020). The Problems Faced by Hotel Security Managers: Antalya Case. *Journal of Tourism and Gastronomy Studies. 8(1)*, 388-403.

Fanelli, C. L. (2016). Protecting Hotel Industry Businesses from Liability for Terror Attacks. *Real Estate Finance. 32(4)*, 1-7.

Feickert, J. V. (2006). Safeguarding Your Customers: The Guest's View of Hotel Security. *Cornell Hotel and Restaurant Administration Quarterly, 47(3)*, 224-244.

Fenge, L. A., Oakley, L., Taylor, B., & Beer, S. (2019). The Impact of Sensitive Research on the Researcher: Preparedness and Positionality. *International Journal of Qualitative Methods. 18,*, 1-8.

Gurtner, Y. (2016). Returning to paradise: Investigating issues of tourism crisis and disaster recovery on the island of Bali. *Journal of Hospitality and Tourism Management. 28*, 11-19.

Hajibaba, H., Boztug, Y., & Dolnicar, S. (2016). Preventing tourists from cancelling in times of crisis. *Annals of Tourism Research. 60*, 48-62.

Henderson, J. W. (2016). *The facility manager's guide to safety and security.* London: Taylor & Francis Group.

Hilliard, T. W. (2008). Safety and security as part of the hotel servicescape for meeting planners. *Journal of Convention & Event Tourism. 9(1),* 15-34. doi: 10.1080/15470t40802t04557.

Hinton, T. (2022, January 14). *Total export revenue of the dairy industry in New Zealand from the financial year 2015 to 2023.* Retrieved from Statista: https://www.statista.com/statistics/1100950/new-zealand-export-revenue-of-dairy-industry/.

Kapuscinski, G., & Richards, B. (2016). News framing effects on destination risk perception. *Tourism Management, 57*, 234-244.

Kekovic, Z. &. (2009). Security as a factor of competitive advantage in tourism. . *Tourism and Hospitality Management. 15(2),* 291-303.

Kim, J. B. (2008). Hotel customer perceptions of biometric door locks: Convenience and security factors. *Journal of Hospitality & Leisure Marketing. 17(1/2),* 162-183. doi:10.1080/10507050801978323.

Marić, D., Marinković, V., Marić, R., & Dimitrovski, D. (2016). Analysis of Tangible and Intangible Hotel Service Quality Components *Industrija. 44(1),*, 7-25. doiI: 10.5937/industrija1-8437.

Mekinc, J. &. (2013). The structure of security and safety crises in tourism. *Journal of Tourism & Services. 4(5/6),* 38-50.

Morakabati, Y., & Kapuscinski, G. (2016). Personality, Risk Perception, Benefit Sought and Terrorism Effect. *International Journal of Tourism Research. 18*, 506-514.

Nwokorie, E. C., & Igbojekwe, P. (2019). Security Challenges for the Hotel Industry: Implications for Selected Hotels in Owerri, Nigeria. *Academica Turistica. 2*, 193-205.

Paraskevas, A. (2013). Aligning strategy to threat: a baseline anti-terrorism strategy for hotels. *International Journal of Contemporary Hospitality Management, 25(1)*, 140-162. doi: 10.1108/09596111311290264.

Ritter, K. (2020, October 1). *Court OK's $800M settlement from MGM Resorts to 2017 Las Vegas Strip shooting victims.* Retrieved from USA Today: https://www.usatoday.com/story/travel/news/2020/10/01/las-vegas-strip-shooting-victims-get-800-million-settlement-mgm/5877222002/.

Sansani, S. (2018). Ethnicity and risk: a field test of the white-male effect. *Applied Economics Letters, 25(2)*, 74-77, doi: 10.1080/13504851.2017.1296540.

Seabra, C., Reis, P., & Abrantes, J. L. (2020). The influence of terrorism in tourism arrivals: A longitudinal approach in a Mediterranean country. *Annals of Tourism Research. 80*, 1-13. https://doi.org/10.1016/j.annals.2019.102811.

Tourism Industry Aotearoa. (2021, March). *Quick facts and figures.* Retrieved from Tourism Industry Aotearoa: https://www.tia.org.nz/about-the-industry/quick-facts-and-figures/#:~:text=Tourism%20was%20New%20Zealand's%20biggest,of%20 New%20Zealand's%20total%20GDP.

Zeman, T. (2020). Soft Targets: Definition and Identification. *Academic & Applied Research in Military & Public Management Science, 19(1),* 109-119.

Chapter 2

COVID-19 Pandemic, Risk-Reduction Strategies and Crisis Management in the Travel Insurance Sector

Bindi Varghese[1,*]
H. Sandhya[1]
and Terrin Thomas[2]
[1]Christ University, Bangalore, India
[2]Credit Assessment Officer, ANZ Bank, Bangalore, India

Abstract

Travel has always been considered to be a risky affair as there are multiple uncertainties associated with it. Though the tourism industry has developed sophisticated methods to manage these risks, there are still certain uncontrollable and unforeseen circumstances that might affect the physical, emotional, and mental state of travellers. The result would be a huge financial burden for the traveller and increased frustration towards the tour operator. The concept of travel insurance was introduced to relieve travellers of such unforeseen risks while travelling. Moreover, the Covid 19 pandemic has instilled a sense of fear and doubt among the minds of travellers which affects their travel decision-making to a large extent. Destinations and tourism suppliers have introduced various risk reduction strategies and methods to resolve this issue. This paper focuses on understanding the concept of risk associated with travel, the various dimensions of risk management, and the key strategies adopted by tour operators and suppliers to minimize such risks.

* Corresponding Author's Email: bindi.varghese@christuniversity.in.

In: Tourism in Crisis
Editors: M.E. Korstanje, V. GB Gowreesunkar and S.W. Maingi
ISBN: 979-8-88697-643-4

Keywords: travel risk, travel insurance, crisis, risk-reduction strategies, ethical dilemmas, agency stewardship

Introduction

In a global and ever-changing world, even if there is a large number of investments by the tourism and hospitality service providers in mitigating risk consequences, not all the potential risks and uncertainties can be controlled. The outcome of the uncertainties will not just be detrimental to the tourism industry but also to the local economy as a whole. The decision to travel largely depends on how the travellers perceive the risk. While some consider risks as an integral part of their travel experience and adapt to them, others try to avoid them by selecting destinations that are safer to travel to and involve less risk. Generally, risks are built on the theory of probability, but they cannot reveal the emotional state of the traveller at a given point in time. Hence, the way the risks are perceived does not reveal the fear of travellers (Larsen, 2007). Based on the age, gender, and staging of family factors of the traveller, certain personalities develop special tolerance or avoidance of risks. These indicators of risk have a direct correlation to how the risks are perceived by the tourists. Validation for this can be stated when a tourist sets on visiting a family or a friend along with their travel being envisaged which means that the tourist destination was seemed to be less risky because it assures travellers a safe expectation about their journey to the destination (Korstanje & George, 2013). The present book chapter interrogates furtherly not only the impact of risk perception in the tourism industry but also the future strategies to be adopted by the industry to achieve safer destinations. Although the literature has extensively expanded over recent years, less attention was paid to the role of insurance in risk perception theory (Korstanje & George 2013). This chapter fills the gap laying the foundations for a new understanding of risk perception theory.

Travel Insurance

Travel insurance is a form of insurance that provides coverage for travel, dental and medical expenses that are incurred during the travel. Under the specified condition of travel that is mentioned in the travel insurance policy, aeromedical evacuation for the traveller is provided. There is a need for travel insurance due to the high cost of medical and dental treatment abroad. As a result of this and to cut down on their medical expenses during their journey all travellers need to understand and be aware of the inclusions and exclusions contained in the policy chosen by them. On average, an estimated amount of 45% of travellers fall ill or face injuries while they are travelling from one place to another (Leggat et al.,1999). International travellers are more prone to injuries that are severe than domestic travellers who travel within the country. As per the study in the UK in 1980, the count of general practitioners is only about 4% in total (Leggat et al.,1999). Following this, the count of GPs in New Zealand is 60% and a total of 39% of travel clinics around the world insist on the need for traveller insurance for any level traveller from domestic to international. 19% of GPs in New Zealand recommend taking travel insurance for their medical guidance whereas 54% of GPs advise travellers to take medical assistance internationally. Travellers are required to purchase an insurance well in advance of their journey. The application forms for travel insurance can be taken from the airlines, travel agents, their doctors, health insurers, and the representative of the travel and tourism industry. Two factors determine the cost of travel insurance: duration of travel and stay; and of course, both are directly associated with the destinations of travel. The discounted policy is at the cost of exclusions of certain coverage and limitations. There are low premium policies available in markets for countries like Asia along with the private medical and dental care cost added too.

Another significant point seems to be that tourists must have realistic expectations of the travel insurance policy. The processing period for a policy is very minimal. The travellers who travel to war zones, the travellers with self-inflicted injuries, who perform acts that are against the law, the travellers infected by various infectious diseases such as AIDS (Acquired Immune Deficiency Syndrome) and other sexually transmitted diseases, the travellers who are pregnant and travellers taking part in a professional sport are not insured by the travel insurance company even at the highest level (Babu et al., 2014). In their travel insurance, an additional charge is paid by the travellers who expect themselves to be involved in any kind of sport that seems to be hazardous. These surcharges are assessed by travel insurance companies on a different case basis. As evidence of their insurance, an insurance card is provided to the travellers. Each card has a policy number printed on it which helps them gain access to dental, paramedical, and medical facilities provided in the abroad countries. Along with the policy number on the card, there is also a toll-free number printed on it to help travellers contact customer care in case of an emergency.

The time, duration, and lifespan of travel insurance are short-term and at times can be made for annual, business, or frequent travel purposes. There is no continuous coverage of travel insurance for internal travel by the tourist. This problem is compensated for by using long-term medical insurance in the host country of the traveller. The availability of aeromedical evacuation should be a must and the registration of the traveller with the local embassy or a local consulate of the traveller's destination should be a checked-upon factor. Whenever an emergency arises with the traveller, the process demands the insurer be informed and contacted on an immediate basis. The tourists must possess a record of original accounts, receipts, and medical reports for any medical or dental treatment as these expenses can be claimed back from a travel insurance policy, employer, or written off against tax (Lawton & Page, 1997). Any conflicts or problems that would arise from the claims can be resolved via a discussion with an official representative from the insurance company that issued the insurance to the traveller. After the discussion with the official, if the customer is not happy about the outcome, then the traveller has the right to take the insurance company to court. But this would turn out to be a very expensive form of dispute resolution. As and when the traveller is unclear about the insurance policy, he should check with the travel agent or travel insurer. Hence travel insurance must not give travellers a false sense of security. They should take every precaution against illness and injury (Leggat et al., 1999).

Beyond Agency Stewardship and Tourism for the Elderly

The aged population has a profound implication for the tourism industry. There is a trend that is followed in the 21st century by Stewardship among agents concerning the ageing factor, the life expectancy of the population, and a fertility decline rate within the population of the country (Travel and Tourism Competitiveness Report, 2017). In the history of tourism and information sourcing related to tourism, the concept of elderly and tourism has gained a mass amount of importance. These are also seen as a major base for marketing the tourism industry and forming company strategies. What brings senior citizens to travel often is their motivation to explore the world. There are a lot of similarities between the two extremes of travellers (Young and Aged) but they do not exhibit uniform behaviour (Lawton & Page, 1997). As a combination of this similarity, "New age elderly" is a differentiated subgroup that focuses on the orientation value rather than the age of the tourists. The people who belong to this subgroup exhibit self-confidence, and activeness and are always open and welcoming to simulation in the surrounding environment. The concept of elderly tourists in the field of tourism is usually neglected by insurance companies. The countries on the European continents, who are the major contributors of tourists in the world, have a special place held for the elderly tourists in their sector. (G, 1997). Schindler (2005) addresses this by focusing majorly on the outbound leading countries, where the tourist company has their business targeted at people who belong to a certain age group such as the retirement age (Allingham, J. D., 2013). They keep their businesses going by offering large discounts to the elderly during the off-peak season of travel. With new companies and organizations emerging, the companies that are now providing these services are expected to face heavy competition shortly. Tourism comes with a tax. There are always some kinds of not-so-familiar stress that a tourist is always subjected to. These are the physical and psychological stresses combined with the ageing process that leads to vulnerable health conditions of older travellers (Lawton & Page, 1997). As a result, with the increased difficulty of older people coping with these stresses, it is not a mandate that the elderly should quit tourism completely. But an alternative to this problem is necessary preparations and counselling for the journey by the elderly tourists (Schindler, 2005).

The travel and tourism industry plays a significant role in spreading awareness of travel health among the population. Knowing the standards of healthcare in the destination makes it very helpful, especially for elderly tourists to plan their holidays and travel itineraries. In previous years, advisory firms related to travel and tourism were not very popular as it was not seen as a major revenue-making sector (Allingham, J. D., 2013). But in recent times, there has been an instant growth in the involvement of health insurance in insurance companies. With the availability of the right information from a dependable source, a complete itinerary of the travel including the transport, accommodation, and fun activities can be planned and formulated taking into account the health and severe medical condition (Leggat & Leggat, 2002). With all these checks in place, elderly tourists can afford to travel with more confidence. They tend to reap the benefits from the travel policy in terms of physical and emotional well-being. Because of the medical health policies in the UK, states companies that are regular in size are elusive as the time their population reaches the late sixties (UN, 2005). Age matters for quotations of travel insurance in their travel. Almost 20% of the population aged about 75 years and 25% of 65 years old refused the need for travel insurance without a second thought. As per a study conducted the main reason for their denial of them is their lack of knowledge of the internet and the information contained in it about the other alternatives to it. Most of the insurance policies issued say about 95% are mostly targeted at the upper age limits of the population. In that one-third of the policies issued did not provide any coverage for tourists aged above 64 years and tourists who were 75 plus years were barred from taking any travel insurance policy in their name. The policies for a traveller's single trip did not include one-third of the people who were aged 65 years and above and 59% of 75 years of age and above. An in-depth analysis of the prices that are charged by the majority of insurers shows how expensive the premium of the insurance gets as the age of the insurance holder increases, sometimes wherein the policies double in its price for a traveller aged 66 years. An elderly tourist with an already existing medical condition is more complicated in obtaining insurance without being rejected. They tend to be potential candidates for partial recovery. However, these coverages can be made available to elderly tourists after special medical screening but at a higher cost than usual which would ultimately be a huge expense for the tourists to pay. Another drawback to this is that elderly tourists are not given insurance to pursue activities like car hire and sports such as winter sports and are automatically cut down on this genre of insurance (L & H, 2003).

The proximity of age and rate and level of claims in insurance is justified by the regulations and rules of an insurer. These proximities are usually connected to the health factors of the traveller which makes it hard for them to provide security for the underwriters. Some of the insurance companies focus more on the services that they provide to the elderly, and age constraints to avail the travel health insurance is immaterial to them (Allingham, J. D., 2013). Despite this, the age and medical health condition of a traveller are taken into account while considering them for insurance (Babu et al., 2014). With the existence of age and discrimination in providing travel insurance, the anxiety factor among uninsured travellers should be taken note of.

The representatives of the insurance companies along with the assorted civil society bodies in collaboration with the insurance companies are working towards developing a new set of processes to guide and help elderly tourists to pick the right kind of insurance which would suit them. To conclude, an effort must be made to understand the simplest of the needs of the elderly senior citizen traveller. These needs should not just be stuck to guiding them to pick the suitable travel insurance but their health needs as a whole. Also, access to obtaining a travel policy should be made simpler and without any burden to promote the growing market of travel insurance in the economy world (Henderson, 2015). Insurance includes a policy, a certificate, an interim receipt, and handwritten evidence of the contract (if the agreement was done orally by the insurer). Law states that insurance must contain: An insurable interest, A risk and a promise of indemnity, and A contract, of the "utmost faith" (Henderson, 2015). Tourism should have an insurance contract as per economic subjects which state that certain situations impose the need for an insurance contract. There are two types of legal insurance in the travel and tourism industry, and they are voluntary (contractual insurance) and legal action (compulsory insurance).

All the vehicles on the road must be insured compulsorily as stated by the Law of Obligatory insurance policy (Henderson, 2015). Not just this, the passengers travelling in public transport need to be insured by the owners of the public transport such as aeroplanes, trains, ships, and buses against accidents caused due to any crisis. Insurance has a major role to play in the development of tourist activities. For risks that are not covered by insurance policies, there is a dire need for voluntary insurance to cover the excluded risk. To be proactive, most tourists tend to take up insurance that covers risks that are otherwise not covered by a regular travel insurance policy. Hence, as a method of precaution, the providers of transport insure themselves. Voluntary insurance is a basic form of regulative insurance. The policy forms of insurance and the associated tariffs define the boundaries of Agency Stewardship with voluntary contract insurance. The entities of business, business materials, and the costs of nonmaterial factors are all the obligations of travellers that cannot be excluded. There are a couple of obligations of the travel agents and hotels which are related to compensation of the damages to the material and immaterial account of service takers which are associated with the development of tourist activities (Allingham, 2013). As a result of this, the tourist companies have their contracts bound to the insurance companies that are responsible for minimizing the compensation amount which is an obligation stipulated in the contract. As a good businessman idea, the tourism industry voluntarily tends to sign contracts for ensuring the risks that are said to be certain of occurrence.

Crisis, Risk Coverage, and Global Practices

The risk coverage covers the general, additional, and supplemental conditions of a risk that are expected to occur in the tourism industry. An example of risk coverage would be to ensure a guest is in the hotel when an accident occurs. The company that covers insurance usually runs a business similar to the hotel business such as in the hospitality sector (Allingham, 2013). As long as the guest who is insured by the insurance company is within or outside the object, it becomes an obligation of the insurer to cover all the risks that the traveller is subjected to. These risks include the risks that are due to accidents caused by the hunting or fishing industry. This coverage of risks applies to only those organizations/companies that are stated in the insurance contract. They ensure their customers during the summer and fall break, especially students. Under special conditions as mentioned in the contract, insurance for skiing, swimming, and diving is offered to its customers. Sometimes insurance is provided for travellers taking public transport (Babu et al., 2014).

In Countries that showcase emissive tourism opportunities, the insurance policy is done keeping in mind the property of the traveller and the personality of the traveller. This is done to mitigate the risks and uncertainties related to a tourist's travel. It is also issued to make sure the traveller feels safe as he/she leaves an environment that is very familiar to him/her and moves into a different environment with unknown dangers. There are several offers issued by tourism and travel organization which includes, coverage for loss of baggage insurance, damage caused by the tourist during their time of travel, and damage by the automobile, ships, or aeroplanes to the passengers during their travel. Insurance is also provided for the sickness of the traveller and the cost of regular repair and service of the transport by which the tourists travel. It also provides insurance for the cost, if the traveller/tourists don't turn up during the trip (Allingham, 2013).

For service receivers, an insurance package is the best alternative which provides the best combinations of different varieties of insurance. The insurance becomes active after the first 24 hours of signing the contract until a different period is specified in the contract. The starting and ending date of insurance needs to be specified in the policy papers. If not specified, each party will take advantage of these and mend the dates as per their convenience. While deciding on what insurance to offer to the customers, the insurance companies need to consider all the potential losses and their consequences. An exposure of loss is defined as when an individual or in this case an organization is vulnerable to any loss, injuries, and damages that are in turn subjected to financial loss. The best way to be prepared for an unpredictable event is to know the complete details of risk and its coverages in and out. Knowing the terms and conditions of the policy issued to the customers and the coverage of those risks under the policy with exclusions that are incorporated with the policy is a big advantage to handling the insurance policy wisely. There are several companies providing insurance policies to their customers with varied customer benefits and risk coverage. These variations are due to changes incorporated by various plans and perils and the responsibility of the tourists of picking the right policy and knowing about what they think is needed for them.

Reading the policy statement clearly in and out without neglecting the fine print on the policy paper is advised for the traveller. As an example, to explain this, we take the airline industry, the insurance policy for flight delays may vary from one insurance provider to another. Some insurers don't cover war terrorism, delays due to strikes, civil riots, or disturbances in the flight schedule due to other operational factors but not due to mechanical reasons. Trip curtailment provides insurance coverage to its traveller once the traveller is abroad(overseas) or in situations where one must reduce the number of holidays planned due to serious reasons such as illness or a family or official emergency (Huang & Tsai, 2003).

It is an important thing to check for the existence of emergency evacuation in the insurance policy when the insured is suffering from an already existing medical condition. As per the law stated by the Financial Industry Disputes Resolution Center (Fidrec), if one needs immediate medical assistance or evacuation, the insurer or the official representative who is authorized by the country the traveller is currently residing in should be contacted. This is done as a result of obeying what is stated in the policy document. The policy document states that the opinion of the insurer must be taken to decide if medical assistance should be given, and that evacuation is necessary from one point of location to the other for treatment purposes. In a scenario where there is a flight delay, a claim can be made on the insurance by the insured only on the condition that the delay is for six consecutive hours or more. A claim is not considered if the delay of the flight is less than six hours. An event that is already known cannot be covered by the insurance policy. This in other words means that when civil riots or natural hazards occur, no coverage is provided by the insurance company. These are mostly published in the airline or hotel tickets or via media news or reports and majorly by the travel advisories run by the government before an insured buys the policy. This helps the traveller make a wise decision while buying the policy. But on the contrary, "the occurrence of the known events' 'happens after the insured buys the policy. In such cases, the claims can be made by cancelling the planned trip but on the given condition that this should have been specified in the contract during the signing process (purchasing of the contract). To be on the safer side, a check on the exclusion clauses is necessary to ensure the claims are as per that which is stated by the Fidrec. Theft coverage is provided by the policy chosen by the insured which covers the accidental loss of personal belongings during the time of travel under special terms and conditions agreed upon by both the insurer and the insured. The process of claiming involves filing a police complaint as theft of one's belongings at the local police station of the traveller's destination because this police complaint report should be provided as a must while submitting documents for the claims of the theft. Most travel insurance like health insurance policies does not provide coverage for already existing medical conditions of the traveller (insured). As a result of this, it is the complete responsibility of the insured to get to know about the exclusions that are present in the policy concerning the health of the traveller. Hence for buying a policy that covers you for your pre-existing medical conditions, you must do complete research about it in the insurance market before buying. An open discussion with the insurer about the complete terms and conditions of the policy and its coverage makes one buy the policy smarter.

The definition for travellers with already existing medical conditions varies from one insurance company to the other. Hence it should be advised to acquire a thorough knowledge of the policy document before purchasing one. This lists any complications that are present or expected to arise before the commencement of the journey. If the insured has been diagnosed with any ailment in the recent period (12 months), then that is a must to be included in the policy document before purchasing.

The working travel medical insurance policy in Singapore shows that, if the insured who is travelling to an overseas country experiences any sickness or meets with an accident, then that person can return to Singapore within 72 hours of the incident and can get medical assistance for free expenses. Whereas in a situation where the insured gets medical help overseas, then that person is given 30 days to recover his expenses as claimed as mentioned and agreed upon in the policy. If an individual is travelling alone then the best option for him is to opt for individual cover. But when you are travelling as a family then it is best advised to go for family insurance which supports everyone including children under the age of 18 years.

The choice of the best insurance plan depends on the nature of the trip. An annual insurance plan is more feasible if you are a regular traveller on almost a weekly basis. This makes it more cost-efficient as annual insurance covers round trips for 12 years. The restrictions to this are, when it comes to overseas travel, the trip cannot extend beyond 90 days at a stretch, and also there happens to be a restriction for a traveller who is aged above 70 years as they can buy only a single trip (Tan, 2017).

The Need for Insurance in Tourism

The need for insurance is very important in any risk management process. For a business that involves a risk management plan along with an emergency response plan in their business structure, there is a must for an insurance plan for its efficient working. The insurance plan of the company along with the risk management strategies, makes the decision regarding the hazards and assets to be insured and about the insurance policy that needs to be sold to its customers (Allingham, J. D., 2013). An important point to be noted is that buying insurance by the traveller will not reduce the occurrence of the risks or doesn't make the activities associated with it any safer than before. Insurance is a post-incident process. It acts mainly as a recovery of the process experienced by the traveller. This does not mean to say that all the customers will be willing to buy the insurance offered by the insurance company.

The types of activities that the travel company is involved in determine the decision-making concerning the purchase of travel insurance. To access the insurance policy obtained by the insured, he /she must carry the policy card along with them during the trip. A large number of properties are accumulated by travel companies who tend to protect their assets through insurance. The decision about whether to buy insurance or not completely depends on internal and external factors such as the quantity terms of coverages that can be purchased, the types and the associated terms and conditions of the insurance policy.

The internal factors also include the level of tolerance of risk that shows the measure of how much the owner is ready to take up the risk. It is very important to study how the insurance obtained by the insured complements the risk of tolerance experienced. Along with this, a keen observation needs to be put to see if business owners are exposed to the loss on a personal level or not, and if they are then they have capable measures to bear the losses experienced by them. Longevity is a very important factor to be taken into account when the business and business structure is studied to see if they provide supportive care to the owners and the assets of the company and the need for insurance is decided to keep in mind the studied business structure of the company. The last but one (the third) factor is to focus on the substitution cost of an asset. The final factor into consideration is the human resources and the shareholders of the company and also the moral and ethical issues of the company and its resources.

After the internal factors, it's now time to explore the external factors. And these statutory requirements also called for legal requirements along with the business requirements of the industry chosen. The insurance plan, the purchase of the insurance that was planned, reading and understanding the policy document of the insurance, maintaining the insurance policies throughout the year from starting till the end, building and maintaining good relationships with the customers and other firms, efficiently dealing with the claims, Building insurance expertise and the recordkeeping of the insurance-related documents, all of these combined form the insurance portfolio (Korstanje & George, 2015). The insurance portfolio also includes records of the accidents that happened during the period of consideration, information about the client, a medical questionnaire about the client, and the registration forms given to the insured at the beginning of the process (Taleski, 2011).

Travel Medical Insurance for Canadians

Travellers to Canada have a significantly high cost for their medical expenses. This makes travel medical insurance a necessity for those who are travelling to Canada. As per the reports of CBC's marketplace, it is seen that clients have coverage for certain risks when they don't own one (Allingham, J. D., 2013). It is believed that travel medical insurance is not just the responsibility of the patient or insured, but also the responsibility of the physicians who help the patients with the claiming process and the application process of the insurance at the initial stages. As physicians have an important role to play, they must stay up to date with travel insurance policies and coverages offered by the insurance company to support their patients.

The GHIP (Government health insurance plan) is an organization that lends a helping hand to travellers (Canadians) in terms of financial support in case of any emergencies while they are away from the country. They target the senior citizens of Canada because they tend to be more prone to suffer from injuries, sicknesses, or accidents of varying degrees. They provide immediate medical assistance to anything that they suffer even including the pre-medical conditions that necessarily may not be included in the policy bought by them. Multiple insurance firms are offering insurance to Canadian citizens for their medical expenses incurred during their travel to and from the country and also for domestic travel within the country. This shows that there are more than a dozen of travel insurance companies in specific that are present in Canada as it is a good area of business for Canadians. The sales made by CIBC as the applications and claims are directed to the Travel Insurance Coordinators (TIC). To name Medipac and Manulife are the two more ruling insurance firms in Canada and have gained significant popularity among the citizens of Canada. There are two types of travel insurance companies, and they are member-based and corporation based. They both work to maximize the profit of the shareholder in general (Allingham, 2013). The main method of the company trying to reduce their risk is to not cover the risks associated with the tourist's pre-existing conditions or accept those risks under special important qualifications. When there is an involvement of a physician in the travel insurance policy, he/she must understand the proper definition of the term "period" before the policy is activated, that is when the medical condition of the traveller who has taken up the insurance is very much in control and is stable. The standard period is for 3 months; however, it can vary from 2 months to one year. These 3 months are called the red zone which is a trouble-free period just before the policy is activated.

Analyzing the stability and control of any disorders can be done with the help of the medication proxy of risk. Any alteration which is done for the type of medication, format, dosage, and prescription and recommendation during the red-zone period, the period even before the insured period begins. The other proxies for stability and control that are relevant are emergencies of the symptoms, testing at the laboratory, and changes in the symptoms of the disorders. It is often assumed that all the applicants of the insurance policies pass the screening test (questions) where the insurance policy is converted into a contract between the insurer and the insured. It is not just a contract as it goes by word but is an agreement that both insurer and the insured come to terms with where the applicant (insurer/traveller) agrees to pay a premium amount for the insurance obtained by the traveller (Council et al., 2017). This is now successful after the agreement has been made and they can be covered by the traveller only when they are claimed under specified conditions.

There happen to be several ways where a person can be uninsured. For travellers with an already existing medical health, a thorough assessment of the individual premium set offered by all the insurance companies in the market must be evaluated to make a wise decision regarding the purchase of insurance at the cost of money and time (Allingham, J. D., 2013). By doing this the traveller will have all the required information at his fingertips. The other useful tip to make a wise decision is to sit along with a physician to complete the application process because, for those with an existing medical condition, it is an unacceptable risk to do it right away at the travel company or agent's office.

Travellers have the right to choose the insurer and it depends on their specific needs. A mixture of various risks that are acceptable along with the different variances that are present in the population and the rates are all required for a healthy and competitively based industry. For any travel insurance company to survive among the others in the market, clear-cut clarity and transparency are needed (Korstanje & George, 2015). These two characteristics are needed to maintain a good rapport and reputation with their clients. It is also one of the best solutions to avoid any sort of conflicts that can occur due to several legal and regulatory laws and actions (Allingham, 2013). In contrast to this, travel insurance in India is still not as popular and efficient as in Canada. This is surely expected to change in the coming future as the perceptions of travellers about travel insurance in India are set to change.

Ethical Dilemmas in the Leisure Business

The majority of travellers buy their travel tickets (e-tickets) online. One of the major reasons for this is because of the variety of discount rates offered for different destinations, schedules, and other additional services. In the airline industry, in particular, travel insurance is generally made available during the booking of air tickets. As a result of fraudulent activities, the Italian Antitrust Authority took major actions against Ryanair and Easyjet airlines with a fine of a large amount. These airline companies who are known for their low-cost travel were in the limelight for lack of transparency about their travel insurance options on their websites (Council et al., 2017). The core problem in transparency was that it did not specify the types of risks that are going to be covered when one takes their travel insurance policy. Several proceedings from January 2013 were concluded with administrative sanctions after numerous complaints from the different associations and customers who opted for their travel insurance policy. When matching as per the breach of laws, articles 20 and 22 of the consumer code were violated. The type of insurance that the company offered to their client was not to be seen mentioned on their website, also the number of exclusions in the policy document that they offered was not mentioned. As an outcome of this, there happened to be very minimal knowledge about the policy procedures and rules among its clients, especially when the policy was bought online. This was a serious issue because the number of exclusions on the medical expenses was almost twice as costly as the value of money of the insurance. There happened to be extra service charges at the airport that the travellers have to pay and they had no idea about it until they reached the airport because they thought these charges were already covered in the travel insurance policy already covered by them. These misleading strategies adopted by the two airlines made it very difficult for travellers to travel via their services and eventually made them lose their trust in their brand.

One of the strategies that Ryanair followed to compel its clients to buy their travel was to make it impossible to deselect the travel insurance option that came along with the booking of tickets. But as an escape from this trap, the travellers had to completely stop themselves from insuring at all by selecting the option that they don't wish to insure themselves. Such commercial practices followed by the airline were very much cruel and disrespectful to its client's liberty. Article (23) of the constitution states that there must be a complete form of transparency and certainty regarding the optional prices. In other words, there has to be an open mode of communication during the booking of their tickets. Customers should be given a choice to select their travel insurance and there must be no compulsion to or their choices. The refunds claimed by the customers are no longer an easy process because of such practices adopted by the airline company (Council et al., 2017). The money that was spent by the clients on compulsion was used by the company to pay off the expenses that were incurred by them to run the airline company. The certification cost was usually much higher than the insurance cost. The other illegal practices that airline companies adopted were to charge the telephonic conversation between the customers and customer-care support to the customers while the call was made to talk about the reimbursement of their cash. This came to an end after most of them claimed reimbursement of their money (Korstanje & George, 2015). Due to the adoption of such complex and fraudulent profit-making strategies that are in place for the reimbursement process, the number of travellers who opt for this option of reimbursement are very low in recent times. The economic and social inflation of the final cost of tickets is due to closed communication between airline companies and their customers. Most of the time the clients are not so sure of the traps they are put into by the airline companies because of their money-making motives. As a lesson learned by the EasyJet Company, they started having a system of booking airline tickets which were very transparent between them and the customers. They adopted an easy process for refunding as well. With these measurements in place by the airline industry, there has been the very little place for any misleading practices with the firm (Berti & Stramacci, 2014).

Advantages of World-of-Mouth

The short form of World of Mouth is eWOM. It is the most common determining factor of different behaviours of consumers. In other words, word of mouth can be defined as the interest showcased by the consumer in a product of the company by bringing it up in his or her everyday conversation. In the tourism industry, eWOM is studied by studying the characteristics of hotels and other accommodation facilities in tourist spots.

Volume and Valence are used to determine the measurement of the word of mouth. These matrices measure the number and nature of messages that are volume and valence respectively. These matrices can be positive, negative, or neutral depending upon the nature of the messages. The number of sales is determined by the volume of the message. The purchase of any product is mostly ruled by the negative value of eWOM. The positive value of eWOM has very little effect on its volume. Utilitarian products are benefited from this negative bias such as the insurance from the insurance company because when the customers plan to buy utilitarian products (insurance) they tend to go more by the negative reviews of the product than the positive ones. The other factor that determines the word of mouth is the matric of density. It is the ratio of the customers that post an insurance company review, (i) in the time (x) to the customers that had already purchased the travel insurance from the same company (i) in the same time (x). This ratio clearly shows the extent to which a product or service has succeeded and failed in the market (P.A & F.W, 2002).

The SquareMouth.com (e-commerce) company has developed a new strategy, which lets the buyers of the insurance compare the travel insurance in the market and then lets them decide to buy the insurance. This made the company outshine the market. This strategy showed that the sales of any travel insurance are mainly dependent on the review of the customers than anything else (Council et al., 2017). In a nutshell, the sales of travel insurance are directly proportional to the number of reviews of the product (insurance). This also at the same time states that when the negativity of the product performance increases (negative reviews), the sales of the same decrease. Therefore, word of mouth negatively impacts greatly the decision-making process of the customers whether to buy the product or not (Amblee, 2015).

Travel Insurance and E-Portal

The satisfaction of the customers is the driving factor in e-portal services. They can be enhanced by focusing on areas such as making easy access to customers on their web page, easy availability of the information of the products such as prices, fast loading of the website, and simple booking steps. All of this would uncomplicate the customer's work of buying travel insurance online (Werthner & Ricci, 2004). Travel insurance has gained an immense amount of popularity in today's world. Every person who travels knows how important insurance is for them. This paves a clear route for the success of e-travel strategies that are budding up in the market. This mainly focuses on an easy life for a person who chooses travel insurance during their travel where any financial loss is recovered by the settlements of refunds. The USA is the major buyer of travel insurance through an e-portal. But in the future, this is expected to decline and there happens to be a rise in the numbers among Asians. In another 5 years, India is going to top the Asian countries who are going to opt for travel insurance, especially for e-portal services (Jeniffer & Chandran, 2016).

E-Portal Customer Satisfaction

Customer contentment is an essential factor when it comes to both insurance and e-portal services. Customer contentment is composed of Attitudes toward the customer, Assurance towards the customer, and Awareness of the customer. The attitudes within the e-portal services tend to evolve over a while. The way of issuing the insurance and the security measures towards its customers and knowledge of accessibility all comprise the attitude of the e-portal insurance (Cave et al., 2016). The customer's attitude towards the e-portal includes the purchase and knowledge of internet usage to buy the insurance policy. It also includes transactional services, and the easy methods of downloads show the attitude of consumers towards e-portal usage in buying travel insurance.

There is a loyalty factor that is very important on an e-portal platform. The main base for marketing e-business is the e-portal. Loyalty along with assurance and reliability is very important in e-portal services. The cost of the product has a direct proportionality with the quality of the product (Jennifer & Chandran, 2016). The more the cost paid the higher the quality of the product. The root of customer contentment is the assurance provided by the insurance company via the e-portal (technology). Reliability is related to the end-user security measures and earning the trust of its customer is known as assurance that is provided by the production company when one buys the product (insurance).

Awareness is a very important part of e-portal customer satisfaction. Awareness of the product and its associated terminologies is very important to deal with problems that arise in terms of claims and customer conflicts (Korstanje & George, 2015). Having faith is very important to the insurer and their products. This comes from building everlasting healthy relationships between them both. Trust is a guiding principle for having and providing good customer satisfaction. This trust comes from having an agreement between them both which asks them to abide by certain rules and regulations. This, in turn, means that there is no gap or hiding between the coverages or exclusions in the policy documents and there is transparent communication between them both. The insurance is mainly done as an alternative that a person or a traveller can depend on when the unfortunate occurs, hence keeping this in mind it is very much necessary to have that trust factor between both. All of this makes customer awareness an important measure of e-portal travel insurance for the best results and to reap all the benefits for both parties (Jennifer & Chandran, 2016).

There is constant and upward growth of the insurance policy in the travel and tourism department. Especially in the 21st century, there has been rapid growth in this industry. They offer a variety of different insurance products and services. There are a lot of mixed and combined forms of travel insurance available in the market these days (Werthner & Ricci, 2004). The risk factors are many during a trip. The demographic regions of the place of travel contribute a lot towards the risks in international travel. The social and health state of a person is a very important criterion to determine the type of risks one can be subjected to. Insurance is a must for people who are pregnant and are travelling (Larsen, S., 2007).

The risk of travel in countries like Malaysia which is the topmost tourist attractive country depends completely on a regulatory framework that is adopted by them. Hence, this kind of policy is purchased by travellers at the early stage of booking to abide by the rules of the country. This is done by the Malaysian government as they care for the lives of their tourists (Hasan & Abdullah, 2014).

Travel Insurance in the Future

EMEA

EMEA is the region that is the most famous for taking travel insurance. Bharath, in his paper, shows that travel insurance companies have a set of separate strategies for giving their customers specialized and custom-made travel insurance. There has been immense growth in travel insurance policy companies in Europe, more than in any other region in the world. There are a lot of emerging and budding vendors in the market who happen to use a direct form of the route into the travel industry to introduce their new products. Because of this, there are a lot of efficient methods of travel insurance methods (Cave et al., 2016). Age is the major driving factor of the insurance company, the popularity, and sales of travel insurance increase as and when elderly people find the motivation to travel around. In countries like Europe and Africa, with a population of seven hundred and forty-two million, there are about one hundred and forty-eight million people of age above 70 years. Hence most of the travel companies in EMEA are having the elderly population as their target for increasing their business (Research, 2016).

APAC

The target for the travel insurance policy in the Asia Pacific region is the growing middle-class population. The ever-increasing population rate in the APAC region, especially India is a boon to these companies. Countries like China and Australia which are major contributors to the GDP growth of the economy are the countries that the travel insurance companies are now targeting to increase their profit. E-portals are quite familiar in these countries to buy any kind of insurance, travel insurance in particular. Most travel insurance companies use banks as a medium to sell their products because people have more trust in banks in general and travel companies tend to take advantage of this. Airlines are another form of medium to sell travel insurance products by travel companies (Research, 2016).

Americas

The American population gives a lot of importance to vacations as a stress buster for them in their hectic work and business life. Travel insurance companies in America take advantage of this trend. The population is more excited to take up high-risk activities in their vacations which makes the travel company take further advantage of this to sell off their products. This lifestyle of Americans when they set out on a vacation makes it very easy for the travel industry to come up with varieties of travel insurance policies to match the needs of their clients (Research, 2016).

Profiling

An assessment of risk, which ensures an event during the event of unfortunate happenings such as accidents. It also includes a claim from a risk that has been insured by the insurance company to the insured. When profiling of risk is done it is nothing but the cost that would be charged for insuring that particular risk by the insurer. There are a lot of parameters in varying concentrations that are used to assess any form of risk by motor insurance companies (Cave et al., 2016). Risk profiling is usually done by the travel insurance company for their insurers. The risk profile built by them heavily depends on expertise, intelligence, technologies, and the assistance provided by the country. The expertise is more about having a good set of manpower working on the travel security of the travellers. Intelligence, on the other hand, is all about mitigating the anticipated risks at the planning phase of the travel and thereby reacting to them, keeping in mind the safety of the travellers (Larsen, S., 2007). The technology part of the risk profiling process depends on the intervention of the travel before the travel such as the online authorization process, the communication process in case an unfortunate event occurs, tracking of the whereabouts of the traveller including their mobile networks and debit/credit card transactions and the feedback from the customers. The final part of the risk profiling is the assistance provided in the destination country which includes medical care, transportation services, etc (Unger, 2015). Risk profiling in a travel organization makes its decision regarding profiling keeping in mind the best-leading safety strategies. While creating a profile, the major concern that is focused is on the threats that are potential to a traveller and the finance that takes to cover if a catastrophe occurs (PIAM, 2017).

Conclusion

By doing the literature review two important criteria regarding the perception of the traveller towards the buying of travel insurance and risk coverages can be seen. The first one is that the purchase of traveller insurance from the buyer completely depends on their trustworthiness, the understanding of the importance of travel insurance for the traveller, and the knowledge of travel insurance. The exchange of travel insurance between the insurer and the buyer for money completely depends on the attitude toward the perception of risk. The selling of travel insurance to the insured is all about the convincing capabilities of the travel insurance company. The purchase of travel insurance by travellers mainly depends on two things, firstly the traveller is aware of the need for travel insurance during their travel and then secondly, they buy it as an obligation. However, the actual reason is not known yet. This may largely depend on the trustworthiness of the company or the type of travel insurance policy that the insured will purchase.

References

Allingham, J. D. (2013). *Travel Medical Insurance.* 819-822.

Amblee, N. (2015). The impact of eWOM density on sales of travel insurance, *Annals of Tourism Research,* 56, 137–140, Indian Institute of Management, Kozhikode, India, Elsevier publication.

Babu, K. V., Gade, J. (2014). *Tourism in India.* 1-18.

Berti, I., & Stramacci, D. (2014). *Travel Insurance: Misleading Practices on Airline*. 229-230.

Cave, M. R., Schatz, S., Wolff, B. S. (2016). *Insurance.* 69-149.

Council, W. T. (2017). *The Economic Impact of Travel and Tourism March 2017.* Inside Cover: Prince Regent National Park, Australia - NASA. Retrieved from IBEF.

Hasan, A. A., & Abdullah, N. C. (2015). Compulsory travel insurance in Malaysia: some regulatory considerations. *Procedia-Social and Behavioral Sciences,* 172, 344-351. https://doi.org/10.1016/j.sbspro.2015.01.375.

Henderson, J. C. (2015). *Tourism Recreation Research.* Population Ageing Tourism and Travel Insurance, 79-82, Ontario.

Huang, L., & Tsai, H. T. (2003). The study of senior traveler behavior in Taiwan. *Tourism management,* 24(5), 561-574. https://doi.org/10.1016/S0261-5177(03)00008-6.

Jeniffer, M. S., & Chandran, A. (2016). Impact of e-travel insurance platforms on customization ventures: An explorative reportage. *International Journal on Global Business Management & Research,* 5(2), 8-15.

Korstanje, M. E., & George, B. P. (2015). What does insurance purchase behavior say about risks? A study in the Argentine context with special focus on travel insurance. *International Journal of Disaster Resilience in the Built Environment.* https://doi.org/10.1108/IJDRBE-09-2012-0030.

Larsen, S. (2007). Aspects of a Psychology of the Tourist Experience. *Scandinavian Journal of Hospitality and Tourism,* 7-18.

Lawton, G., & Page, S. (1997). Evaluating travel agents' provision of health advice to travelers. *Tourism management,* 18(2), 89-104. https://doi.org/10.1016/S0261-5177(96)00104-5.

Leggat, P. A., & Leggat, F. W. (2002). Travel insurance claims made by travelers from Australia. *Journal of Travel Medicine,* 9(2), 59-65.

Leggat, P. A., Carne, J., & Kedjarune, U. (1999). Travel insurance and health. *J Travel Med,* 6(4), 243-248.

Schindler, K. J. (2005, July). Travel counseling for the elderly traveler. In *Nursing forum* (Vol. 40, No. 3, pp. 107-115). Malden, USA: Blackwell Publishing Inc. https://doi.org/10.1111/j.1744-6198.2005.00015.x

Travel and Tourism Competitiveness Report (2017) Industry trends. World economic forum. Retrieved from Industry trends: http://reports.weforum.org/travel-and-tourism- competitiveness-report-2017/industry-trends/.

Werthner, H., & Ricci, F. (2004). E-commerce and tourism. *Communications of the ACM,* 47(12), 101-105.

Chapter 3

Struggling to Move: The Effects of COVID-19 and the Radical Transformation of Tourism, Argentina as a Case Study

Maximiliano E. Korstanje*
Department of Economics, Buenos Aires, Argentina

Abstract

At the end of December 2019, a new virus outbreak baptized by scientists as COVID-19 (SARS-CoV2) paralyzed global commerce generating millionaire losses in the world. The virus was rapidly disseminated to the western cities through international travel and the tourism industry, a problem which led governments to cancel international flights while closing the airspace. The WHO (World Health Organization) recommended energetically the imposition of strict lockdowns and keeping social distancing as two valid forms to mitigate the pandemic. In the question of months, the virus wreaked havoc in the main economies of the world grinding the tourism and hospitality industries to an unparalleled halt. To put things straight, to date, more than 37 million people have been infected and one million have perished. Afrgentina, a southern Latin American country, which adopted a stricter and longer lockdown in the beginning, was gradually escalating to seventh place in the number of infected people (894.206) seconded by Peru and France. The socio-economic effects of COVID-19 on the tourism industry are not only manifold and complex but also denote a multifaceted dynamic. While some voices have alerted on the urgency to develop more resilient and eco-friendly forms of consumption, others have emphasized the need of changing the current research towards multidisciplinary methods. In

* Corresponding Author's Email: mkorst@palermo.edu.

In: Tourism in Crisis
Editors: M.E. Korstanje, V. GB Gowreesunkar and S.W. Maingi
ISBN: 979-8-88697-643-4

the pre-pandemic days, tourists were valorized as an ambassador of "civilization," real global knights widely admired and objects of curiosity while nowadays tourists are negatively seen as potential enemies or carriers of a mortal disease, so to speak widely feared and demonized as never before. In this context, the present chapter discusses conceptually the effects and changes of the tourism industry in Argentina, particularly but with some broad strokes that illustrate the ways the industry is changing in the world.

Keywords: tourism, travel behaviour, fear, COVID-19, pandemic, feudalization process

Introduction

The end of December was the moment that exactly marked the start of a nightmare for policy-makers, specialists and professionals in the tourism and hospitality industries. The outbreak of a new version of SARS –SARSCOv2- known as COVID-19 (Coronavirus disease) shocked and paralyzed global trade affecting negatively some service sectors like hospitality, tourism, recreation, restaurants, theatres, events and festivals only to name a few (Prayag, 2020; Prideaux, Thompson & Pavel 2020). The paradox lies in the fact the industry served not only as a facilitator of the contagion but at the same time operated for a rapid recovery in a post-pandemic context. Worried by the fast dissemination accelerated by international travel and tourism, governments unilaterally disposed of countless restrictive measures associated with the closure of borders and airspace. These steps were unfortunately accompanied by a strict lockdown to impede the free circulation of streets (Sigala, 2020; Rogerson & Baum, 2020). The WHO (World Health Organization) extended a set of suggestions which oscillated from social distancing to the wearing of masks. Despite these initiatives, in the question of months, the pandemic wreaked havoc in the largest economies of the world grinding tourism to an unparalleled halt. To put things straight, to date, more than 37 million people have been infected and almost one million have invariably perished. Among the most affected countries, we have the US (219.933 victims) followed by Brazil (150.555), India (109.894), Mexico (83.781), the UK (42.875), Italy (36.000), Spain (33.124), Peru (33.305), France (32.779), and Argentina (27.000) only to new a few.

In the mid of this mayhem, the present chapter narrates and describes the case of Argentina, a Southern Latin American country which initiated a strict and long lockdown which affected its socio-political administration, if not gradually escalating in the number of infected cases and victims positioning in the seventh-place seconding Peru and France. This point suggests not only do we have much to learn from this virus but also the future of tourism remains –at least- uncertain. To some extent, the lack of standardized protocols or programs by the side of WHO obscured the medical diagnoses and programs of control. At the same time, each country encouraged assorted –but different- measures to mitigate the pandemic. Beyond this controversy, it is noteworthy that a whole portion of global economies slumped down because of COVID-19 creating serious durable effects. To cut the long story short, COVID-19 led the tourism industry towards its worse crisis in history (Radic et al. 2020).

Let's comment to readers that the paper was mainly organized into three parts. In the first section, we discuss the interplay between virus outbreaks and tourism, the ebbs and flows of literature as well as its strengths and weaknesses. The second section is reserved to evaluate a methodological discussion and sampling details. The third and fourth sections enumerate the research results, limitations and challenges for a Post COVID tourism industry.

Tourism and Virus Outbreaks

Initial Discussion

Over recent days, tourism-related scholars devoted their efforts and attention to deciphering the complexity and dynamic of the phenomenon evaluating to what extent the industry has possibilities to subsist (Zheng, Hog & Wen 2020). Theories and works revolving around the effects of COVID-19 on the tourist system abound but they can be very well classified into two clear-cut families. Some studies alert on the need of developing more resilient and eco-friendly destinations to resolve the problem of climate change (Gossling, Scott 6 Hall, 2020; Prayag, 2020; Prideaux, Thompson & Pabel, 2020). Other voices acknowledge the urgency to embrace new multidisciplinary research to overcome the next obstacles (Wen, Wang & Kozak 2020; Wen et al. 2020). It is important not to lose sight of the fact that the discipline cultivated a strange fascination for the figure of the tourist as a key player of the system while probably other agents have been relegated to the dust of oblivion. Scholars certainly acknowledge –citing A. Franklin- that the tourist-centricity which stems from the economic-based paradigm- has some problems to study tourism in a world without tourists. The question whether of John Urry (1992) imagined "the tourist gaze" as a motivational force of global capitalism (consumption), the COVID-19 sets the pace for a new feudal world where a new version of this tourist gaze prevails. We have dubbed this the "wicked gaze" to symbolize the demonizing process and hostility shown against foreign –if not Chinese or Asian- tourists in the West. In the days earlier than the virus outbreak tourists were esteemed as "ambassadors of peace and prosperity" whereas now they are seen as "ambassadors of the disaster," potential carriers of a fatal disease (Korstanje 2020).

Having said this, the present chapter explores the substantial changes in the tourism industry in Argentina while laying the foundations towards a new radical understanding of the role played by the alterity in the stage of new normality.

As the previous backdrop, the term pandemic is often associated with the presence of infectious disease, most probably because of a virus outbreak, which cannot be contained and rapidly expands to infect people in multiple continents and countries. Pandemics usually made significant changes in culture and the economic organization of society. History witnesses how pandemics not only accelerate conquests but also the rise of chauvinist expressions and nationalism. The radical transformations of pandemics open the doors to new situations and contexts. In this context, scholars should trace back to the history of pandemics to mitigate their negative aftermaths (Hall, Scott & Gossling, 2020). The nature of crisis often captivates the attention of scholarship on some risks while relegating other major risks (Hall 2010), in which case a clear diagnosis of the situation is always due. As Cass Sunstein (2005) puts it, the term risk is a concept very hard to grasp but also human emotions distort the causalities of tragedies. We are educated to maximize some minor risks –echoing our emotions- while others are minimized. The net of experts, jointly with the authorities, should make future decisions with a firm basis in scientific reports. The role of activists, and pressure groups should be at least undermined. In a hyper-connected and globalized world, the virus travels with us. Needless to say that this applies very well to the virus outbreak and spreading of COVID-19, which today affects not only the tourism industry but also global commerce as never before (Qiu, et al. 2020; Sheller 2020; Gossling, Scott & Hall, 2020; Zenker & Kock, 2020; Higgins-Desbiolles, 2020). What is more important, this global emergency evinces the urgency to adopt new strategies and methods leading the current epistemology towards a more hybridized form, or so to speak a multidisciplinary perspective

(Gretzel et. al 2020). Furthermore, affordable digital technologies allow new forms of virtual tourism where social contact and physical movements are dispensable. If the future of tourism research was originally marked by technology no less true is that COVID-19 potentiates interesting novel fields of exploration in Artificial intelligence (Zeng, Chen & Lew, 2020), information technologies (Xian, Fesenmaier, Werthner 2020; Cai, Mckenna & Wassler 2020), virtual tourism (Kwok & Koh, 2020; Sigala 2020) and so forth.

Tourism, Mobilities and Virus Outbreaks

As the previous argument is given, the high levels of mobility which characterized global capitalism pave the ways for innovation and economic progress but at the same time shortens travel timeframe. This means that far-away geographical points can be touched in hours, a fact that probably revolutionized the travel industry. To some extent, the same means of transport which energize the global economy act as carriers of the virus (Hall 2010; Korstanje 2019). Social distancing, as well as the closure of borders and international travel, was a radical measure adopted by almost all governments leading the industry next to collapse (Gretzel et al. 2020; Fernando 2020). As Bob McKercher (2003) puts it, the world should be prepared to face a great variety of virus outbreaks resulting from the global expansion of tourism without mentioning the overcrowded cities and the current conditions of life in urban areas. Different studies have eloquently documented the impacts of SARS and H1N1 on the tourism industry and local economies worldwide (McKercher 2003; McKercher & Chon, 2004; Monterrubio 2010; Novelli, et al. 2018). In this perspective, experts call attention to developing reliable methods of research which help policymakers to mitigate the effects of pandemics, reducing not only the global threats but also giving some insight into the sensibility of the industry to pandemics. As above discussed, the cancellation of international travel and tourism activity seems not to be new, similar measures have been promoted in past outbreaks such as SARS or Swine Flu. This happens simply because tourism rests on a philosophical paradox. At the same time, the industry needs social contact and mobilities to prosper in the same way the virus is widely disseminated. Killing the virus means killing tourism (Jamal & Budke, 2020; Nepal 2020). In consequence, countless administrations dispose of border closures, and the suspension of commercial activities to protect their respective health systems. What is equally important, those economies which depend exclusively on tourism are more affected than others which are more diversified. This is exactly one of the troubling aspects of lockdowns in classic tourist destinations (Mariolis, Rodousakis, & Soklis, 2020; Polyzos, Samitas & Spyridou 2020). The dimension of the crisis varies by country and economy. The effects are particularly different in the First and the Third worlds. While scholars in the global North have taken an active position in writing theoretical essay reviews to expand the current understanding of the impacts, in the global South fieldworkers are limited to evaluate specific study cases giving the flesh to the bones (Niewiandomski 2020; Karim et al. 2020; Edwards 2020). The urgency of under-developing economies to stop the contagion while leaving the lockdown was of vital importance for the survival of the tourism industry (Karim et al. 2020). Rogerson & Rogerson (2020) analyze the socioeconomic impacts of COVID-19 on the African economies. Centring on South Africa as a main study case, they allude to the idea that some spaces of vulnerability created by persistent inequalities bear serious material losses because of the pandemic. To put the same bluntly, these so-called areas of vulnerability depend exclusively on tourism to control poverty. In the same way, those metropolitan areas which adopt tourism as the main actors are not only more vulnerable but face the most devastating effects leading the industry toward an unparalleled crisis. In consonance with this, Gaffney & Eeckles (2020) affirm that those countries dependable on the tourism economy are more sensitive to the negative effects of a global quarantine or the closure of borders. Tourists are vivid agents of prosperity and economic wealth fare for some under-developing countries but at the same time the carriers of the virus. This creates a contradictory situation which is very hard to resolve. To expand the understanding of this quandary, the authors suggest the enumeration of low and high-risk countries affected by the pandemic. In consonance with this, Farzanegan et al. (2020) hold the thesis that those nations characterized by high levels of mobility are prone to experience more deaths and infected cases than low-mobile countries. Those economies dotted with inbound and outbound international travel had serious problems coping with the virus outbreak. The denial to close airports, borders and airspace aggravated the situation accelerating inevitable mass contamination. To wit, Sah et al. (2020) validate these assumptions in Nepal while Korstanje (2020) proffers the case of Argentina where thousands of tourists stranded abroad were expatriated to Buenos Aires. In Nepal, the virus placed the health and tourist industry in jeopardy increasing the health budget to 6% for the coming fiscal year (Sah et al. 2020). In Argentina, the tourism industry went through a paralleled crisis which slumped down almost 80% of accommodation offers. At a closer look, tourists are being demonized and suspected to disseminate the virus whereas chauvinist and racist expressions against neighbouring migrants emerged in the core of metropolitan Buenos Aires (Korstanje 2020). To the devastating economic effects of COVID-19, scholars claim that new racist expressions or discourse against Chinese communities have been brought into the foreground. Racism situates as a major danger not only to human rights but also to the future of tourism (Yu et al. 2020; Carr 2020). The incipient literature seems to be clear about the untrammelled expressions of a much deeper hostility against Chinese tourists in western cities (Park, Kim & Kim 2020; Zheng, Hoh & Wen 2020). Sometimes these discourses are affirmed by misleading news about foreign tourists while in other long-dormant geopolitical disputes or rivalries –among neighbouring countries- are certainly revived. The present chapter discusses the different discourses of tourism staff, tourists most of them stranded abroad or expatriated who were forced to come back to their homes because of the pandemic. This descriptive research should be understood in the limits of an exploratory approach and course not extrapolated to other universes. Anyway, we are confident the results are illustrative and innovative.

Methodology

On 20 March 2020, Argentinean President Alberto Fernandez ordered the lockdown closing not only borders, public transport and commercial activity but airspace. In consequence, thousands of Argentinean tourists were stranded in the world, pressing the Ministry of Foreign Affairs to conduct a program of repatriation at a higher cost absorbed by the government. The presidential decision included not only the cancellation of flights but the closure of universities, schools and public edifices generating serious economic impacts. At the same time, the government bailed out many corporations absorbing part of the workers´ salaries. Many hotels were recycled as hospitals to give attention to infected patients with mild symptoms. These measures were similar in the entire world less -for this case- some Argentines turned a deaf ear to the presidential decree flying abroad in the lapse of time between the ends of March to May of 2020. As a result of the restrictive measures, thousands of Argentinean tourists were stranded abroad while foreign tourists who spent their time vacationing were trapped in the country. In social media, foreign tourists and expatriates were demonized as potential carriers of the virus while popular opinion claimed Alberto Fernandez to adopt stricter steps of control at airports and borders. In this way, police –supported by migration officers- were encouraged to scrutinize travellers who potentially violate the lockdown. All incoming visitors who come from Brazil, the US or Europe should be confined to 14 days of lockdown. The first point of entry in this discussion appears to be the figure of the tourist as a new *undesired guest.* The question of whether John Urry coined the term tourist-gaze to denote the rise of a new form of consumption based on ocularcentrism sets the pace to a new conception, where gazing was simply banned. This was called a "wicked gaze" (Korstanje 2020). The "Other" is any more an object of curiosity in these new times; rather it is a clear source that inspires hostility and fear. Doubtless, the right of traveling in the territory was temporarily suspended while the country plunged into a state of chaos where the provinces (States) closed their internal frontiers. The lack of standardized protocols and programs of mitigation associated with an extreme panic led governors to adopt different measures which oscillated from new requisitions and documents to the rejection of Argentinean travellers coming from other states. To date, almost 4.000 persons are stranded in the borders between Chaco and Formosa. In the days of COVID-19 the provincial borders, at least as they are drawn in the law, suffered radical transformations. We come across a type of feudalization process which suggests a political condition of segregation where units move with autonomy respecting the central administration. COVID-19 ignited a feudalization process marked not only by racism and chauvinism but for separatism. This, so to speak, goes from barricades to migratory expenses and restrictions for the entrance of outsiders, a point considered unconstitutional by experts. Each Province (state) not only reserved the rights of police but surely contradicted the constitution, each one regulated the borders at their discretion. States such as San Luis, San Juan and Mendoza banned the entrance of other Argentinean tourists and travellers. Only food transport, which was tightly scrutinized, was permitted to enter to leave out the state during the day. The Province of Formosa remains impermeable to receive travellers –no matter their profession- even to date. Some lawsuits were presented before the Supreme Court of Justice because of the unconstitutionality of travel-ban local dispositions. Hundreds of Argentinean tourists, drivers and travellers were stranded in Provinces for months without assistance, shelter or food. In other cases, drivers were subject to strict protocols of control and surveillance. In the third stage, some states, which were pressed to boost their local economies through the tourism industry, opened their frontiers but with strict travel bans or migratory requisitions. Whereas visitors should present the respective COVID test certifying they are healthy, other requirements such as an all-inclusive tour or round-trip tickets without mentioning a certificate of residence or health insurance for travels were strongly requested upon arrival. In normal conditions, all these noted measures are requisitions for travelling abroad but hitherto applied for domestic tourists.

In this chapter, we employ the neologism *of pandemic tourism* to denote the decision or curiosity to travel to destinations seriously affected by COVID-19 and other pandemics. *Pandemic tourism* should be understood as a new trend of tourists who travel to zones affected by pandemics or highly infected by the virus(es) to get an outstanding experience. Although the results of this research should not be extrapolated to other scenarios, no less true is that they apply to other study cases associated with SARS, H1N1 or Ebola. Methodologically speaking, we have selected 55 participants (from 25 to 55 years old) divided among 30 males and 25 females. The participants were organized into two samples: a) those who have been stranded abroad by tourism or for working purposes (i.e. pilots, cruise workers, postgraduate students and businessmen, only to name a few) and b) those who voluntarily overlooked the risks of COVID19 and started a journey abroad ignoring the presidential decree. Both were named cluster A and cluster B. The Snowball method was used as the main criterion of sampling. Because of confidentiality issues, the real names of the interviewed people have been changed. It is important to mention that the obtained outcomes, far from being extrapolated to other universes, should be understood within the limits of the sample.

Findings and Discussions

Because of the lockdown remains, personal meetings –or face-to-face interviews- are not allowed in Argentina. Hence, the used method was snowball while the interviews were conducted through Zoom and Skype. Both samples keep commonalities and serious differences. The first common-thread point in both samples is "the fear of being infected by COVID-19 abroad." This suggests the impossibility to receive the correct medical support and follow-up, in a foreign country. Claudio (male, 27 years old) is a flight attendant and says "*I have a great experience in travelling and particularly I am not afraid to be sick out of Argentina, but in this case, I was terrified to think in the odds of being infected by COVID-19. If you ask me, hospitals and health system in the UK suddenly collapsed and the information was poor, we know nothing when and under what conditions we would return home.*" A similar testimony is found in Maria (female 39 years old) who works as a historian and was surprised while attending to a Conference in Spain: "*I was surely terrified when Covid19 spread; we had neither information to the details of flight to Buenos Aires nor any idea if the government will open the airspace to allow our repatriation. What is worse, all this resembles a horror history and apocalyptic genre where the bottom days are around the corner.*"

In sharp contrast to panic sentiment, those who flew after the lockdown showed a manifest indifference to "Coronavirus disease" which was accompanied by political hostility against President Fernandez. Carlos (male, 37 years old), who works as an agricultural engineer, travelled to Paris accompanied by his sons:

> "I have no fear, this is an invention of China and the media to paralyze the industry in the West, this is like little flu which is being magnified by journalism. I do not share the decision of President Fernandez to close the airspaces, I have rights, and have the right to move as I want, from here to there, he is a dictator and this virus allowed him to impose a regime in my country. I made the decision to travel anyway and I am proud of that, this is an act of resistance!

The second element, which distinguishes the two samples, is the worries about losing the job or the company falling into bankruptcy. Interviewed participants in cluster A showed a much deeper concern about being laid off once returned home. This sentiment is particularly observed in tourism or hospitality workers. As Joaquin eloquently remarks:

> "Unemployment is one of my greatest fears, I am a tour operator in Buenos Aires, and COVID-19 evinces the end of tourism. The lockdown not only limits public circulation but also mobilities and tourism. The system should face a serious crisis, probably like we have in 2001 in Argentina. Thousands and Thousands of Argentineans will be impoverished because of COVID-19. The government should assist rapidly in the industry and implement efficient policies of recovery... the enemy is not the virus but poverty.

Rather, in cluster B, the worries stem from the possibility to weaken the democratic institutions taken advantage of the fear, the crisis generates. Fabiana (female, 27 years old) utters: "*I am afraid of the Argentine government, not the virus. The fear, this government is manipulating, facilitates things to undermine the check and balance forces that make democracy strong, Fernandez wants to impose fear and the lockdown because his policies are not to be widely rejected. Like in the case of terrorism, where the "terrorist" is demonized to impose economic policies that in other circumstances will be rejected, now Fernandez is adopting the lockdown to impoverish the private sector and in this way, introducing Chavism expropriating private fortunes, and properties (like in Venezuela now in Argentina).*

Both testimonies agree poverty caused by the economic crisis is an important factor of COVID-19, but they differ in their reactions. Fabiana seems to adopt a partisan (if not ideological) position blaming President Alberto Fernandez for the crisis, while Joaquin signals the risks of collapse in the tourism industry as well as service sectors. For both something is in danger. Joaquin alludes to the economic factor while Fabiana to the democratic institutions.

The third factor of analysis appears to be linked to the need to feel special experiences. Like in post-disaster or dark tourism, there is a segment of thrill-seekers who move to zones of disaster, war or conflict only to feel outstanding experiences. Almost 10 participants of cluster A replied that they were suddenly trapped after March and never would fly abroad after the lockdown while 12 in Cluster B were enthused to travel to understand what was happening in the world. This is the case of Juan (male, 45 years old), a sociologist, who acknowledged that:

> "COVID-19 offers an apocalyptic scenario where things will not be normal any longer, this is an outstanding time, I loved to live. I am not frightened to travel abroad, I needed to be closer to this dark experience I needed to feel the adrenaline to be in destinations highly infected by COVID-19. My first destination was China, preferably Wuhan but it was impossible, so I bought a ticket towards New York. I am not an unconscious guy... this historical event should be lived with great intensity!.

Instead, Adriana (a postgraduate student) offered a different viewpoint: "these are sad days, I was studying anthropology in Australia when this happens. I thought I would never come back to my country, to be with my parents and sisters. This event will change me forever I will not see travel and tourism, in the same way, I loved to travel and study worldwide, understand other cultures and nations, and be in contact with different people. Now, I have suffered from insomnia, and some irrational phobias to take a bus or a train. I stay at home now, and probably will be a long time without planning holidays.

Another interesting sub-cluster, which we have not typified in this note of research is reserved for the expatriates –which means professionals -who even if working abroad- opted the decision to come back to Argentina. This is the case of Emanuel who is the hotel´s concierge in Portugal. He gives a romantic answer when this interviewer asked for what he felt once expatriated.

> "Difficult to say I am sad, the feelings on my side are mixed ... I decided to study tourism in Europe and this goal was successfully achieved, but COVID-19 allowed me to come back to my home. Believe me, though you work hard, you will be never a European guy. An expatriate feels a half side is emptied, you are happy with your achievements but here is not your home, they do not speak your tongue, and they do not think like you, after all, you will be always a stranger. I note my compatriots are very tough when they return to Argentina. They come back temporarily on holidays or to visit friends and take a lodge at a hotel or rent a car. They scornfully treat badly to the staff, often comparing the service in a third-world country with first-world ones. To your question, I must confess, now I reckon they are hostile to them because they hate they will never be native of the society they admire, their half remains emptied. I am complete and it is a merit of COVID-19."

After further review, this chapter innovatively explores the emotions and expectations of expatriate tourists who remained abroad for days or weeks just after the lockdown affected thousands of Argentinean tourists. The information permits us to draw off an exploratory model centred on three different characters (so to speak or forms of adaptation to a risky situation) which are detailed: *Stranded tourists, Pandemic seekers, nostalgic travellers or expatriates.*

Dilemmas and Limitations

To sum up, and in an exploratory dimension, the gathered preliminary results evince a promising hypothesis which may be very well continued in a future approach. However, these outcomes cannot be extrapolated to other universes and situations. The obtained outcome permits to draw of three different grids or psychological characters, which are based on the factors that remain coadjuvant to deciding to travel in a pandemic context:

1. Stranded tourists: this segment represents all tourists who were involuntarily trapped by the global lockdown administered by the nation-state because of COVID-19. These tourists develop a "precautionary character" with serious problems to bear the uncertainty.
2. Pandemic seekers-deniers: this segment is mainly drawn by those tourists who are motivated to defy the government or to be closer to the infected epicentre, and make the decision to travel abroad despite the imposed travel bans. These tourists develop a "defying character." They bode well with the climate of uncertainty.
3. Nostalgic expatriates: the segment is formed by expatriates who work abroad but are emotionally or economically forced to return home. These tourists emotionally instil a "relational character."

Last but not least, the present research ignites a new discussion –that starts a novel methodological insight- in the fields of post-COVID-19 contexts. The specialized literature was historically marked by the interplay of tourists vs. locals, but little attention was paid to expatriate or stranded travellers, this investigation intends to be an initial contribution.

Conclusion

COVID-19 has not only changed global commerce and the world but also placed the tourism industry upside down. Experts and colleagues of all pundits agree tourism research should coordinate efforts on a clear diagnosis that helps to mitigate the economic effects of the pandemic as well as the opportunities to reverse climate change. It is safe to say that the pandemic ushered the industry into a state of crisis and chaos as never before. However, less attention was given to the psycho-sociological effects of the pandemic. These include racism and separatism to a much deeper hostility against foreign tourists. To fill the gap, the present chapter reviewed not only the incipient literature –in its infancy- but also the behavioural changes in travel patterns. Last but not least, three sub-segments have been identified: *stranded tourists* who developed a precautionary logic, *pandemic deniers* who are often associated to be critical of President Alberto Fernandez, and *Romantic expatriates,* a cluster characterized by a sentiment of nostalgia to be forced to return to their country. Each one has developed different tactics to deal with risk and uncertainty. Although illuminating –if not fresh- to some extent, the obtained outcomes cannot be extrapolated to other cases and universes.

References

Bauman, Z. (2017). Tourists and vagabonds: Or, living in postmodern times. In *Identity and social change* (pp. 19-32). Abingdon, Routledge.

Cai, W., McKenna, B., Wassler, P., & Williams, N. (2020). Rethinking knowledge creation in Information Technology and Tourism. *Journal of Travel Research*, 0047287520946100.

Carr, A. (2020). COVID-19, indigenous peoples and tourism: a view from New Zealand. *Tourism Geographies*, 1-12.

Derrida, J., & Dufourmantelle, A. (2000). *Of hospitality*. Stanford, Stanford University Press.

Dixon, D. P., & Jones III, J. P. (2015). The tactile topologies of Contagion. *Transactions of the Institute of British Geographers*, *40*(2), 223-234.

Edwards, R. B. (2020). Bubble in, bubble out: Lessons for the COVID-19 recovery and future crises from the Pacific. *World Development*, *135*, 105072.

Farzanegan, M. R., Gholipour, H. F., Feizi, M., Nunkoo, R., & Andargoli, A. E. (2020). International Tourism and Outbreak of Coronavirus (COVID-19): A Cross-Country Analysis. *Journal of Travel Research*, 0047287520931593.

Fernando, J. L. (2020). The Virocene Epoch: the vulnerability nexus of viruses, capitalism and racism. *Journal of Political Ecology*, *27*(1), 635-684.

Gaffney, C., & Eeckels, B. (2020). COVID-19 and Tourism Risk in the Americas. *Journal of Latin American Geography*, *19*(3), 308-313.

Gössling, S., Scott, D., & Hall, C. M. (2020). Pandemics, tourism and global change: a rapid assessment of COVID-19. *Journal of Sustainable Tourism*, 1-20.

Gretzel, U., Fuchs, M., Baggio, R., Hoepken, W., Law, R., Neidhardt, J., & Xiang, Z. (2020). e-Tourism beyond COVID-19: a call for transformative research. *Information Technology & Tourism*, 1.

Guidotti-Hernández, N. M. (2011). Unspeakable violence. *Remapping Us and Mexican National Imaginaries*. Durham, UNCS Press.

Hall, C. M. (2010). Crisis events in tourism: subjects of crisis in tourism. *Current issues in Tourism*, *13*(5), 401-417.

Hall, C. M., Scott, D., & Gössling, S. (2020). Pandemics, transformations and tourism: be careful what you wish for. *Tourism Geographies*, 1-22.

Higgins-Desbiolles, F. (2020). Socialising tourism for social and ecological justice after COVID-19. *Tourism Geographies*, 1-14.

Jamal, T., & Budke, C. (2020). Tourism in a world with pandemics: local-global responsibility and action. *Journal of Tourism Futures*.6(2): 181-188.

Jayathilaka, G. K. (2020). The Worldmaking Agency of the Sri Lankan Travel Blogger. *Tourism Culture & Communication*, *20*(2-3), 117-127.

Karim, W., Haque, A., Anis, Z., & Ulfy, M. A. (2020). The movement control order (mco) for covid-19 crisis and its impact on tourism and hospitality sector in malaysia. *International Tourism and Hopitality Journal*, *3*(2), 1-7.

Korstanje M. E (2017) *Tourism, Terrorism and the End of hospitality in the West.* Basingstoke, Palgrave Macmillan.

Korstanje, M. E. (2018). *The Challenges of democracy in the War on terror: the liberal state before the advance of terrorism.* Abingdon, Routledge.

Korstanje, M. E. (2019). Interrogating on the Essence of the Zombie World. In *Terrorism, Technology and Apocalyptic Futures* (pp. 19-43). Cham, Palgrave Macmillan.

Korstanje, M. E. (2020). Passage from the tourist-gaze to the wicked-gaze: a case study on COVID19 with special reference to Argentina. *International Case Studies in the Management of Disasters: natural–manmade Calamities and Pandemics. In George B & Qamar-ud-Din Mahar. Wagon Lane, Emerald Group Publishing*.

Kwok, A. O., & Koh, S. G. (2020). COVID-19 and Extended Reality (XR). *Current Issues in Tourism*, 1-6.

Lashley, C. (2008). Studying hospitality: Insights from social sciences. *Scandinavian Journal of Hospitality and Tourism*, *8*(1), 69-84.

Lynch, P, Germann-Molz J, McInthosh A, Lugosi, P & Lashley C. (2011). "*Theorizing hospitality." Hospitality & Society,* 1(1): 3-24.

Lyon, D., & Bauman, Z. (2013). Liquid surveillance: A conversation. *Cambridge, Malden: Polity*.

Mariolis, T., Rodousakis, N., & Soklis, G. (2020). The COVID-19 multiplier effects of tourism on the Greek economy. *Tourism Economics*, 1354816620946547.

McKercher, B. (2003). SIP (Sars induced Panic) a greater threat to Tourism than Sars (Severe acute respiratory Syndrome. *E-revise of Tourism Research (ERTR)*, *1*(1), 17-18.

McKercher, B., & Chon, K. (2004). The over-reaction to SARS and the collapse of Asian tourism. *Annals of tourism research*, *31*(3), 716-730.

Monterrubio, J. C. (2010). Short-term economic impacts of influenza A (H1N1) and government reaction on the Mexican tourism industry: an analysis of the media. *International Journal of Tourism Policy*, *3*(1), 1-15.

Nepal, S. K. (2020). Travel and tourism after COVID-19–business as usual or opportunity to reset?. *Tourism Geographies*, 1-5.

Niewiadomski, P. (2020). COVID-19: from temporary de-globalisation to a re-discovery of tourism?. *Tourism Geographies*, 1-6.

Novelli, M., Burgess, L. G., Jones, A., & Ritchie, B. W. (2018). 'No Ebola… still doomed'– The Ebola-induced tourism crisis. *Annals of Tourism Research*, *70*, 76-87.

Park, E., Kim, W. H., & Kim, S. B. (2020). Tracking tourism and hospitality employees' real-time perceptions and emotions in an online community during the COVID-19 pandemic. *Current Issues in Tourism*, 1-5.

Polyzos, S., Samitas, A., & Spyridou, A. E. (2020). Tourism demand and the COVID-19 pandemic: an LSTM approach. *Tourism Recreation Research*, 1-13.

Prayag, G. (2020). Time for reset? COVID-19 and tourism resilience. *Tourism Review International*, *24*(2-3), 179-184.

Prideaux, B., Thompson, M., & Pabel, A. (2020). Lessons from COVID-19 can prepare global tourism for the economic transformation needed to combat climate change. *Tourism Geographies*, 1-12.

Qiu, R. T., Park, J., Li, S., & Song, H. (2020). Social costs of tourism during the COVID-19 pandemic. *Annals of Tourism Research*, *84*, 102994.

Radic, A., Law, R., Lück, M., Kang, H., Ariza-Montes, A., Arjona-Fuentes, J. M., & Han, H. (2020). Apocalypse now or overreaction to coronavirus: The global cruise tourism industry crisis. *Sustainability*, *12*(17), 6968.

Ritzer, G. (2019) *Inhospitable hospitality*. In *Experiencing hospitality. Rowson, B & Lashley C.* Hauppauge, Nova Science Pp. 73-91.

Rogerson, C. M., & Baum, T. (2020). COVID-19 and African tourism research agendas. *Development Southern Africa*, 1-15.

Rogerson, C. M., & Rogerson, J. M. (2020). COVID-19 and tourism spaces of vulnerability in South Africa. *African Journal of Hospitality, Tourism and Leisure*, *9*(4), 382-401.

Sah, R., Sigdel, S., Ozaki, A., Kotera, Y., Bhandari, D., Regmi, P, & Dhama, K. (2020). Impact of COVID-19 on tourism in Nepal. *Journal of Travel Medicine*, *27*(6), taaa105.

Selwyn, T. (2000). An anthropology of hospitality. *In search of hospitality: Theoretical perspectives and debates*, Lashley C & Morrison, A. (eds), Oxford, Butterworth-Heinemann, 18-37.

Selwyn, T (2019) "Hostility and Hospitality: connecting Brexit, Grenfell and Windrush." In *Experiencing hospitality. Rowson, B & Lashley C.* Hauppauge, Nova Science Pp. 51-72.

Sheller, M. (2020). Reconstructing tourism in the Caribbean: connecting pandemic recovery, climate resilience and sustainable tourism through mobility justice. *Journal of Sustainable Tourism*, 1-14.

Sigala, M. (2020). Tourism and COVID-19: impacts and implications for advancing and resetting industry and research. *Journal of Business Research 117: 312-321.*

Sunstein, C. R. (2005). *Laws of fear: Beyond the precautionary principle* (Vol. 6). Cambridge, Cambridge University Press.

Tzanelli, R., & Korstanje, M. (2020). Introduction: Critical Thinking in Tourism Studies. *Tourism Culture & Communication*, *20*(2-3), 59-69.

Urry, J. (2002). *The tourist gaze*. London, Sage.

Wen, J., Wang, C. C., & Kozak, M. (2020). Post-COVID-19 Chinese domestic tourism market recovery: potential influence of traditional Chinese medicine on tourist behaviour. *Anatolia*, 1-5.

Wen, J., Wang, W., Kozak, M., Liu, X., & Hou, H. (2020). Many brains are better than one: the importance of interdisciplinary studies on COVID-19 in and beyond tourism. *Tourism Recreation Research*, 1-4.

Yu, M., Li, Z., Yu, Z., He, J., & Zhou, J. (2020). Communication related health crisis on social media: a case of COVID-19 outbreak. *Current Issues in Tourism*, 1-7.

Zeng, Z., Chen, P. J., & Lew, A. A. (2020). From high-touch to high-tech: COVID-19 drives robotics adoption. *Tourism Geographies*, 1-11.

Zheng, Y., Goh, E., & Wen, J. (2020). The effects of misleading media reports about COVID-19 on Chinese tourists' mental health: a perspective article. *Anatolia*, *31*(2), 337-340.

Xiang, Z., Fesenmaier, D. R., & Werthner, H. (2020). Knowledge Creation in Information Technology and Tourism: A Critical Reflection and an Outlook for the Future. *Journal of Travel Research*, 0047287520933669.

Zenker, S., & Kock, F. (2020). The coronavirus pandemic–A critical discussion of a tourism research agenda. *Tourism Management*, *81*, 104164.

Zheng, Y., Goh, E., & Wen, J. (2020). The effects of misleading media reports about COVID-19 on Chinese tourists' mental health: a perspective article. *Anatolia*, *31*(2), 337-340.

Chapter 4

East African Tourism Policies Review and Crisis Preparedness in Pandemic Situations

Keziah Odemba[1,*], PhD
and Shem Wambugu Maingi[2,†], PhD
[1]National Director Ministry of Tourism Kenya, Nairobi, Kenya
[2]School of Business, Economics and Tourism, Kenyatta University, Nairobi, Kenya

Abstract

The COVID-19 pandemic has had a profound negative impact on the economies of the Eastern Africa Region and particularly the tourism sector which contributes hugely to the GDPs of these countries. The shock of the pandemic has already reduced growth in service sectors related to tourism and caused massive job losses. Under the current conditions, Ministries of Tourism were confronted with various challenges that will impact long-term development and set the agenda for public policy action. The chapter seeks to address the challenge in the East African Region which requires broad mitigation measures to counteract the consequences of the outbreak as well as specific policies to support local tourism-related businesses and affected communities. The study will examine the preparedness of the region in handling pandemics and offer various scenarios of possible interventions. This chapter addresses this problem by drawing on literature from different literature to recommend generic strategies for crisis preparedness during pandemic situations. The study situates the current outbreak within prior

* Corresponding Author's Email: kizzyod@yahoo.com.
† Lecturer, Author's Email: maingi.shem@ku.ac.ke.

In: Tourism in Crisis
Editors: M.E. Korstanje, V. GB Gowreesunkar and S.W. Maingi
ISBN: 979-8-88697-643-4

pandemics and offers some directions for research and practice. Due to the human desire for travel, pandemics affecting the sector will manifest when least expected. It is the role of every government to be ready and reduce its impact by implementing progressive policies.

Keywords: crisis, East Africa, pandemic, policy, preparedness

Introduction

Over the past decades a growing number of natural hazards and disasters, caused by the susceptibility of tourism to biosecurity risks and health scares. As observed by Cioccio and Michael (2007) it is the nature of the tourism environment which is often hazardous or offers experiences in volatile settings. Despite the increasing threat of natural disasters to tourism businesses and destinations, few tourism destinations were prepared to handle the impacts of such threats (Cassedy, 1991), yet disaster planning is a core competency of tourism managers (Faulkner, 2001; Hystad & Keller, 2006). According to the Worldometer (2020) globally, the COVID-19 pandemic has led to 446,707 deaths, 8,290,232 confirmed cases as of 18th June 2020, an unprecedented decline in international tourism as well as travel restrictions globally, therefore sparking fears of global economic recession, large-scale quarantines and crises, (Worldometer, 2020; Nicola et. al., 2020). During the pandemic period, movement control orders (MCOs), widespread suspension of transport connectivity, travel restrictions and national lockdowns have grounded the tourism industries to a halt, therefore, providing a very negative effect on the tourism and travel sectors globally. The World Health Organization has noted with concern that despite the preventive measures, most of the countries affected were not adequately prepared for the COVID-19 pandemic in terms of limited testing capacities and public health control measures, therefore increased human-to-human infections as well as diminished effectiveness of response measures, (World Health Organization [WHO], 2020). At the global scale, the level of tourism preparedness has been problematic owing to the reported disparities in destinations' socio-economic abilities to cope with and recover from the COVID-19 pandemic, (United Nations Development Programme [UNDP], 2020). The Global Health Security Index collaborates these findings by noting that an overall GHS index score of 40.2 out of 100 in terms of international preparedness for the COVID-19 pandemic in terms of Anti-microbial resistance (AMR), biosecurity, biosafety, early detection, rapid response, health sector capacity, financing and risk environment, (Global Health Security Index [GHSI], 2020).

In the African context, the virus had been confirmed to have spread to Africa on the 14th of february 2020. Currently, the pandemic has resulted in 348,871 infected cases and 9,098 deaths as of 26th June 2020, [African Centre for Disease Control and Prevention, (Africa CDC, 2020)]. Before the COVID-19 pandemic African healthcare systems and infrastructure had been in a deplorable state as indicated by African nations were working towards slowing down and ultimately halting the spread of the virus through a coordinated and integrated approach as guided by the AU Africa CDC Emergency Preparedness and Response Programmes and Plans. Most of these pandemics historically such as the Influenza, SARS, bird flu, bubonic plague, swine flu, and Ebola were zoonoses and arise from chimeric viruses spread from wild animals to humans, (Waltner-Toews, 2020). Supply and Demand shocks related to the COVID-19 pandemic were expected to slow down GDP growth in many countries in the African context. Studies by Ozil, (2020) show a significant disconnect between the socio-economic impact of the COVID-19 pandemic as well as the policy responses in African countries. An analysis of the Global Health Security Index in 2019 by the Nuclear Threat Initiative in collaboration with the Centre for Health Security, John Hopkins Bloomberg School of Public Health, NTI, (2019) shows that all East African countries were not fully prepared for pandemics or epidemics (NTI, 2019). In terms of epidemics preparedness, the report indicated that Kenya has a comparatively higher capacity in terms of epidemic preparedness within the region with a GHSI score of 45.9 compared to Uganda (GHSI index score of 42.7), Rwanda (GHSI index score of 33.8) and Tanzania (GHSI index score of 33.5) respectively. Similarly, in terms of early detection and reporting of epidemics, Kenya has had higher GHSI index scores compared to the other respective countries in the region. However, in terms of rapid response and mitigation of the spread of epidemics, the report noted that Uganda has had higher GHSI index scores compared to the other respective countries in the region.

The Problem in East African Context

Over the recent past, large-scale natural and human-induced crises have increased in frequency and impacted the disappointment of governments around the world. (Becken & Hughey, 2013; Buchanan & Denyer, 2013; Mair, Ritchie, & Walters, 2016; Ryu et al., 2013). During periods of crisis, governments have an integral role to sustain tourism which contributes 7.5% to 10% to the GDP of the East African States. Currently, measures of Disaster response in East Africa are yielding temporal results as compared with the huge costs related to the COVID-19 pandemic. Despite tax and fiscal relief measures as well as the extensive National Disaster preparedness fund allocations, the tourism economy in the East African region had been hard hit. In 2019, Kenya's tourism sector risks losing a sector worth KES 163.6 bn, 1.6 million jobs and 8.8% of Kenya's GDP while Ethiopia risks losing USD 3.6 bn, 1.1 million jobs and 5% of Ethiopia's GDP, while Tanzania supports 1.5 million jobs and a sector worth 6.5% of the country's GDP and Uganda's tourism sector risks losing 700,000 jobs in the sector and about 7.7% of Uganda's GDP, (Delloite 2020; Government of Tanzania, 2022). The general observation is the lack of local-level preparedness, which results in interruptions in normal operations and damage to tourists' sense of destination safety and appeal (Biran, Liu, Li, & Eichhorn, 2014; Paraskevas & Altinay, 2013). The specific problem is that during the ongoing COVID-19 pandemic, the governments of the East African region unfortunately lacked strategies for crisis preparedness that could reduce business interruptions and improve their destination's image.

The Concept of Crisis and Pandemic Preparedness in the Tourism Sector

The term pandemic crisis arises from certain triggered viral outbreaks within a society. It presents itself as a significant disruptor to the economic and social organizations of a society, (Jordan-Meier, 2011). Crisis preparedness during pandemic situations has become a fundamental concern for most tourism enterprises and local communities worldwide. In the wake of recent global crises, crisis preparedness has become a key part of destination planning, (Pennington-Gray et al., 2014). Different studies focused on the different approaches towards effective crisis preparedness. Conaghan and Hanrahan, (2009) and Harris, (2007) focussed on supply-side certification systems, Lew (2013) advocated for resilience planning as an effective approach to crisis preparedness, Morakabati, Page and Fletcher, (2020) centred on emergency management paradigms in tourism. Crisis preparedness is all about developing capacities and capabilities in terms of personnel, logistics, national legislation, technologies, resources, equipment and funding that were all aimed at reducing the impacts of the pandemic crisis on a region. In the realm of pandemic preparedness, the scale and scope of preparedness are further escalated by the recurring nature of the outbreak. There have been organizations such as the World Health Organization in 2018 which developed essential steps for developing a national influenza-like pandemic preparedness plan, (WHO, 2018). However, as noted by Glaesser (2020), the tourism industry is characterized by a subjective risk perception factor, where tourism products are information products that are highly immaterial and produced in future and therefore highly vulnerable to negative information during the pandemic. Visitors were also not prepared for extended quarantine stays and unfamiliar with the risks and emergency systems within the destination and therefore were highly vulnerable to pandemic-related restrictions. It is worth noting that there is an increasing number of studies in the tourism field on tourism disaster management. However, most have highlighted and indeed researched, reactive response and recovery efforts of the tourism industry at the expense of reduction and readiness strategies and initiatives. Yet more proactive, and more strategic planning approaches to tourism crisis and disaster management have been proposed (Ritchie, 2004). The lack of focus on tourism disaster planning by researchers is a concern, especially considering that reduction and readiness strategies have been the focus of the natural hazards and emergency planning field for some time. In this regard, tourism managers must change their thinking from a reactive approach to tourism disaster management toward a proactive planning approach. Furthermore, researchers should focus more effort on understanding the current level of industry reduction and readiness efforts as well as potential barriers or impediments in tourism disaster planning to ensure more effective planning and management were undertaken. According to Nickelson and Robinson (2014) there has seen an intense focus worldwide in the last two decades towards global action on disaster risk reduction and preparedness. The World Conference on Natural Disaster Reduction, held in Yokohama, Japan, from the 23rd to 27th of May 1994 provided more of the beacons for disaster prevention, mitigation and preparedness which will make a significant contribution towards sustainable development futures. These aspects were noted in the strategy for the year 2000 and beyond that is focused on developing a global culture of prevention as an essential component of disaster reduction and the adoption of the policy of self-reliance in each country and community.

Tourism Policy Reviews in East Africa

Attempts to analyze policy were made complex not only by decisions, actions, and events, but by the knowledge that there is no coherent or universally accepted theory of public policy processes, and no single means of explaining events' (Hall & Jenkins, 2004, p. 527). Policy development involves ideological beliefs and political philosophy. All tourism stakeholders operate within the ideological beliefs and political philosophy of the government; therefore, this ideology determines whether tourism development will be given financial support; it can set the style of tourism, and the nature and extent of government involvement. Normally the ideology reflects the national political culture and political parties (Elliott, 1997, p. 56). As these ideologies change, a government's tourism policy 'will differ in forms and means in relation both to the form of political economy that prevails in the country and to the degree of development reached' (Sessa, 1976, p. 238). Thus, policy and the policy process will change over time, and what is a 'good' policy must be determined by argument, not scientific information. The policy implementation process may also require several other steps such as administrative coordination and policy coordination (Hall, 1999, p. 278) as well as support from effective legislation. Policy implementers require the power to 'make and enforce decisions which were binding upon their members', they have responsibilities which were interpreted by ideologies in shaping objectives (Elliott, 1997, p. 56). Swain (1999, p. 1008) suggests that the study of policy and power in tourism 'includes a broad range of concepts from ideology to exchange rates and visa control'. Thus, policy involves the exercise of power (Marzano & Scott, 2009). Currently, there is only a small methodological literature concerning tourism policy. There is some agreement that the study of tourism policy involves complexity, dynamism and change, and as a result, Stevenson, Airey and Miller (2008) recommend the use of multiple approaches to understanding policymaking. Tourism policy involves collective action and how collective choices were made, implemented and enforced in and for society (Buhrs, 2000). The tourism policies in the East African nations were similar. The government has set the tone and therefore has the power to decide which areas to support. All the governments have not supported crisis preparedness and indeed, Uganda and Tanzania do not have crisis management in their tourism policies. On the other hand, Kenya has a crisis management policy statement with suggested interventions. The policy involves actions, decisions, politics, values and ideological beliefs, and social processes involving communication and outcome such as legislation and implementation. This is complex and requires strategic collaboration locally, regionally and internationally. A combination of regional pandemic policies and crises in tourism research studies and online resources were used to demonstrate the importance of preparedness before pandemics and ready-to-use tourism-specific policies to reduce the impact on tourism businesses. This chapter provides a context and viewpoint on the possible implications of post-COVID-19 reflection for pandemic preparedness and policies for the East Africa region in the future. This viewpoint chapter captures only the East African region in a broad sense, a snapshot of rapidly emerging online perspectives but at the same time draws together relevant research that emphasises the importance of preparedness during a pandemic.

Post-Pandemic Tourism Policies

The tourism industry is one of the most directly affected sectors in this current crisis and this calls for immediate and long-term responses. In the case of China, the first country to go through the various stages of the COVID-19 pandemic, McKinsey and Company (2020b) found consumers were regaining confidence, and interestingly, a greater interest in environmentally friendly products. Again, the demand from clients, who are tourists, should compel governments to include sustainability practices in tourism policies across the region. Currently, all policies mention sustainability but the practice is negligible. According to Downs (1972), the modern public cyclically attends to many issues. A problem "leaps into prominence, remains there for a short time, and then, though still largely unresolved, gradually fades from the centre of public attention" (1972, p.38). The 2003 SARS outbreak illustrates this well, as tourism growth in Asia picked up very quickly once the perceived threat diminished (McKercher& Chon, 2004). Tourism policies in the region were not consistent or long-term. Tanzania is now reviewing their tourism policy in 2020 since the 1980s. Domestic tourism is expected to play an important role in leading the initial recovery phase, given the uncertain outlook for international travel. Countries, where domestic tourism is developed, were likely to see recovery in the sector more quickly than countries that were heavily dependent on international tourism flows. Many countries, and the tourism sector, have moved to promote domestic travel and cater to visitors from their own countries. At the regional level, the East African Tourism strategy needs to factor in response to crisis and preparedness and also how to capture neglected markets after crises, notably their domestic markets and then the regional market. Regrettably, none of the East African countries has a strategy to promote the region to each other's citizens, yet South Africa promotes their country specifically to each East African country, with specific tailor-made marketing strategies.

Since pandemic impacts were felt throughout the tourism ecosystem, reopening and rebuilding destinations require a collaborative approach, (Gowreesunkar, et al., 2022; Gowreesunkar, et al., 2021). Tourism businesses and workers were benefiting from economy-wide stimulus packages, with many governments also introducing tourism-specific measures. In late August 2020, Kenya was awarded the "Safer Tourism Seal," this was done under the Rebuilding Travel umbrella, a global pro-tourism industry group composed of members of tourism boards, ministers of tourism, professional associations, industry stakeholders, researchers and academics as well as travellers. Countries were currently taking steps to introduce tourism-specific measures to address the immediate impacts on the sector and to facilitate its recovery. Governments were also adjusting the measures put in place to take better address the needs of tourism businesses, and the sector as a whole. The travel and tourism industry governments of the East African region should continue to reinforce their coordination mechanisms to accompany the businesses, notably the smallest ones, and the workers. The Governments should also consider the long-term implications of the present COVID-19 crisis, and stay ahead of the digital curve by supporting a low-carbon transition, and promoting the structural transformation needed to build a stronger, more sustainable and resilient tourism economy. This crisis is an opportunity to rethink tourism for the future. It has been a concern to governments that there is a risk of as many as 50% collapses of SMEs across the globe. This has been the case in the East African region as well. This widespread occurrence could have a strong impact on these fragile economies. Most governments have been quick to acknowledge the specific circumstances of SMEs, and have put in place policies to support them; health measures, and information on how to adhere to them, measures to address liquidity by deferring payments, measures to supply extra and more easily available credit to strengthen SME resilience, measures to avoid the consequences of lay-offs, and structural policies. These general SME measures have also been accessible to SMEs in the tourism sector. During health pandemics, there should be cooperation between tourism and the health sector to support the containment effort. In Kenya, on several instances, the hospitality sector supported the medical personnel with meals, helped the needy with food and provided spaces for people needing quarantine. The pandemic has brought about opportunities with the potential to develop the previously unseen sector. The current crisis is accelerating the digital transformation of the sector. Digital solutions were being developed to create virtual tourism experiences. There is a need for policy in this area and a code of ethics to pre-empt any underhand dealings by cyberspace criminals. Domestic tourism numbers have gone up in the region and notably in Kenya judging from the influx of locals at Masai Mara National Reserve to witness the Wildebeest migration. This is due to new entrants in the Domestic tourism business and collaboration with tour operators and hotels and lodges. Government should identify these opportunities and pitch them to the local population to encourage them to invest in tourism.

Crisis Preparedness in the East Africa Region

Kenya, Tanzania and Uganda have been dealing with one another under the umbrella of one regional entity or another for more than a century. There was a customs union between Kenya and Uganda in 1917, an East African High Commission from 1948 to 1961 and an East African Common Services Organisation from 1961 to 1967. As one of the fastest-growing regional blocs in Africa, the EAC has a population of approximately 168.2 million people with a combined GDP of US$155.2 billion. The three countries share similar cultures and histories with minor variations. Currently, there are concerted efforts to make the region fully integrated. Kenya and Uganda are members of the Common Market for Eastern and Southern Africa (COMESA), which has 385 million consumers, while Tanzania belongs to the Southern African Development Community (SADC), which groups 13 countries with 215 million people. Concerning the current pandemic, projections indicate that economic growth in the region will decline from 2.4 per cent in 2019 to between -2.1 to -5.1% in 2020 (World Bank predictions) depending on the measures taken to mitigate the pandemic's effects. Other estimates show that the pandemic is costing the region between US$37 billion and US$79 billion in output losses. The result of business closures means mass losses of livelihoods. In aviation, tourism and hospitality industries, entire sector value-chains have been rendered indefinitely dysfunctional. Indeed, when the pandemic broke out in early March 2020, the East African governments were caught unawares. This means that lessons have not been learnt from past pandemics. Looking at the Tourism Policies of the East African Region, there is no mention of how to handle pandemics, although security is covered slightly in the policies of Tanzania, Rwanda and Uganda but nothing on crises and pandemics, (Kimunio and Maingi, 2022). In the Kenyan tourism policy, the issue of security and crisis are covered. All the policies do not contain pandemic, disaster or crisis preparedness. This is a gap that needs to be addressed to reduce the vacuum created in decision-making when a crisis occurs. After the outbreak, it would have been comforting and calming to citizens if they saw their leader meet their counterparts from the region, however, there was no urgent meeting of the leaders to chart a way forward together. Instead, each leader worked independently. A lack of synergy and a common approach to working as a team against a common enemy was observed. This tends to create a hostile environment affecting all sectors of the economy. During the current pandemic of COVID-19, it was clear that the governments of the east african region were not working together. While some were sharing crucial data on numbers, other countries were withholding data or not testing for infections. This causes hostilities to flare up. This has been a work in progress since normalcy has yet to be restored. Timely sharing of data can help in decision-making for the region. Instead, each country closed itself in and looked inwardly. A pandemic should be confronted and dealt with openly regardless of missing knowledge. This is a position of strength. This would have been the opportune time to revive the East African regional crisis committee to guide the various heads of state as they waded through the pandemic while trying to keep their citizens safe. However, it was clear that there was no continuous dialogue between the regional leaders. During the crisis of both ebola, terrorism bombings and COVID-19, people of the region experienced contradicting policies from the different governments coming from their ministries of health and ministries of tourism. Many issues were shrouded in mystery and there was a lack of clear communication from the media of the three countries. Even during the current pandemic, there was no data from two countries except Kenya. Uganda shared data later on but Tanzania has not been free to share data. As mentioned earlier, tourism and movement act as a vector for the distribution of the virus locally, regionally and globally. This shows that tourism indirectly supports pandemics. Tourists are large consumers of food and many businesses purchase their food from global markets. Tourism, therefore, supports industrialized food production. Also, tourism is a major source of greenhouse gases, which impact climate change, affecting the environment with ensuing floods and drought further increasing the risk of pandemics. It follows then, that any policy developed for these areas will affect tourism, hence the need for synergies and harmonization. Despite an increase in meetings to deliberate on matters of environment, health, tourism, infrastructure and others in the East African region; positive results have remained few and far apart. There seems to be a lack of commitment from the East African countries on how to act on the United Nations Sustainable Development goals and integrate them into their policies. Although frequently mentioned and talked about in meetings and conferences, currently, there is no evidence-based strategy for climate change mitigation or for achieving the SDGs. Instead, there is an overall silence regarding pandemics and other risks the global tourism system imposes on itself and the global economy (Scott et al., 2019).

The current COVID-19 pandemic should lead tourism stakeholders to critically reconsider the much-talked-about volume growth model for tourism. This perspective has already been criticized and questioned in the context of the global financial crisis (Hall, 2009) and as the challenges of over-tourism, climate change and the COVID-19 pandemic further illustrate, this perspective is outdated. Volume growth agendas are driven by individuals and large businesses profiting from such growth models. This specifically includes international tourism organisations, the platform economy (e.g., Booking and AirBnB), aircraft manufacturers such as Boeing and Airbus, national Destination Management Organisations, and individual large tourism corporations. Sadly, the UNWTO is responsible for advancing the SDGs in their entirety, yet in its current form, represents a growth advocacy platform (Gössling et al., 2016; Hall, 2019). Decisions by policymakers will play an important role in shaping the tourism sector in the post-COVID-19 context. As recovery plans were being designed, countries identified key priority areas and ensuing challenges. One of them is re-thinking the tourism sector. The pandemic has allowed tourism leaders and experts to rethink the tourism system for a more sustainable and resilient future. Policy interventions will be required to address structural problems of the sector, avoid the return to issues of tourism management (e.g., over-tourism), and advance key priorities, such as encouraging new business models, embracing digitalization and promoting connectivity. The other key area is rebuilding destinations and the tourism system. This will take time; therefore, support and recovery measures will need to be comprehensive across the value chain that contributes to the tourism experience. Accessibility, connectivity and transport should be high on the agenda just as accommodations, restaurants, resorts, events, travel associations, travel tech companies, tour operators, and tourism associations. Another key area is Innovating and investment in tourism. Government policies here should ensure that the sector is ready to resume and keep on innovating and transforming. Investments will be needed to make structural and physical changes to address health requirements and visitors' expectations in the first phase of recovery and the long term. Some countries have also put in place measures to support innovation in SMEs to ensure stronger long-term economic resilience.

Conclusion

In conclusion, governments need to take a proactive role in matters crisis management in tourism. The East African experience has shown that, to restore traveller confidence and stimulate tourism demand, governments need to collaborate with the private sector and put in place new recommended standards of safety, hygiene, testing, and procedures. At the same time, governments will need to take steps to ensure that the destination community were comfortable that the benefits associated with the return of visitors outweigh any concerns over the potential health risks. Kenya has been currently developing a war-room strategy for the sector especially during crises and pandemics. This strategy enables leadership to make critical decisions without full information. The next market for tourism lies with Regional and Domestic tourism. Governments need to develop specific tourism strategies for these previously ignored markets. This calls for diversification of markets and transformation of marketing methods and styles. Further, the tourism policies of all the countries should be reviewed to reflect the new reality. Crisis and pandemics in tourism should be addressed and a Crisis preparedness strategy developed. Beyond the immediate responses needed, policymakers will need to learn from the lessons of the COVID-19 crisis, to improve crisis management strategies to better prepare destinations and the sector more broadly to respond to future shocks. The COVID-19 pandemic provides striking lessons to the tourism industry, policymakers and tourism researchers about the largely ignored effects of global change.

References

African Centre for Disease Control and Prevention, Africa CDC, *(2020) COVID-19 African CDC Dashboard Infections and Death Rates*. Assessed through: https://africacdc.org/covid-19/.

Becken, S. & Hughey, K, F. D., (2013). Linking tourism into emergency management structures to enhance disaster risk reduction, *Tourism Management,* 36, 77–85. doi: https://doi.org/10.1016/j.tourman.2012.11.00.

Biran, A., Liu, W., Li, G., & Eichhorn, V. (2014). Consuming post-disaster destinations: The case of Sichuan, China. *Annals of Tourism Research*, 47, 1–17. doi: https://doi.org/10.1016/j.annals.2014.03.004.

Buhrs, T. (2000). The environment and the role of the state in New Zealand. In P. A. Memon & H. Perkins (Eds.), *Environmental Planning and Management in New Zealand (pp. 27-35).* Palmerston North: Dunmore Press.

Cassedy, K. (1991) *Crisis Management Planning in the Travel and Tourism Industry: A Study of Three Tourism Destinations and a Crisis Management Planning Manual*, San Francisco, CA: PATA. [Google Scholar].

Cioccio, L. and Michael, E. J. 2007. Hazard or disaster: Tourism management for the inevitable in Northeast Victoria. *Tourism Management*, 28: 1–11.

Conaghan, A., and J. Hanrahan. (2009). "Global Conformity of Indicators for Eco-Certification Programs." *Tourism and Hospitality Research in Ireland Conference: Dublin Institute of Technology*.

Downs, A. (1972). Up and down with ecology – the issue attention cycle. *Public Interest*, 28, 38–50. [Google Scholar].

Elliott, J. (1997). *Tourism, Politics and Public Sector Management.* London: Routledge.

Faulkner, B. 2001. Towards a framework for tourism disaster management. *Tourism Management*, 22: 135–147.

Glaesser, D. (2020) Pandemic Preparedness Planning for Travel and Tourism. *World Tourism Organization (UNWTO)* Assessed through: https://www.icao.int/SAM/Documents/2009/MEDSEM/Pandemic%20Prep%20Planning%20for%20T%20and%20T%20v4%20UNWTO.pdf.

Gössling, S. (2002). Global environmental consequences of tourism. *Global Environmental Change*, 12(4), 283–302. https://doi.org/10.1016/S0959-3780(02)00044-4 [Crossref], [Web of Science ®], [Google Scholar].

Government of Tanzania, (2022) *Tourism Policy and Strategies in Tanzania.* Retrieved from: http://www.tanzaniagateway.org/docs/tourismpolicyandstrategies.pdf.

Gowreesunkar, V. G., Maingi S. W., Roy H. and Micera R. (2022) Rebuilding tourism post pandemic – Policy recommendations from global case studies [version 1; not peer reviewed]. *Emerald Open Res* 2022, 4:2 (document) (https://doi.org/10.35241/emeraldopenres.1114919.1).

Gowreesunkar, V. G., Maingi, S. W., Roy, H. and Micera, R. (2021), "Conclusion: Rebuilding Tourism Post Pandemic: Some Reflections on Destination Management Solutions!," Gowreesunkar, V. G., Maingi, S. W., Roy, H. and Micera, R. (Ed.) *Tourism Destination Management in a Post-Pandemic Context* (*Tourism Security-Safety and Post Conflict Destinations*), Emerald Publishing Limited, Bingley, pp. 329-334. https://doi.org/10.1108/978-1-80071-511-020211023.

Hall, C. M. (1999). Rethinking Collaboration and Partnership: A Public Policy Perspective. *Journal of Sustainable Tourism*, 7(3/4), 274-289. Kerr, W. (2003).

Hall, C. M. (2009). Degrowing tourism: Décroissance, sustainable consumption and steady-state tourism. *Anatolia*, *20*(1), 46–61. https://doi.org/10.1080/13032917.2009.10518894 [Taylor & Francis Online], [Google Scholar].

Hall, C. M. (2019). Constructing sustainable tourism development: The 2030 agenda and the managerial ecology of sustainable tourism. *Journal of Sustainable Tourism*, 27(7), 1044–1060. https://doi.org/10.1080/09669582.2018.1560456 [Taylor & Francis Online], [Web of Science ®], [Google Scholar].

Hall, C. M. (2020). Biological invasion, biosecurity, tourism, and globalisation. In D. Timothy (Ed.), *Handbook of globalisation and tourism* (pp. 114–125). Edward Elgar. [Google Scholar].

Hall, C. M., & Jenkins, J. (2004). Tourism and Public Policy. In A. Lew, C. M. Hall & A. Williams (Eds.), *A companion to tourism* (pp. 425-540). Oxford: Blackwell.

Harris, S. M. (2007). "Green Tick™: An Example of Sustainability Certification of Goods and Services." *Management of Environmental Quality: An International Journal,* 18 (2): 167-78.

Jordan-Meier, J. (2011) *The Four Stages of Highly effective Crisis Management: How to manage the media in the digital age*. CRC Press, Taylor and Francis Group, LLC.

Kerr, W. (2003). *Tourism Public Policy, and the strategic Management of Failure*. New York: Pergamon.

Kimunio, I. and Maingi, S. W. (2022), "A Markov regime-switching (MS) approach to modeling the effects of fiscal policies and COVID-19 pandemic on tourism destination competitiveness in Kenya," *Journal of Hospitality and Tourism Insights,* Vol. ahead-of-print No. ahead-of-print. https://doi.org/10.1108/JHTI-09-2021-0245.

Lew, A. (2014) Scale, change and resilience in community tourism planning, *Tourism Geographies*, 16:1, 14-22, doi: https://doi.org/10.1080/14616688.2013.864325.

Mair, J., Ritchie, B. W., & Walters, G. (2016). Towards a research agenda for post-disaster and post-crisis recovery strategies for tourist destinations: A narrative review. *Current Issues in Tourism,* 19(1), 1–26. doi: https://doi.org/10.1080/13683500.2014.932758.

Marzano, G., & Scott, N. (2009). Power in destination branding. *Annals of Tourism Research*, 36(2), 247–267.

McKinsey and Company. (2020b). *Cautiously optimistic: Chinese consumer behavior post-COVID-19.* Retrieved April 6, 2020, from https://www.mckinsey.com/business-functions/marketing-and-sales/our-insights/global-surveys-of-consumer-sentiment-during-the-coronavirus-crisis. [Google Scholar].

Morakabati, Y. Page, S. J. and Fletcher, J. (2020) Emergency Management and Tourism stakeholder responses to crises: AA Global survey. *Journal of Travel Research*, 56 (3), 299-316.

Nickelson, G. and Robinson, R. (2014) Yokohama and Hyogo: A springboard for Caribbean action in disaster risk reduction, *Association of Carribbean States (ACS).* Assessed through: https://www.preventionweb.net/news/view/42112.

Nicola, M., Alsafi, Z., Sohrabi, C., Kerwan, A., Al-Jabir, A., Iosifidis, C., Agha, M. and Agha, R. (2020) The socio-economic implications of the coronavirus pandemic (COVID-19): A review. *Int J Surg.* 78 (2020): pp. 185–193.

NTI, (2019) Global Health Security Index: Building Collective Action and Accountability. *NTI and John Hopkins Bloomberg School of Public Health*, USA.

Pennington-Gray, L., Schroeder, A. Wu, B., Donohoe, H. and Cahyanto, I. (2014) Travelers' perception of Crisis Preparedness Certification in the United States, *Journal of Travel Research. Vol.* 53 (3), 353-365 doi: https://doi.org/10.1177/0047287513496470.

Scott, D., Hall, C. M., &Gössling, S. (2019). Global tourism vulnerability to climate change. *Annals of Tourism Research, 77*, 49–61. https://doi.org/10.1016/j.annals.2019.05.007 [Crossref], [Web of Science ®], [Google Scholar].

Sessa, A. (1976). The Tourism Policy. *Annals of Tourism Research,* 3(5), 234-247.

Stevenson, N., Airey, D., & Miller, G. (2008). Tourism Policy Making: The Policymakers' Perspectives. *Annals of Tourism Research*, 35(3), 732-750.

Swain, M., Brent, M., & Long, V. (1999). Annals and Tourism Evolving: Indexing 25 years of publication. *Annals of Tourism Research,* 25(Index to Volume 25), 991-1014.

UNWTO. (2020a). *COVID-19: UNWTO calls on tourism to be part of recovery plans.* https://www.unwto.org/news/covid-19-unwto-calls-on-tourism-to-be-part-of-recovery-plans. [Google Scholar].

Waltner-Toews, D. (2020) *On Pandemics: Deadly Diseases from Bubonic Plague to Coronavirus Greystone Books.*

World Health Organization, (2020) 2019 Novel Coronavirus (2019-nCoV): Strategic Preparedness and Response Plan. *World Health Organization.*

Worldometer (2020) *Global Coronavirus cases as at 17th June 2020,* Worldometer. Assessed through: https://www.worldometers.info/coronavirus/

Chapter 5

New Morbid Forms of Tourism: The Case of Dark Tourism in Perspective

Maximiliano E. Korstanje*
University of Palermo, Argentina

Abstract

The COVID-19 pandemic not only whipped the Western countries affecting seriously the GDP and the economic performance, but also interrogated on the nature of the tourism industry. The tourism industry was the main carrier but at the same time the main victim of the COVID-19. Having said this, the present proceeding concentrates efforts in discussing the effects of virus outbreak in the industry as well as laying the foundations towards a new understanding of safety and security in tourism. Over the recent years, the precautionary logic which culturally enrooted in the Western reasoning, punctuated on the importance to detect and eradicate those threats which affect the industry. This leading paradigm which opened the doors for the adoption of risk perception theory, so to speak just after the attacks to WTC (2001) set the pace to a new aradigm. Nowadays, as many specialists alert, the concept of precaution has been replaced by adaptancy. New forms of tourism such as Dark tourism, Thana tourism, post disaster tourism speak us of a new (morbid) taste where the "Other`s pain" situates as the main commodity to exchange. In my earlier book (Korstanje 2016), this epoch has been baptized as "thana-capitalism." These new forms or faces of the industry are mainly marked by a consumption given just after the tragedy takes hit.

---

* Corresponding Author's Email: mkorst@palermo.edu.

In: Tourism in Crisis
Editors: M.E. Korstanje, V. GB Gowreesunkar and S.W. Maingi
ISBN: 979-8-88697-643-4

Keywords: risk perception theory, dark tourism, consumption, security, adaptancy

Introduction

Dark tourism has become a more than interesting topic and object of study for many academic circles worldwide. Doubtless, dark tourism situates as a leading point of debate in top-ranked journals. As Hooper & Lennon observe, one of the problems of dark tourism seems to be associated with higher levels of fragmentation, which means a dispersion in the used definitions. What is more important, different circles use different academic paradigms in applied research (Hooper & Lennon 2016). Philip Stone (2012) has convincingly argued that dark tourism represents an anthropological attempt to domesticate one of the mysteries of life, death. Per his viewpoint, "the Other´s finitude" speaks to us of our own life calling attention to the proper expectancies. To put this simply, dark tourism serves as a catalyst instrument which helps us imagine our death through the lens of the "significant Other." Over recent years, some voices have emphasized the need of defining dark tourism as a type of dissonant heritage (Light 2017; Hartmann 2016) or a significant sacred pilgrimage that builds a bridge between the past, the present and the future (Olsen & Korstanje 2019). Having said this, dark tourism is many things and at the same time, something very hard to precise (Korstanje 2016).

As the previous backdrop, some studies have focused on dark tourism as an efficient instrument for economic revitalization in a post-disaster or conflict context. At a first look, dark tourism not only enhances resiliency but also accelerates the post-disaster recovery timeframe (Isaac, Cakmak & Butler, 2019; Tucker, Shelton & Bae, 2017; Kelman & Dodds, 2009). Although these works are not new simply because some of them have seen the light of publicity earlier than the turn of the twentieth century (Seaton, 1996; Lennon & Foley 1999), their proliferation has been witnessed just after 2010. Like post-disaster tourism, dark tourism occupied a central position in the planning process assisting policymakers to put the obliterated areas in further value. Furthermore, dark tourism was certainly implemented as a mechanism of resiliency very helpful for the recovery facet (Dresler 2022; Sy & Yu Park 2022). In this vein, some scholars have proclaimed the commonalities between dark tourism and post-disaster tourism (Pottorf & Neal 1994; Lin, Kelemen & Tresidder, 2018). At a closer look, dark tourism engages with thanatosis which (like post-disaster tourism) put the visitors directly before the "Other`s pain"

(Martini & Buda 2020). To some extent, the change of paradigm which situated dark tourism as a main object of study has invariably remained as untouched. In a recently-released book, Maximiliano Korstanje (2020) holds the thesis that dark or thana-tourism is far from being a new trending topic but the scholarly-given attention has been triplicated just after 2010. Public opinion has been captivated by this new niche igniting a hot debate within scholarship. While some voices alert on the ideological distortion of dark tourism discourses, others applaud enthusiastically dark tourism as a valid instrument to enhance resiliency. The fact seems to be that the triumph of dark tourism as a dominant paradigm entails the failure of risk perception theory to give a firm conceptual background to policymakers. The risk perception doctrine (which emerged from cognitive psychology) has been borrowed from the fields of tourism research just after the 2001s. The attacks on the US as well as other global risks such as natural disasters and recent virus outbreaks led policymakers to question to what extent the industry is still safe. Risk perception theory rested on the precautionary doctrine which punctuates the importance to use forecasting and planning to detect and eradicate global risks which threaten the industry. The escalation of these global risks in an ever-changing world has resulted in the adoption of a new paradigm where mass destruction is taken as usual. This is the context where the post-disaster studies emerge from (Korstanje 2020). In the mid of this debate, the present book chapter interrogates the nature of dark tourism as well as the necessary conditions to replace the precautionary logic with other paradigms. With the benefits of hindsight, the book chapter holds the thesis that post-disaster studies certainly exhibit the failure of risk perception theory to understand and prevent the negative impacts of global threats in the tourism industry (Korstanje & Olsen 2020).

The first section is a short companion on the changes accelerated by the terrorist attacks in 2001. The risk perception theory, a leading paradigm in the cognitive psychology, was widely adopted in the tourism research. Unfortunately, the failure of risk perception theory to give answers to the global threats led scholars in the need to employ new paradigms such as post-disaster and dark tourism. The second and third section explore the commonalities and differences between dark tourism and post-disaster tourism respectively. It is not otiose to say both paradigms have strengths, and weaknesses. The conclusion gives a snapshot for applied research in the fields of dark tourism for the next years to come. Of course, this is a theoretical approach which should be empirically validated in future studies.

Terrorism, Risk Perception Theory and the Turn of the Century

As stated in the earlier section, the turn of the twentieth century witnessed the multiplication of countless risks, which include terrorism, natural disasters, virus outbreaks as well as the rise of a climate of political instability without mentioning economic crisis globally (Ritchie 2009; Laws, Prideaux & Chon, 2007). The tourism research adopted the concept of crisis management as well as risk perception as the main leading paradigms (Yang & Nair, 2014; Fuchs & Reichel, 2006). Although the risk perception doctrine is far from being new simply because it was alive in cognitive phycology for more than four decades, no less true was that the turn of the century and the terrorist attack perpetrated by the radicalized cell Al-Qaeda to the US paved the pathways for the introduction to the notion of risk in tourism (Jonas et al. 2011). The theory was certainly based on the precautionary principle which means that rational planning helps policy-makers to detect and eradicate those global dangers which can threaten the industry. At the same time, the risk perception theory expands the current understanding of travel behavior as well as the consumers` reactions to certain risks (Korstanje 2009). What is equally important, demographic characteristics, features or affiliation as well as the psychological character explain why some consumers are prone to risk perception while others are more insensitive. From its outset, the goals of risk perception theory were twofold. On one hand, it is inscribed in the urgency of anticipating the potential dangers -earlier than they happen-. On another, it predicted the effects and tendencies of the market in a new stage of complexity and danger. Those consumers or segments oriented to bear higher levels of uncertainness are less sensitive to risk perception than other groups (Liu-Lastres, Schroeder & Pennington-Gray, 2019; Floyd et al, 2004; Reisinger & Mavondo, 2006). At a first glimpse, the risk perception doctrine was a fertile ground which populated the content of leading tourism-related journals from 2001 to 2010 (Chen et al. 2022). However, since 2010 year, this hegemonic paradigm sets the pace for a new theoretical background, post-disaster tourism (Korstanje 2016; Tzanelli 2016).

As the previous argument is given, the complexity of an ever-changing and globalized world or a much deeper chaotic scenario, makes the risk perception theory fall short. Far from placating, the effects of climate change have been accelerated by greenhouse gas emissions. Besides, the action of radicalized groups and terrorism affected not only the US but entire Europe expanding the violence to countries such as Germany, France, Spain and the UK. Recently, the COVID-19 virus outbreaks have wreaked havoc in the global trade as well as in the tourism and hospitality industries. To some extent, it is important to add, that the precautionary logic -as an old-fashioned paradigm- needed serious changes. Just after 2010, some scholars claimed that the current academic paradigm does not suffice to give firm answers to the problems of the industry (Miller 2008; Korstanje 2020). One of the grounding differences between post-disaster tourism and risk perception theory rests on the capacity for adaptation (not prevention) (Cakar 2020). The tourist experience is created just after the disaster takes a hit. Also, the process of consumption is certainly determined by the urgency to recover the affected zone, not to prevent the aftermaths of the traumatic event. This means that post-disaster tourism and dark tourism operate in the shades of tragedy providing not only a lesson to survivors (heritage) but also the material resources to fasten the recovery stage (Miller, Gonzalez & Hutter, 2017). It is important not to lose sight of the fact that the natural curiosity of visitors seems to be an essential part of the resilient mechanism as well as relief in a post-disaster context (Zhang 2021). Having said this, natural and man-made disasters occupy a central position in the configuration of human and in-group identity (Zhang 2022). Some studies suggest that disaster tourism is an inherent part of the dark tourism spectrum (Rucinska, 2016) or dark heritage formation (Roberts & Stone 2014; Biran, Poria & Oren, 2011). The question of identity and tragedy has no clear guidelines though it offers a fertile ground for future layouts (Farmaki 2013). Quite aside from this controversy, dark tourism and post-disaster tourism have inherently some basic differences which need to be discussed in the next lines.

Dark Tourism Studies

Although there is a serious discrepancy revolving around the origin, nature and evolution of dark tourism, as well as its homogeneity with other associated terms, it is safe to define dark tourism as a new tendency originated in secular societies which helps visitors to understand the proper finitude through the "Other`s death" (Stone & Sharpley, 2008; Dale & Robinson 2011; Ryan & Kohli 2006). Visitors, so to speak, to these dark sites look not only for outstanding and authentic experiences but also understanding of their own lives (Barton & Brown 2012; Stone 2012). Some voices have recognized that dark tourism is mainly associated with heritage consumption or sacred pilgrimage. Visitors are culturally motivated to move to traumatic spaces to deal with their troublesome past. Since dark consumption cements national heritage, it is safe to say culture, heritage and dark consumption are inextricably intertwined. To put the same in other simpler terms, dark tourism engages with a spiritual journey symbolically enrooted in a much deeper traumatic landscape, where the self certainly debates between the past and the present (Light 2017; Hartmann 2014; Strange & Kempa 2003; Collins Kreiner, 2016; Olsen & Korstanje 2019). In some of her earlier works, Maria Buda acknowledges that dark tourism has a polysemic nature mainly marked by its association with other derived topics which include prison tourism, thana tourism, and mourning tourism (only to name a few). Doubtless, dark tourism captivated the attention of countless scholars in recent years. However, as she alerts, the nature of dark tourism, as well as the profound psychological motivations of visitors, remain unclear. In this respect, psychoanalysis plays a leading role in unpacking the nature and evolution of this social phenomenon. Psychoanalysis has indeed been overlooked systematically by the applied research in the fields of tourism. In this vein, dark tourism should be contemplated as a part of effective tourism simply because it gives the opportunities to visitors to dive into their emotional inner world. The self often moves between love and death drives, in which case, the curiosity for death is naturally intricated in our psychology. Having said this, dark destinations are selected or rejected according to our biography and the emotional world which looks for answers that explain death. She gives a convincing argument alluding to dark tourism as a conflictive ritual where the emotionality before death confronts with pleasure (Martini & Buda, 2020; Prayag, Buda & Jordan, 2021; Cave & Buda, 2018; Buda 2015). In consonance with this, Philip Stone (2006) develops a conceptual model to understand the spectrum of dark sites. Per his viewpoint, dark sites oscillate between lightest to darkest typologies. This spectrum is given not only by the type of infrastructure disposed to welcome visitors but also by how fresh the memory is. Those sites characterized by extreme pain or mourning are often oath to be open to mass tourism (unlike fun dark factories). The shared emotionality occupies an important space in the configuration of shared discourse. The interplay between demand and supply in dark tourism has been widely explored in different works (Sharpley 2006; Farmaki 2013; Stone & Sharpley 2008). This point leads other authors to discuss the issue from the lens of critical sociology. As Joy Sather-Wagstaff (2016) eloquently observes, beyond the hegemony of the economy, dark tourism appeals to human reciprocity. Based on her auto-ethnography on Ground-zero, she argues that death not only jolts culture from a lingering complacency but also opens the doors to solidarity with victims. The intervention of the state to impose a fabricated discourse (heritage) of the traumatic event leads to ideological forms of distortion, where the real reasons behind the disaster remain covert. At the same time, dark heritage situates as a complex space of conflict and politics. Last but not least, Rodanthi Tzanelli, Senior Professor at Leeds University (UK). Per Tzanelli, dark tourism moves in the shades of a much deep colonial discourse where first-world tourists are unfamiliar with the crimes and brutalities perpetrated by European nations in the colonial period. Following this, dark tourism should be seen as an ideological mechanism of indoctrination that affirms the centre-periphery dependency culturally forged in the colonial expansion. For Tzanelli, dark tourism and post-disaster tourism can be used exchangeable as similar terms. In the next section, we will discuss the commonalities and differences between post-disaster tourism and dark tourism.

Post Disaster Tourism

Like dark tourism, post-disaster tourism is not a new term but scholarship paid attention to this emerging topic just after the 2000s decade. Post-disaster tourism is framed into the constellations of disaster management or disaster resilient management (Rahayu, Haigh & Amaratunga, 2018; Korstanje & Ivanov, 2012). At a closer look, the aims of post-disaster tourism are threefold. Firstly, it offers a conceptual framework useful to policymakers to accelerate the recovery facet just after a disaster (Seraphin, Korstanje, & Gowreesunkar, 2020). Secondly, it enhances the collective resiliency supporting locals to rememorate their victims while laying the foundations for a new re-start. Resilience should be understood as the capacity proper in each human group or culture to deal with traumatic events (Korstanje & Ivanov, 2012; Kato 2018). Third, post-disaster tourism enacts new gentrification processes which re-cycle the old-fashioned urban dynamism and social maladies. Most certainly, post-disaster consumption attracts new foreign investors interested in funding local communities (Katsinas, 2021). Chew & Jahari (2014) lament that there is a certain disconnection between risk perception theory and post-disaster studies. This happens simply because the promotion of risky destinations or destinations whipped by disasters is relatively new in the planning process. To this end, Chowdhury, Prayag & Orchiston (2018) said overtly that relational capital, which means the skills and capacities to show empathy for the "Other", has a direct impact on adaptative resiliency while optimizing business performances. Tucker, Shelton & Bae (2017) hold that tourism assists locals to transform traumatic experiences into hope. This change appeals to a process of transition where narratives are moulded by a combination of destruction and renewal. To some extent, this type of empathy for the victims is what has in common with dark tourism and post-disaster tourism. Zhang (2021) equates dark tourism to disaster tourism insofar as both are successfully employed as a part of economic relief while placating the devastating effects of trauma. Per his obtained outcomes, disaster ignites cognitive and emotional dimensions which lead to the creation of relational experiences. Like dark tourism, post-disaster consumption revolves around the "Other`s pain" engaging with the victims. The second element in common lies in the fact both construct a shared narrative (heritage) which is packaged, commoditized and exchanged with visitors. Dark tourist sites offer a lesson about the disaster which is cannot be forgotten. Dorota Rucinska toys with the belief that post-disaster tourism is part of the dark tourism spectrum. There is a wide range of niches which are psychologically motivated to gaze at spaces obliterated by disasters and catastrophes. This thanatological drive is commoditized and channelized by specialized tour operators which makes disaster a cultural product. Jordan & Prayag (2022) evince how disasters often are thought of within the fields of dark tourism attractions representing a limonoid space where locals and tourists interact with each other. Even if the intensity of the experience in these sites varies on culture and time, no less true seems to be that dark tourism empowers and stimulates consumption with positive direct consequences on the locals` lives. However, both views depend on how the event is interpreted. For tourists, the dark side is seen as a lesson of what can happen in their societies, while for survivors it is a space of mourning and emotional engagement. Sometimes, communities affected by disasters are not empathic with the idea of developing tourism. In consonance with this, Korstanje & Baker (2018) have explored the case of Cromañon and ESMA in Argentina. Both sites are spaces of memory dedicated to the victims of an accident and the violent repression of the Juntas in the 70s decade. In both cases, survivors are reluctant to accept mass tourism because they strongly believe the economic factor played a vital role in the traumatic event. It is safe to say that mass tourism, far from being a healing instrument (at least for them) is part of the problem because it ignites corruption and conflict. These findings very well coincide with Stone`s darkest spectrum widely described in many other studies (Stone 2006; Biran & Hyde 2013; Raine 2013; Huermann & Chhabra 2014).

As the previous argument is given, this does not authorize to say that all dark tourism sites are related to disaster consumption. Some cemeteries, prisons, concentration camps, and spaces of mass death are not strictly associated with natural disasters. Not surprisingly, the main difference between dark tourism and disaster tourism rests on the fact that dark tourism harps on the "significant Other`s death", no matter the context whereas disaster tourism operates in the shadows and clouds left by a natural or made-man disaster. Lastly, Richard Butler (2017) focuses on the concept of resiliency as the touchstone of post-disaster tourism. This element which leads to responsibility and ethics not necessarily is present in dark tourism consumption. Echoing this, Isaac, Cakmak & Butler (2019) alert the fact the category of dark tourism is very complex and hard to grasp. Some of the elements are circumscribed to suffering, but not limited to. The motivation of dark tourists ranges from curiosity about mass death and destruction to heritage consumption. This is not exactly what occurs in disaster tourism. Last but not least, Korstanje (2020) exerts a caustic critique of dark and post-tourism studies. Methodologically speaking, the obtained results are derived from the administration of open or closed-end questionnaires, where the visitors are seen as the main source of information. This seriously confronts a basic assumption in applied research which says that subjects often lie to protect their interests or are unfamiliar with their inner world. As he puts it if I ask a gangster about his profession, what does he supposedly answer? he surely will say I am a respectable businessman, but is he a businessman? Interviews -unless combined with other methods - rarely show a scientific correlation among variables (Korstanje 2016; 2020). Farfetched as it may sound, other derived problems in both (dark and post-disaster tourism) are associated with the urgency towards economic alleviation. The commoditization of dark sites (which makes tragedy an exchangeable product) paves the way for a kitschification of the tragedy (Potts, 2012) prone to create a spectacle. When this happens, not only the real reasons for the event are forgotten or biased but also the probability to face a new tragedy turns higher. What is more important, the vital -if not ethical- the question is whether post-disaster tourism and dark tourism need human suffering to prosper, in which case some scholars call attention to the dependency between death and profits. To put the same bluntly, dark and post-disaster sites are systematically orchestrated around the "Other`s suffering" as the main commodity, to what extent does this means that the structural conditions that led to disaster are corrected is a point of discrepancy that exegetes of post-disaster tourism fail to respond. At the time these dark spaces multiplicate less intention to change the cultural background that made the disaster possible. As a result of this, -it is not simplistic to say- disasters [far from being reduced] are sold and exchanged as commodities in a macabre form (Korstanje 2016; Tzanelli 2016; Bowman & Pezzulo, 2009).

Conclusion

Without any doubt, the present chapter has discussed the vulnerability of the tourism industry to external threats. Since 2001, several dangers have placed the industry in jeopardy. In this context, the risk perception doctrine emerges as a leading paradigm that helped policymakers to identify and eradicate global threats. The escalation of violence and the systematic failures to deter the effects of climate change has invariably led to the adoption of new paradigms mainly linked to post-disaster consumption. Dark tourism and post-disaster tourism are certainly inscribed as new niches oriented to make from the disaster the main commodity. The present chapter explored the ebbs and flows of both trends while laying the foundations for a new understanding of what we dubbed the spectacle of the disaster. In the first section, we shed light on the 11 Sept of 2001 as a foundational event that marked a new epoch. The terror and political violence traversed all nations worldwide. The failure of risk perception theory sets the pace for a new paradigm centered on adaptancy and resiliency. However, the question of adaptancy has some ethical problems which beg the question: to what extent we can solve the conditions that generate disasters if we adapt to them? Or how we can fix the background that led to a state of disaster if the reasons are biased or theatricalized? There is no clear answer to these questions, in which case they represent the launching platform for the next layouts or interrogations.

References

Barton, A., & Brown, A. (2012). Dark tourism and the modern prison. *Prison Service Journal*, *199*, 44-49.

Biran, A., Poria, Y., & Oren, G. (2011). Sought experiences at (dark) heritage sites. *Annals of tourism research*, *38*(3), 820-841.

Biran, A., & Hyde, K. F. (2013). New perspectives on dark tourism. *International Journal of Culture, Tourism and Hospitality Research*. 7(3): 191-198.

Bowman, M. S., & Pezzullo, P. C. (2009). What's so 'dark'about 'dark tourism'?: Death, tours, and performance. *Tourist Studies*, *9*(3), 187-202.

Buda, D. M. (2015). *Affective tourism: Dark routes in conflict*. Abingdon, Routledge.

Butler, R. W. (2017). *Tourism and resilience*. Wallingford, CABI.

Çakar, K. (2020). Investigation of the motivations and experiences of tourists visiting the Gallipoli Peninsula as a dark tourism destination. *European Journal of Tourism Research*, *24*, 2405-2405.

Cave, J., & Buda, D. (2018). Souvenirs in dark tourism: Emotions and symbols. In *The Palgrave handbook of dark tourism studies* (pp. 707-726). Palgrave Macmillan, London.

Collins-Kreiner, N. (2016). Dark tourism as/is pilgrimage. *Current Issues in Tourism*, *19*(12), 1185-1189.

Chen, S., Xu, Z., Wang, X., & Škare, M. (2022). A bibliometric analysis of natural disasters and business management in tourism. *Journal of Business Economics and Management*, *23*(2), 305-326.

Chew, E. Y. T., & Jahari, S. A. (2014). Destination image as a mediator between perceived risks and revisit intention: A case of post-disaster Japan. *Tourism management*, *40*, 382-393.

Chowdhury, M., Prayag, G., Orchiston, C., & Spector, S. (2019). Postdisaster social capital, adaptive resilience and business performance of tourism organizations in Christchurch, New Zealand. *Journal of Travel Research*, *58*(7), 1209-1226.

Dale, C., & Robinson, N. (2011). Dark tourism. In *Research themes for tourism* (pp. 205-217). Wallingford UK: CABI.

Dresler, E. (2022). Dark souveniring: just a souvenir or something more complex. *Journal of Marketing Management*, 1-21.

Farmaki, A. (2013). Dark tourism revisited: A supply/demand conceptualisation. *International Journal of Culture, tourism and hospitality Research*. 7(3): 281-292.

Floyd, M. F., Gibson, H., Pennington-Gray, L., & Thapa, B. (2004). The effect of risk perceptions on intentions to travel in the aftermath of September 11, 2001. *Journal of Travel & Tourism Marketing*, *15*(2-3), 19-38.

Fuchs, G., & Reichel, A. (2006). Tourist destination risk perception: The case of Israel. *Journal of Hospitality & Leisure Marketing*, *14*(2), 83-108.

Hartmann, R. (2014). Dark tourism, thanatourism, and dissonance in heritage tourism management: new directions in contemporary tourism research. *Journal of Heritage Tourism*, *9*(2), 166-182.

Hooper, G., & Lennon, J. (2016). *Dark tourism*. London, Taylor & Francis.

Heuermann, K., & Chhabra, D. (2014). The darker side of dark tourism: An authenticity perspective. *Tourism analysis*, *19*(2), 213-225.

Isaac, R. K., Çakmak, E., & Butler, R. (Eds.). (2019). *Tourism and hospitality in conflict-ridden destinations*. Abingdon, Routledge.

Jordan, E. J., & Prayag, G. (2022). Residents' cognitive appraisals, emotions, and coping strategies at local dark tourism sites. *Journal of Travel Research*, *61*(4), 887-902.

Jonas, A., Mansfeld, Y., Paz, S., & Potasman, I. (2011). Determinants of health risk perception among low-risk-taking tourists traveling to developing countries. *Journal of Travel Research*, *50*(1), 87-99.

Kato, K. (2018). Debating sustainability in tourism development: Resilience, traditional knowledge and community: A post-disaster perspective. *Tourism Planning & Development*, *15*(1), 55-67.

Katsinas, P. (2021). Professionalisation of short-term rentals and emergent tourism gentrification in post-crisis Thessaloniki. *Environment and Planning A: Economy and Space*, *53*(7), 1652-1670.

Kelman, I., & Dodds, R. (2009). Developing a code of ethics for disaster tourism. *International Journal of Mass Emergencies and Disasters*, *27*(3), 272-296.

Korstanje M. E (2009). "Re-visiting risk perception theory in the context of travel." E-Review of Tourism Research, 7(4): 68-81

Korstanje M. E (2016) *The Rise of Thana Capitalism and Tourism.* Abingdon, Routledge.

Korstanje, M. E. (2020). The dark tourist: Consuming dark spaces in the periphery. *Tourism, terrorism and security*. Korstanje M. & Seraphin H (eds). Bingley, Emerald Group Publishing.

Korstanje, M. E., & Baker, D. (2018). Politics of dark tourism: The case of Cromanon and ESMA, Buenos Aires, Argentina. In *The Palgrave Handbook of Dark Tourism Studies* (pp. 533-552). London, Palgrave Macmillan.

Korstanje, M. E., & Ivanov, S. H. (2012). Tourism as a form of new psychological resilience: The inception of dark tourism. *CULTUr-revista de Cultura e Turismo*, *6*(4), 56-71.

Korstanje, M. E., & Olsen, D. H. (2020). Negotiating the intersections between dark tourism and pilgrimage. *Dark Tourism and Pilgrimage*, Olsen D & Korstanje M. (eds), Wallingford, CABI, 1-15.

Martini, A., & Buda, D. M. (2020). Dark tourism and affect: Framing places of death and disaster. *Current Issues in Tourism*, *23*(6), 679-692.

Miller, D. S. (2008). Disaster tourism and disaster landscape attractions after Hurricane Katrina: an auto-ethnographic journey. *International Journal of Culture, Tourism and Hospitality Research*. 2(2): 115-131.

Miller, D. S., Gonzalez, C., & Hutter, M. (2017). Phoenix tourism within dark tourism: Rebirth, rebuilding and rebranding of tourist destinations following disasters. *Worldwide Hospitality and Tourism Themes*. 9(2): 196-215

Laws, E., Prideaux, B., & Chon, K. S. (Eds.). (2007). *Crisis management in tourism.* Wallingford, Cabi.

Lennon, J. J., & Foley, M. (1999). Interpretation of the unimaginable: The US Holocaust Memorial Museum, Washington, DC, and "dark tourism." *Journal of Travel Research*, *38*(1), 46-50.

Liu-Lastres, B., Schroeder, A., & Pennington-Gray, L. (2019). Cruise line customers' responses to risk and crisis communication messages: An application of the risk perception attitude framework. *Journal of travel research*, *58*(5), 849-865.

Light, D. (2017). Progress in dark tourism and thanatourism research: An uneasy relationship with heritage tourism. *Tourism management*, *61*, 275-301.

Lin, Y., Kelemen, M., & Tresidder, R. (2018). Post-disaster tourism: building resilience through community-led approaches in the aftermath of the 2011 disasters in Japan. *Journal of Sustainable Tourism*, *26*(10), 1766-1783.

Olsen, D. H., & Korstanje, M. E. (Eds.). (2019). *Dark tourism and pilgrimage*. Wallingford, CABI.

Potts, T. J. (2012). 'Dark tourism'and the 'kitschification'of 9/11. *Tourist Studies*, *12*(3), 232-249.

Pottorff, S. M., & Neal, D. D. M. (1994). Marketing implications for post-disaster tourism destinations. *Journal of Travel & Tourism Marketing*, *3*(1), 115-122.

Prayag, G., Buda, D. M., & Jordan, E. J. (2021). Mortality salience and meaning in life for residents visiting dark tourism sites. *Journal of Sustainable Tourism*, *29*(9), 1508-1528.

Rahayu, H., Haigh, R., & Amaratunga, D. (2018). Strategic challenges in development planning for Denpasar City and the coastal urban agglomeration of Sarbagita. *Procedia engineering*, *212*, 1347-1354.

Raine, R. (2013). A dark tourist spectrum. *International Journal of Culture, tourism and hospitality Research*, *7*(3), 242-256.

Ritchie, B. W. (2009). Crisis and disaster management for tourism. In *Crisis and Disaster Management for Tourism*. Bristol, Channel View Publications.

Roberts, C., & Stone, P. (2014). Dark tourism and dark heritage: Emergent themes, issues and consequences. In *Displaced Heritage: response to disaster, trauma and loss. Covenry I*, Corsane G & Davis P. (eds). Newcastle, Newcastle University Press. 9-18.

Rucińska, D. (2016). Natural disaster tourism as a type of dark tourism. *International Journal of Humanities and Social Sciences*, *10*(5), 1458-1462.

Ryan, C., & Kohli, R. (2006). The Buried village, New Zealand–An example of dark tourism?. *Asia Pacific Journal of Tourism Research*, *11*(3), 211-226.

Sather-Wagstaff, J. (2016). *Heritage that hurts: Tourists in the memoryscapes of September 11*. Abingdon, Routledge.

Seaton, A. V. (1996). Guided by the dark: From thanatopsis to thanatourism. *International journal of heritage studies*, *2*(4), 234-244.

Sharpley, R. (2006). Travels to the edge of darkness: Towards a typology of "dark tourism." In *Taking tourism to the limits* (pp. 239-250). Abingdon, Routledge.

Séraphin, H., Korstanje, M., & Gowreesunkar, V. G. (Eds.). (2020). *Post-disaster and post-conflict tourism: Toward a new management approach*. London, CRC Press.

Stone, P. R. (2006). A dark tourism spectrum: Towards a typology of death and macabre related tourist sites, attractions and exhibitions. *Tourism: An International Interdisciplinary Journal*, *54*(2), 145-160.

Stone, P. R. (2012). Dark tourism and significant other death: Towards a model of mortality mediation. *Annals of tourism research*, *39*(3), 1565-1587.

Stone, P., & Sharpley, R. (2008). Consuming dark tourism: A thanatological perspective. *Annals of tourism Research*, *35*(2), 574-595.

Strange, C., & Kempa, M. (2003). Shades of dark tourism: Alcatraz and Robben Island. *Annals of tourism research*, *30*(2), 386-405.

Su, R., & Yu Park, H. (2022). Negotiating cultural trauma in tourism. *Current Issues in Tourism*, 1-17.

Tucker, H., Shelton, E. J., & Bae, H. (2017). Post-disaster tourism: Towards a tourism of transition. *Tourist studies*, *17*(3), 306-327.

Tzanelli, R. (2016). *Thanatourism and cinematic representations of risk: Screening the end of tourism*. Abingdon, Routledge.

Yang, C. L., & Nair, V. (2014). Risk perception study in tourism: Are we really measuring perceived risk?. *Procedia-Social and Behavioral Sciences*, *144*, 322-327.

Zhang, Y. (2021). Unpacking visitors' experiences at dark tourism sites of natural disasters. *Tourism Management Perspectives*, *40*, 100880.

Zhang, Y. (2022). Experiencing human identity at dark tourism sites of natural disasters. *Tourism Management*, *89*, 104451.

Chapter 6

Selection, Adaptation and Survival: A Case Study on the Impact of the COVID-19 Pandemic on the Tourist Sector of Juiz de Fora (MG)

Thiago Duarte Pimentel*
Elias Mediotte
Paulo Rodrigues Cerqueira
Marcela Bifano Costa de Oliveira
Mariana Pereira Chaves Pimentel
and Stella Freesz
State University of Juiz do Fora, Brazil

Abstract

This book chapter aims to analyze the impacts of COVID-19 Pandemic on the tourism sector in Juiz de Fora (Brazil) based on the perspective of organizational ecology. The main argument developed here is that the pandemic has imposed a new condition over all the existing firms through two main forms: 'selecting' the survival firms through an extreme and severe scarceness of resources by a long period, and then, acting over the remaining firms imposing them a diverse set of strategies and actions to 'adapt' themselves to the 'new conditions. A field research was conducted between October 2020 and August 2021 focusing on the inter-organizational relationship among some

* Corresponding Author's Email: thiago.pimentel@ich.ufjf.br.

In: Tourism in Crisis
Editors: M.E. Korstanje, V. GB Gowreesunkar and S.W. Maingi
ISBN: 979-8-88697-643-4

important structural components of the tourism supply chain (lodging, food, travel agencies, cultural equipment, and transportation firms). Methodologically, a case study method was used to guide the mixed research, with a random but not stochastic sample of 66 firms, whose data were analyzed qualitatively by Content Analysis and quantitatively by Descriptive Statistics. The results show that 15% of the firms have closed the operations [selection variable] due to the pandemic; all remaining firms needed to adapt themselves in terms of legal compliance (restrictive laws), managerial practices (human resources and labor routines) and strategies (new technologies and new markets) [adaptation variable]; also, all of the remaining firms have kept their business in online mode, total or partially, even in the current period of pandemic decline [retention variable]. We conclude that all companies needed to reinforce their attention on the external environmental impositions to a greater or lesser degree.

Keywords: COVID-19, tourism, supply chain, Organizational Ecology Theory/OET, Judge of Fora-MG, Brazil

Introduction

Over decades, researchers dedicated to the theme of tourism needed to give numerous proofs of its theoretical and practical importance in order to counterbalance the scenario imposed by the *Doxa* of an apparent superficiality and absence of seriousness that, consequently, was refracted in the eyes of a commonsense observer (Krippendorf, 1999). Nowadays, however, the importance of tourism is out of the question. This activity crosses the four corners of the world, and is settled in both the economically central and peripheral countries of the capitalist system, involving labor and income generation, ideological and political borders, as well as different forms of border establishment, social markers and distinctions in the ways that ordinary citizens use their free time (Pimentel, 2022).

Despite this, the world has been invited - or better, was imposed- to reflect on the role of tourism in contemporary society, due to its continuous growth (of more than 56 times) since the decade of 1950 (Our World in Data, 2022[1]) However, the tourism activity has been reduced to virtually zero in the short

[1] The United Nations World Tourism Organization (UNWTO) estimates that internationally there were just 25 million tourist arrivals in 1950. 68 years later this number has increased to 1.4 billion international arrivals per year. This is a 56-fold increase. (see: https://ourworldindata.org/tourism).

period of nearly 2 years precisely in the emergency, growth, peak and decline of the global COVID-19 pandemic (Baum & Hai, 2020; Gössling, Scott & Hall, 2020). Studies in all areas of knowledge have been discussing the underlying issues, assumptions, and conditioning factors related to impacts of this pandemic as well as prospections of future scenarios to deal with its impositions. In this sense, several terms have been coined, and, among them, one is perhaps the best to capture today's *zeitgeist*: the 'new reality'. (Korstanje, 2020; Korstanje & George, 2021; Mediotte et al., 2021).

Thus, among all the productive activities, tourism was perhaps the most impacted by the pandemic started in China in 2019 (Flaxman et al., 2020). Directly dependent on the mobility of people, both nationally and internationally, the impacts were immediately seen through the movement of closing borders to contain the pandemic and, hinder its spread, to control its outbreaks by restricting mobility (Niestadt, 2020; UNWTO, 2020).

Brazil was not aside from this scenario, being, instead, one of the central places where the pandemic was developed in its greatest severity, computing today almost 687,962 deaths (Our World in Data, 2022[2]). The peak of the pandemic in this country occurred precisely between the years of mid-2020 to mid-2021, when worldwide health agencies recommended measures of social distancing and/or isolation, stoppage of the tourist trade, suspension of events, postponement of travels, and the establishment of sanitary barriers. In addition, Brazil has witnessed the largest outbreaks of spreading disease and increasing death tolls (Mediotte et al., 2021), exactly when measures were adopted by the national, state and municipal governments to restrict work in companies as well as the operation of these (Brazil, 2022[3]).

Taking into account the aforementioned context, the present study focuses on the analysis of the impacts of the COVID-19 pandemic on the tourist sector of the city of Juiz de Fora, taking this as a case study in a way it represents a synthesis of a reasonably common context in Brazil due to the size of the city, turnover, number of inhabitants, and the intermediate degree of development of the tourism sector (Pimentel, 2022).

Specifically, this paper aims to analyze the impacts of COVID-19 on the tourism sector in Juiz de Fora (Brazil) based on the perspective of Organizational Ecology Theory (OET). The main argument developed here is that the pandemic has imposed new conditions on all existing companies in

---

[2]https://ourworldindata.org/coronavirus/country/brazil?country=~BRA#what-is-the-cumulative-number-of-confirmed-deaths

[3] https://www.gov.br/cgu/pt-br/coronavirus/governo-federal

this sector and, in doing so, has mainly impacted them in two ways: first, by 'selecting' the surviving companies through an extreme and severe scarcity of resources for a long period; and second, by imposing on them a diverse set of strategies and actions to 'adapt' to the 'new conditions.

From the theoretical point of view, this study is justified because the perspective of OET is particularly interesting to analyze this context, since its emphasis lies precisely on the influences of environmental variables on organizations, in this case, taking into account the amplitude and magnitude of the disruptive event of the COVID-19 pandemic, which universally and intensely 'stopped' the whole world. So, this became 'the' event of the greatest importance, worthy of being analyzed in a way that it could heuristically represent the apex of the force of environmental selection over a given niche.

The OET lays mainly into the following premises: on the analysis of a multidimensional space (Liu; Van Witteloostuijn, 2020; Carrol et al., 2002; Hannan; Freeman, 1989, Hutchinson, 1978), the constant changes in scenarios (Koller, 2016), and the various components and factors of the environment that intensify the integration/ competition among organizations, resulting in their survival or failure. Thus, the OET is understood as a theory that defends the multiplicity of organizations that *must* to adapt to the environment in different aspects (social, economic, among others) to survive in the market and deal with competition through alliances with other companies with similar processes. The theory also contradicts the perspective that the management should only be focused (just or mainly) on internal factors because the external pressures determine the environmental conditions in which organizations behave and, in doing so, their possibilities of action, including their eventual (need for) restructuration in order to adapt to the changing conditions.

From the empirical point of view, even before the pandemic, there was already a pattern, in terms of the performance of the tourism sector on screen, showing "[...] existence of a traditional, mechanical production process with low added value and the possibility of stagnation" (Pimentel, 2020b, pp. 1-2), that, in the case, could be aggravated by a situation of crisis and exacerbated by restriction of resources, operating capacity and customers. In this sense, the study intends to shed light on the new 'standard' of operation imposed on companies that is marked by a minimum level of efficiency, and check how it was implemented, as well as the economic survival strategies adopted by the companies analyzed.

Organizational Ecology in Perspective

The twentieth century was the century of organizations, both from a practical and theoretical point of view. Several organizational theories emerged and developed in this period[4]. However, a special attention is deserved to those arisen from the late 1950s and early 1960s, because this period is marked by an intense economical restructuration based on the post-Fordist mode of production (*lean production*) (Harvey, 2008), with unprecedented implications for the accumulation of capital.

Since the 1960s, organizations have been subsumed into a rationalized and automated system of mass production and consumption of material goods (Harvey, 2008). At the theoretical level, organizational theories substantiated by the ideas of structural-functionalism and economic determinism emerged to support the reproduction of this new scenario, as in the case and the predominancy of the Institutional Theory, Contingency Theory and OET (Lounsbury & Ventresca, 2003), in attempts to articulate the efficiency of the network of actors and the combination of several behavioral and structural factors (Motta, 2001). All these theories have in common a relationship with the organizational environment[5].

The OET arose influenced by biological models on natural selection, adaptation and survival, appropriating them to the structural analysis and the view of complex systems in the post-industrial administration stage, characterizing itself as a postmodern discursive approach. As Montoya Restrepo et al. (2012, p. 47) ponder, the "concept of organizational ecology was coined to confirm the fact that all organizations are essentially complex ecological systems characterized by social interdependence and changes in

---

[4] Several classifications have been made and can serve as a reference for organizational theories and their approaches (cf. Angeloni; Fernandes, 1999; Pimentel, 2012).

[5] Organizational Ecology has similarities with other theories created contemporarily to them, such as, for example, the (a) Contingency Theory, which departs from environmental assumptions to show how this environment (the environment) draws the organizational structure, which appeared in the '60s, with the evaluation of factors that directly interfere in the structure. In this theory, the most effective structures to achieve the organization's objectives are evaluated. Therefore, the factors of the environment are related to the most appropriate techniques of management; (b) the theory of organizational economics where the functionalist character, exposes the rationalism and positivism present in organizational thinking, whereas the Economist theory focuses on the analysis of competitive advantages (Vasconcelos; Cyrino, 2000) and in it, the organization is seen as an arrangement of contracts (Caldas; Cunha, 2005); and also with institutional theory (Oliveira; Heber, 2020) institutional theory, which arises as a response to the external environment and permeates processes and strategies for interaction and adaptation to the environment (Selznick, 1996; Santos, 2011), although this appears poorly defined in Organizational Ecology theory.

physical systems." Many aspects of contingency can be considered evaluation factors of the response of organizations to external environmental factors such as age, size and the internal distribution of tasks. In this sense, the OET can be seen as a model of selection while the theory of contingency is more focused on models of adaptation (Zapata Rotundo & Mirabal Martinez, 2011), even if, in essence, they show more similitudes and complementarities than divergences.

The *Theory of Population Ecology of Organizations* emerged in the wake of this process, in the 1970s. It is traditionally credited to the work '*The Population Ecology of Organizations*' by sociologists Michael T. Hannah and John Freeman (1977). These authors were inspired by biological models on the selection and adaptation of species populations to seek explanations about the causes of the wide diversity of population fields of organizations and their variations in density, focusing on the impacts of environmental causalities (whether they being social, economic or political nature) in determining and complexing the field, and the structures of opportunities and competition for scarce resources, in which organizations arise, enter, develop, or even become extinct (Hannan & Freeman 1989; Hannan & Carroll 1992; Carroll & Hannan, 2000).

The basic premise underlying *Population Ecology* is that of Darwin's natural selection law (Aldrich and Pfeffer, 1976; Morgan, 2002; Yoshida, 2011) defending that organizations operate in specific niches (market segments) performance levels vary according to the internal structure of a niche in which they operate. This selection process assumes that organizations adapt to the different contexts to which they are inserted, to respond to the demands of society, and, in these concrete responses, survive (Hannah & Freeman, 1977). Therefore, they defend the natural selection model as an examiner of the distribution of resources in the environment, a factor that, when evaluated, involves an environmental perspective that generates, as a consequence, better adaptation of the organization to the environment, which, in the end, selects those organizations 'more able' to it.[6]

---

[6] In biology, the Darwinist Theory "[...] it is constructed from three basic phenomena: reproduction (replication), selection and mutation. For evolution to occur, a given population of individuals needs to reproduce." (Silva Junior, 2014: 16), admit going, therefore, two orders of facts: "1) existence of small organic variations, which occur in living beings at regular intervals of time and which, by the law of probabilities, can be advantageous for the individuals who present them; 2) Struggle for life that living individuals, which is due to the tendency of each species to multiply according to a geometric progression." (Caputo, 2011: 23).

In this theoretical framework, the environment exerts a *suis generis inertial pressure*[7] on organizations settled in a particular niche, sector or institutional field, that occurs in a relatively homogeneous and inescapable way (Geroski, 2001; Morgan, 2002; Holzmann, 2009), and pushes organizations to improve their internal policies, to specialize personnel and equipment, as well as to improve the information passed on to managers (Morgan, 2022). This may lead to inflexibility of some organizations (Holzmann, 2009), but it can also -and more frequently- be seen as being derived from their success in the market since organizations that are in leadership positions are less likely to persist for a long time since the demand for innovation is intermittent (Geroski, 2001).

Thus, OET emphasizes the dynamics of population growth and decline and has the Darwinian model of selection as the examining principle of the distribution of resources in the environment (Sutherland et al., 2013), appropriated in three types of analysis: (1) that focusing the organizations as an analysis unit *per se*, (2) that related to the environment and (3) and which uses multiple populations in a competition character (Whole & Brittain, 1986).

To Aldrich and Pfeffer (1976), this model of natural selection consequently generates a better adaptation of the organization to the environment, which is a theme of greatest concern of the Contingency Theory. However, many aspects associated with contingency are taken as evaluation criteria of the organization's responses to external environmental factors by authors of OET, such as the impacts of age, size and the internal distribution of tasks. Thus, although the OET predominantly focuses on 'selection' processes, while contingency theory prioritizes adaptation, there are more similarities and complementarities between them than divergences (Zapata Rotundo & Mirabal Martinez, 2011), and both ends dealing, to a greater or lesser extent, with both sides of the question.

Although much is said about selection in the OET, it is perceived that adaptation is also an important concept. Whole and Brittain (1986) point out that the OET research's strategy focuses on specialization, that, in turn, collaborates with the emergence of adaptive strategies. Hannan and Freeman (2005) see the perspective of adaptation in the literature on management as an influencing factor in the survival of the organization and consequently the

---

[7] According to Xu (2020), OET treats legitimacy as a central factor and focuses on competition inter-organizational in the research of the legitimacy of the social enterprise. In addition to this idea, Carrol & Hannan (1989) point out that the OET emphasizes that organizational legitimacy originates from structural characteristics of the context, such as the number of similar organizations, and the so-called population density.

selection of the organization to remain in the market. Therefore, adaptive advantage arises from the responses to environmental imperatives, and induces strategic behaviors that help the organization's survival because "[...] organizations need to adjust to face the challenge and align their internal resources with the external demand in the organization's attempt to increase the company's growth and adaptability in survival." (Koller, 2016, p. 839). The authors argue, from the perspective of adaptation, that:

> subunits of the organization - usually coalitions of managers or dominant coalitions - scan the relevant environment for opportunities and threats, formulate strategic responses, and adjust the organizational structure appropriately. [...] Contributors to this usually assume a hierarchy of authority and control that determines decisions regarding the organization as a whole at the top. It follows, then, that organizations are affected by their environments according to how managers or leaders formulate strategies, make decisions, and implement them. (Hannan; Freeman, 2005: 71).

Briefly, three characteristic themes of OET stand out, which are evidenced by the authors (Hannah; Freeman, 1977; Baum, 2012; Rocha, 2015) as being central: the demographic process – since this information is taken based on the failures of a given organizational population –; ecological processes – as they serve as the basis for the analysis of the relationship between the environment and the organization –; and, finally, environmental processes – which deal with the effects of institutional environments on a given organizational population. Additionally, Hannan and Freeman (1984) highlight some characteristics of OET: high rate of variation between forms of organization; high rates of organizational mortality, high competition in the sector; and non-abundant sources. According to Baum (1998), OET authors raise and use data about the creation and death of populations in order to understand that demographic process including their birth, development and failure. He adds that three indicators should be considered when dealing with OE analysis: the diversity, the difficulty and the instability of the organizations. In Table 1 (below) the main points of OET are summarized.

In addition to these factors, the need for adaptive advantage (Koller, 2016) is visible in the analysis of the strategic behavior adopted by managers to seek for the organization's survival. As Smith & Sidorova (2003) point out, there are some factors related to organizational survival within the theory of OET, namely: reliability, which is defined as the production capacity of collective products capable of attracting critical resources; size, because larger organizations transmit greater reliability than the smaller ones (Peli et al., 1994); age, because the older the time of existence tends to be related to a greater the credibility given to managers, employees and clients, especially in the case of service organizations; niche, because the competition acts as the main factor where those with characteristics less suitable to a given target are eliminated. Thus, OET is seen as an evolutionary perspective regarding the adaptability of organizations. One of the main forms that the theory proposes, throughout the study of Hannah and Freeman (1977), is the coupling of individual and organizational intentions transforming them into one.

Table 1. Main points of Organizational Ecology Theory (OET)

Scope	**Population of Organizations**
Central question	Why are there so many types of organizations?
Analysis unit	Population
Population concept	Organizations with the same form of resource-use; populations are likely to be delimited by market segment.
Population analysis	In three dimensions: (1) belonging to an industry (i.e., producing the same product) and limited by market segment; (2) sharing the same resource-rich fundamental environment; (3) sharing the same organizational attribute (Hannan and Freeman 1987; Hannan and Carroll 1995; Carroll and Hannan 2000).
Measures and criteria	Shape, density and diversity
Basic idea	The environment influences the organization's disposition
Study objective	Variation of the population of organizations (birth, growth and mortality), diversity, size and density of organizations, as well as structural inertia of the field and forms of selection, adaptation and retention
Main characteristics of the group	Diversity among organizations; difficulty in adapting to the environment by organizations; variability in organizations.
Basic change process	Variation; retention; competition.
Main assets	Structural inertia; Changes; density of organizations; use of resources; competitive and legitimizing factors; institutional environments; technological cycles.

Source: Own elaboration from the literature review, especially based on Hannah & Freeman (1977), Holzmann (2009) and Halpin (2015).

Looking outside organization, to the environment, OET is founded on a multidimensional space (Liu; Van Witteloostuijn, 2020; Carrol et al. 2002; Hannah; Freeman, 1989, Hutchinson, 1978), given the constant changes in scenarios (Koller, 2016), to the various components of the environment where organizations are established beyond the various factors that intensify the integration/ competition between them and result in their survival or failure. Carroll (1984) completes this idea by defending that there are three levels of analysis within OET and that they are respectively: the organizational level- which is based on the perspective of development; the population level – which uses the selection approach and finally the Community level, which handles macro-evolution as a strategy. In the author's view, the OET emphasizes the multilinear and probabilistic nature of evolution.

Complementarily, Aijie (2011) argues that OET is done through the following composition: internal structures (organizations are an organic unit with complex group relationships); composition of species (equal or related industrial economic units that form clusters); sharing of resources (results from associations between companies, companies and research institutions and services and intermediaries, in addition to the production and trade relationship between suppliers and customers and users of the *ecological chain of upstream* and *downstream*); external environment (a cluster-filled environment is a fertile space for rapid business growth) and, ultimately, dynamic resources.

Table 2. Variation and characteristics of Organizational Ecology Theory (OET)

Possibilities for generating the environment	Key points of each variation
High rate of variation between forms of organization	As individuals learn about the past, they better adapt to the future by making individual behavior interfere with the characteristics of the organization, differentiating them from each other as a result. Therefore, there is a coupling of individual and organizational intentions.
High organizational mortality rates	Organizations respond relatively slowly to the occurrence of threats and opportunities in their environments. Thus, due to the structural inertia in the skeleton of the organization, such a response often does not occur under the time required by the external environment, causing many organizations not to resist.
High competition in the sector	With non-adaptation over time, new organizations are created by increasing competition between existing ones.
Non-abundant sources	The resources – raw material, labor, use of political support – according to the authors are scarce and organizations that have more access to them are the ones that have the greatest reliability and the greatest influence in the market, thus limiting the use of resources.

Source: Own elaboration (2022).

In this analysis of organizations, the niches are seen as complementary to each other and are classified into three dimensions, i.e., space dimension (that is responsible for the size and life cycle of companies), resource dimension (that determine the use of internal and external environment resources) and role dimension (that determine the functions of organizations) (Hutchinson, 1978). Therefore, according to Oliveira & Heber (2020, p.103) the virtue of this multidimensional field's analysis lays in the fact that "organizational foundation and failure are influenced by environmental, demographic and ecological processes. Environmental processes, specifically, are categorized as institutional and technological."

In this sense, Hannan (2022, p. 5) emphasizes the impressive diversity of themes and the generality of studies that were influenced by authors and applied the analytical structure of OET, that to several organizational populations: "airlines, auditors, automobile producers, banks, breweries, credit unions, electricity suppliers, electronics producers, labor unions, life insurers, newspapers, semiconductor producers, social movement organizations, social service agencies, software producers, terrorist organizations, venture capital groups and wineries."

Currently, the influence of the OET has been furthered in the United States, followed by the Netherlands, England, Germany, Australia, Canada and France. In Brazil, and other Latin American countries, this influence is beginning to gain space. In developed countries, the theory has been used in environmental science studies, mainly focused on sustainability factors of organizations. In Brazil, researchers are centered on the scope of organizational management[8]. Thus, OET has been applied in the perspective of the "ecology of governance organizations", which seeks to identify what is or what is not governed, what are the legitimate powers of a governor and how their political preferences can be instantiated in rules (Lake, 2020).

Several authors (Dawkins, 1976; Hawley, 1986; Palmaka, 2010), as well as Silva Junior (2014), understand that the OET deals with the theme of variation, selection and retention. On Morgan's perspective (2002), the internal pressure itself is the trigger for the development of the organization itself, which causes it to improve internal policies, the specialization of personnel and equipment, and the information passed to managers. Such

[8] In the 171 records of studies related to OET overviewed in the bases Web of Science and Scopus, only 4% refer to the Brazilian context Available At: https://www-webofscience.ez25.periodicos.capes.gov.br/wos/woscc/analyze-results/f92d4f96-7b3b-466c-9751-14eb8748ac8d-482eabe4, access on 11/08/22.

pressure can be understood as the inflexibility of organizations (Holzmann, 2009).

Geroski (2001) corroborates the idea of inertial pressure by understanding that it can derive from the success of the organization in the market, and that market leadership positions have fewer possibilities to persist for long since innovation is always occurring. Holzmann (2009) complements this by addressing that the factors that create inertia can be sources of competitive advantages, and Caldas & Cunha (2005) see inertial pressure as a facilitating mechanism for the survival of organizations.

Gathering the conceptualization of previous authors, Lopes (2017, p.249) argues that "organizational ecology seeks to understand a set of factors that explain organizational success or failure, considering that companies are seen from the perspective of the organizational population". Melo (2002) adds to this discussion arguing that OET is based on the principles of self-regulation opposed, consequently, to hierarchical, centralized and external factors. As Melo (2002, p.8) points out

> Socio-ecological regulation is based on the interdependence of organizations, which, to survive in an environment with a high degree of uncertainty, need to rely on a constant negotiation of roles, objectives and mutual advantages, defined from shared values. This is achieved with the support of a learning process.

While OET has been useful to analyze the influence of the environment on organizations, it has, on the other hand, not without its critics. According to Oliveira (2016), the decisions of organizations obey a deterministic and conservative order that is negotiated, emphasizing normative aspects, enabling consensus and reacting to divergent interests. Conversely, Miguel Cunha (1999), sharing Donaldson's (1995) ideas, understands OET as an *anti-management perspective*, as it highlights the functions of the external environment and diminishes the functions of the manager. Managers, according to the author, are not necessarily 'heroes', as shouldn't be treated as 'anti-heroes': they are organizational actors constrained by context, but not to the point that their action is determined "by the external environment" (Cunha, 1999, p.5).

In addition, Caldas & Cunha (2005) argue that change, although possible at the organizational level, is an eminent population phenomenon, instead of a continuous adaptation process directed to individual organisms. To the authors (Caldas; Cunha, 2005, p. 66), "this supra-organizational view of change repositions the role of managers, exposing the limitations of their actions".

Thus, this theory analyses a multiplicity of organizations that are apt to the environment in different aspects (social, economic, among others) so that these organizations can survive in the market, and deal with competition through alliances with companies that deal with similar processes. The theory also contradicts the perspective that the management of a company is only about internal factors because external pressures determine the organizations to restructure and suit the new conditions of the environment.

Therefore, based on literature above reviewed, it is possible to realize that the OET has several implications for practice. However, many of them are directly linked to the adaptation of the organization to the environment. This research becomes plausible if there is the understanding that the theory of OET helps to analyze several factors that influence an organization's survival in the market and the environment in which they are included, in addition to the competitive factors among the organizations.

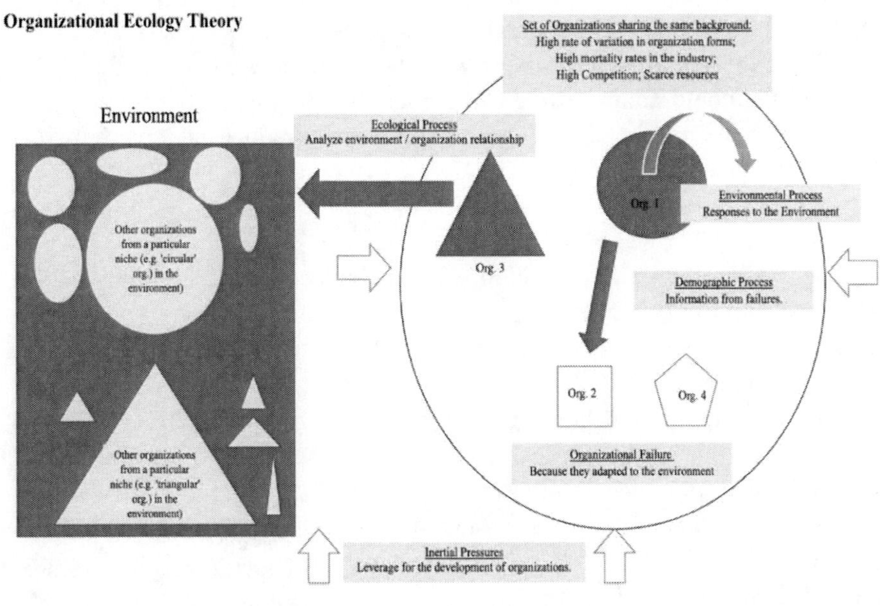

Source: Reproduced from Freesz & Pimentel (2022: 6).

Figure 1. Characteristics of OET about the environment.

Thus, the set of categories listed above is present in Figure 1, above, provides an overview of the main characteristics of OET about the environment. Through them, it is possible to identify the processes that mark the relationship between an organization and its environment, respectively in the ecological, environmental and demographic levels. In addition, the inertial pressures and situations of organizational failures are involved and verified by the impact of the pandemic on the tourism sector of Juiz de Fora, which is the central focus of this study.

Methodology

Characterization of the Research

Given the drastic and unprecedented impacts of the global pandemic crisis of COVID-19 in the history of humanity, and the absence of reasonably stable and valid parameters of previous situations on which to rely this study, we opted to use the method of *grounded theory*, because it prioritizes empirical data as a starting point for research guidance, gives its necessary flexibility and allows the researcher to investigate the phenomenon in its course. By doing so, we could adapt different methods and data collection techniques, ways of contacting the actors and identify the practices adopted by the companies (Glaser & Strauss, 1967; Strauss & Corbin, 1998; Bryant & Charmaz, 2007; Bianchi & Ikeda, 2008; Bryant & Charmaz, 2019; Morse et al., 2021).

The event of COVID-19 required rapid answers in terms of policies, strategies, and actions from public and private organizations to maintain standard operations. In this context, this article focuses on the impacts of this event on the companies of the tourism sector and this sector in general, particularly in the period between October 2020 to August 2021. A mixed research method of qualitative-quantitative character was used, but the general methodological approach was based on *the grounded theory*. In a way, the case study combined the specific techniques and procedures of a semi-structured questionnaire for data collection, Content Analysis for the qualitative analysis and Descriptive Statistics for the quantitative one.

Characterization of the *Locus* and Object of Study

As a *locus* and empirical object of study, we used the analysis of the case of the tourist sector[9] of Juiz de Fora (Minas Gerais, Brazil)[10], only as an illustrative example of the dynamics that are believed to be taking place, in other realities, in a reasonably similar way, even with different extensions and intensities. Additionally, it is believed to be this "[...] a very representative case of the dynamics and profile of medium and small supply chains in the context of domestic tourism in Brazil." (Pimentel et al., 2022:98).

Juiz de Fora is located in southeastern Brazil, in the state of Minas Gerais (Figure 2). It is a medium-sized city, with 516,247 inhabitants (IBGE, 2021), and has a high Human Development Index [HDI] – reached 0.778 according to IBGE (2010) – so it is considered a representative city in the region, with high economic development capacity. Among the industrial sector, the main activities are the production of textile products, food and beverage processing, metallurgy, furniture manufacturing and vehicle assembly (JFMinas, 2022). Specifically, the city is one of the main commercial centers of Minas Gerais. Similarly, it has a concentration of important services, mainly health and high school services.

In terms of tourism, Juiz de Fora has a large number of services and tourist offers and is considered one of the inducing destinations of Minas Gerais (SETUR, 2017). Your reputation can be witnessed in several ways, as you're seeing according to different stakeholders, governments, and outside agencies:

> It is ranked 11th among the Brazilian cities that receive the most international fairs and events (PMJF). According to studies by the Convention Visitors Bureau de Juiz de Fora, the Brazilian Institute of Geography and Statistics (IBGE) and the Getúlio Vargas Foundation (FGV), the city is ranked as one of the 100 best in the country for investments. Currently, it is in the process of updating the municipal tourism plan, according to the basic instrument of planning and management of tourism activities created by the Ministry of Tourism and SETUR (MG), intending to offer a quality service to visitors and the juiz-forana community (Pimentel, 2020, p. 20).

---

[9] Structural Standards of Tourist Services deal with aspects of lodging, food, travel agencies, cultural equipment and transportation. This delimitation was previously stipulated by taking into account the classification of essential tourism activities of the Ministry of Tourism (Brazil - Ministry of Tourism, 2015).

[10] This study is tributary of a series of previous researches conducted by the Economic and Social Observatory of Tourism (UFJF) on the tourist sector of Juiz de Fora (Minas Gerais, Brazil). It is based on a previously existing data set from an industry database, that were already formed by previous studies, and periodically expanded by the aggregation of new data.

The tourist system of Juiz de Fora was officially made up of about 337 organizations in 2021. However, empirical data suggests that this number may be underestimated. This universe is formed by individual entrepreneurs (8.6%), micro-enterprises (74.8%), small businesses (10.4%) and other types of business (6.2%) (Cadastur, 2021). Its components include lodging, food, travel agencies, cultural equipment and transportation services.

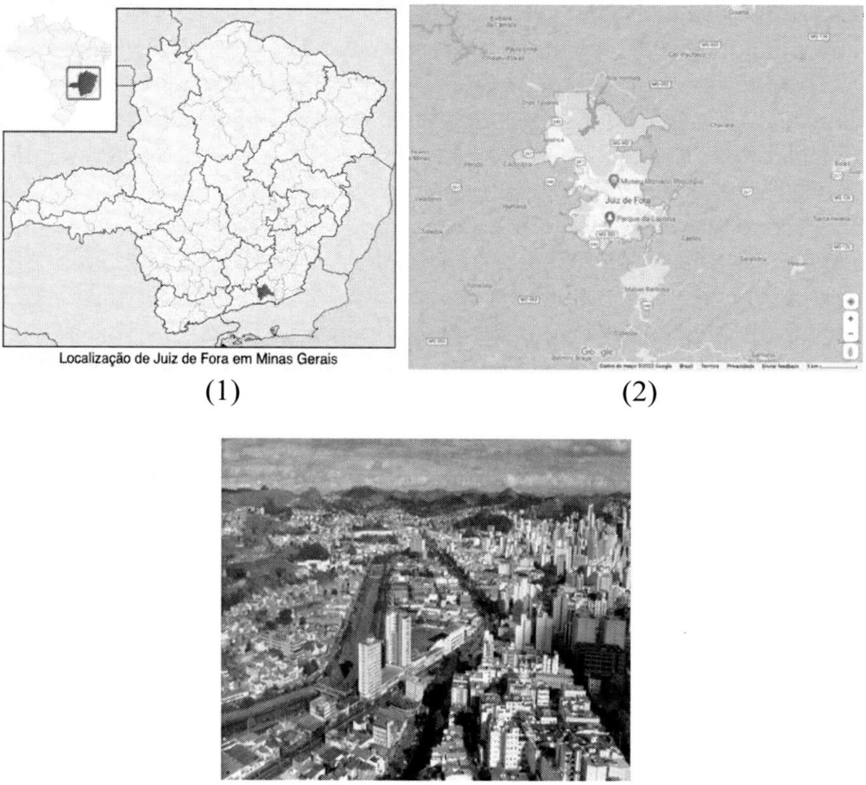

Source: Mosaic composition of images based on (1) Abreu (2006), (2) Juiz de Fora on *google maps* at the scale of 5km, (3) Municipality of Juiz de Fora (2022), reproduced from Pimentel et al. (2022:99).

Figure 2. Location of the city of Juiz de Fora.

Concerning the subsectors of tourists, transport is the most representative (29.7%). The tourist agencies are very significant (27.9%) among the tourist business, which means that the destination is also a generator of tourist flows to other locations. The services provided to tourists themselves are distributed among restaurants and other food services (16.3%), events (9.2%), tour guide services (8.6%), lodging (4.7%) and services especially related to entertainment (3.6%).

Table 3. Tourism subsectors that make up the production chain

Tourist components	Frequency	Percentage
Events (cultural equipment)	31	9.2
Accommodation	16	4.7
Other services (entertainment-related)	12	3.6
Restaurants (food services)	55	16.3
Tourism agency	94	27.9
Tour guide services*	29	8.6
Transportation services	100	29.7
Total	337	100.0

Note: * Tour guide services were presented disaggregated from the services of the tour agency.
Source: Cadastur (2021).

Data collection occurred between October 2020 and July 2021 and counted a random, non-representative and convenience-selected sample consisting of 66 companies in the on-screen tourism sector, that was submitted to a semi-structured electronic questionnaire (research instrument), consisting of 65 open and closed questions, divided into 6 blocks, namely: (i) General profile of the company; (ii) Management operations; (iii) Inter-organizational relationship; and (iv) Internal Management Process (Table 3).

Data Analysis: its Logic and Structure

According to the list of data presented in the methodology, the analysis of this study was structured according to the 4 steps described in the following and represented in Figure 3, below.

In this sense, the first step was the presentation of the blocks related to the organization and structuring of the article, that refer to the analysis of the empirical study. These blocks were dimensioned into 6 types of institutional Profiles: –1 - Sociodemographic Profile of the Interviewee; –2 - Organizational Demographic Profile; –3 - Employee Profile; –4 - Economic Profile; –5 - Production and Logistics Management Profile; 6 – Interorganizational Relations.

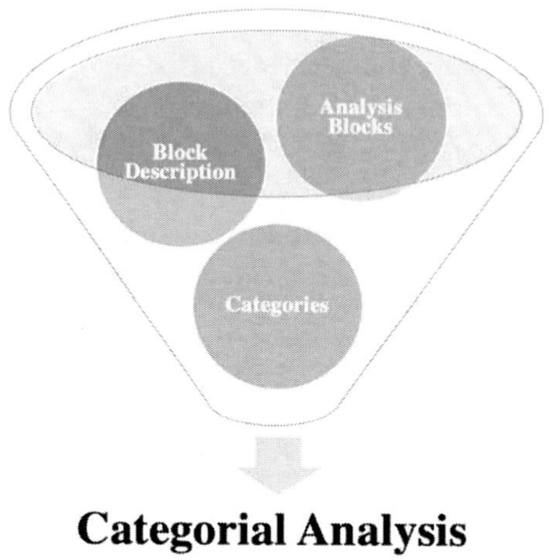

Source: Own elaboration from the research data.

Figure 3. Data analysis structure.

The second step was the presentation of the description of the Blocks, based on the answers obtained by the representatives of the organizations mapped to this study. Therefore, the dimensions and constituent variables of each Analysis Block are displayed. Regarding the dimensions, we relate–1 - Sociodemographic Profile of respondents (Data of Representatives);–2 - Organizational Demographic Profile (Institutional Data);–3 - Employee Profile (Human Resources);–4 - Economic (Financial) Profile;–5 - Production management and logistics profile (Management);–6 - Interorganizational Relations (Strategic). In this sense, the variables are the details of each dimension, both presented in graphs and/or tables.

In the third step, we approached the constitution of categories (and subcategories), followed by their specific questions to the context of the study, relating them to the OET, focusing on the 3 main indicators: *selection, adaptation and survival.*

In the end is performed the Categorial Analysis, presenting the primary data of the research through graphs and statistical percentages, that were based on the sample collected and on the discussions about the context of the pandemic and its impacts on the tourism sector in Juiz de for in the period analyzed. In Table 4, the Analysis Blocks that originated the categories (and subcategories) of this study are presented.

Table 4. Blocks of analysis and scope of study dimensions/variables

Blocks	Description	Dimensions	Variables
Block 1	Sociodemographic Profile	Representative data	Age
			Gender
			Education
			Professional Occupation
Block 2	Organizational Demographic Profile	Institutional Data	Market Time
			Operation Branch
			Specific Subarea
			Space Type
			Size (qt. It worked)
			Coverage (Local x National)
Block 3	Employee Profile	Human resources	Employment Situation
			Average Remuneration
			Training
			Place of Residence
Block 4	Economic Profile	Financial	Billing
			Market Share
			Sales Volume
			Products Sold
Block 5	Production and Logistics Management Profile	Management	Operations Control
			Planning
			Stock Replacement
			Disclosure
Block 6	Interorganizational Relationships	Strategic	Innovations
			Partnerships
			Shares

Source: Own elaboration from the research data.

Analysis and Discussion

Data Presentation

Because the research sample is consisted of a mapping of 16 companies directly and indirectly linked to the tourism activity in Juiz de Fora, it is necessary to demonstrate, as an illustration, the composition of the interviewees, namely Representatives [Block–1 - Sociodemographic Profile], as well as their organizations of origin [Block–2 - Institutional Data]. It is important, therefore, to recognize these profiles and their nuances, and correlate them with the then pandemic scenario so that we could demonstrate their impacts on the aspects stated in the following Blocks. In this way, we start with Block–1 - Sociodemographic Profile, presented in the following Figure 4.

Source: Own elaboration based on the empirical data of research.

Figure 4. Representatives' Sociodemographic Profile.

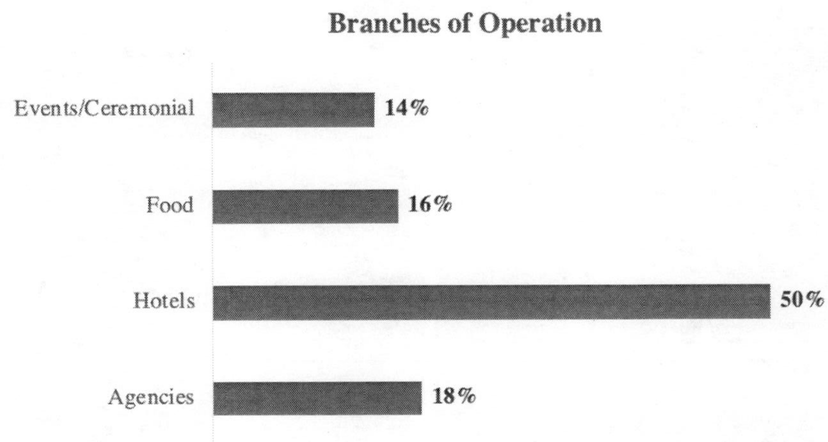

Source: Own elaboration based on the empirical data of research.

Figure 5. Branches of operation of the companies.

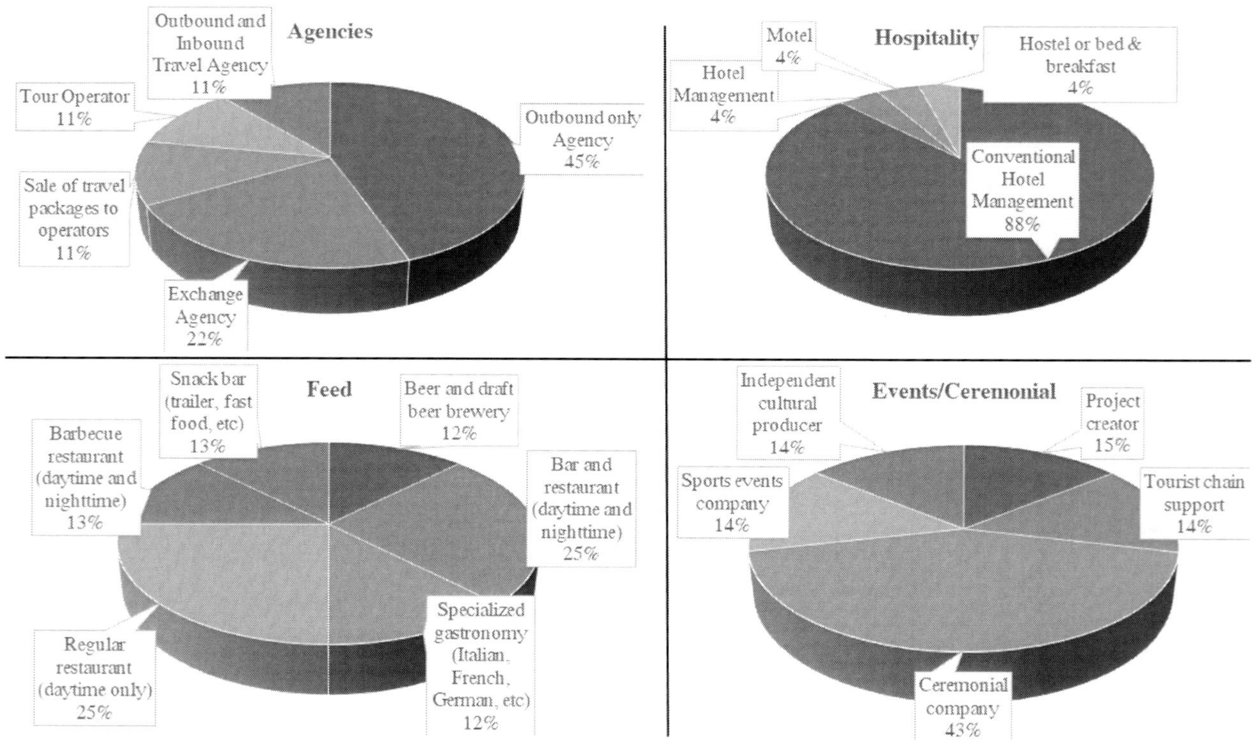

Source: Own elaboration based on the empirical data of research.

Figure 6. Subareas of companies' operations.

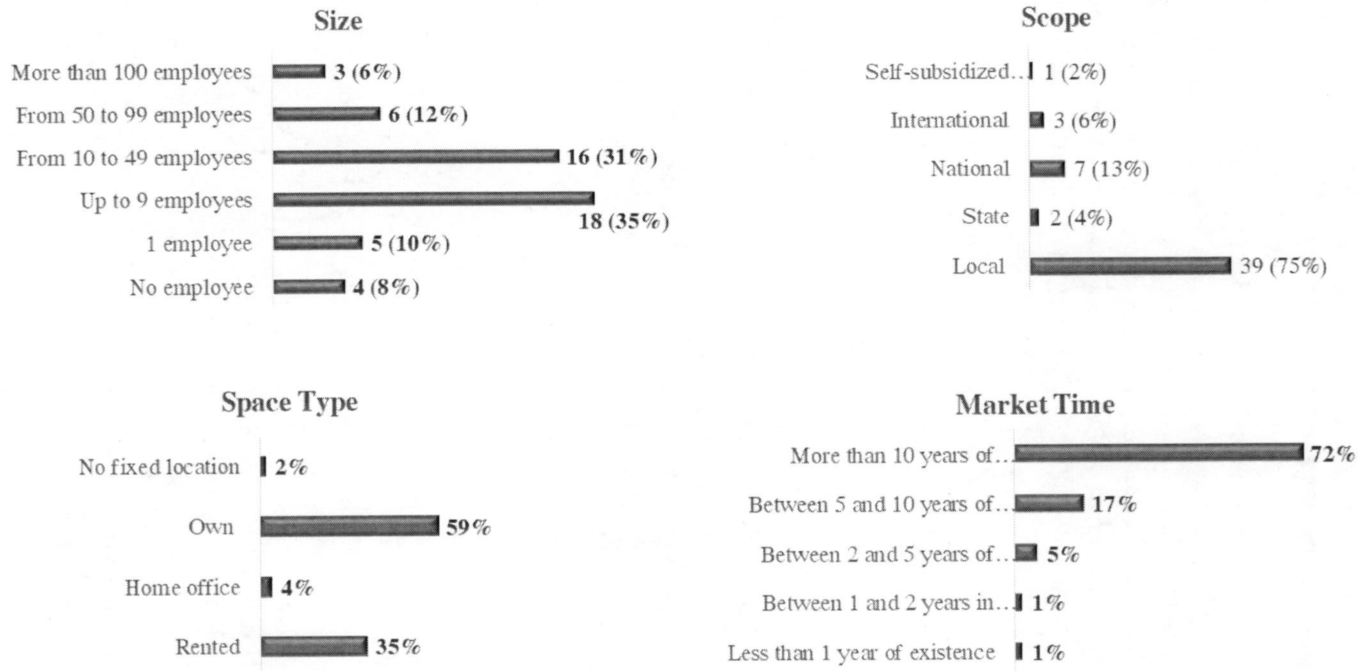

Source: Own elaboration based on the empirical data of research.

Figure 7. Size and scope of the analyzed companies.

It was observed of the total of 61 respondents, 37 of them are female, which corresponds to 60% of the sample, and their main age is around 40 years. The sample of male respondents consists of 24, totalizing 40%, and their main age is around 41 years. Regarding the list of positions held in the companies, 43% of them hold a university degree of formation and 34% have a master in business administration (MBA). Furthermore, it is perceived that the degree of specialization of women is higher than that of men, reflecting, mostly, the occupation of executive (CEO), strategic and managerial positions in the companies analyzed. In general, 49% of them hold executive positions, 39% hold managerial and strategic positions– while 11% are occupying operational positions.

Next, we present Block–2 - Organizational Demographic Profile. First, we highlight, in Figure 5, the variable Operation Branch.

According to the sample obtained, of the total of the companies mapped, 50% belong to the hospitality industry. The others show the following rates: 18% consisting of travel agencies, 16% of food companies and 14% of companies that operate with Events/Ceremonial. Graph 2 situates the subareas of these companies' activities (Figure 6).

As observed, the Agencies subarea has a higher concentration in the Exchange Agencies (22%), while the majority corresponds to half of this, especially for Emissive and Receptive Tourism Agencies, with 11%. In the Hotel industry, we identified that the performance in Conventional Hospitality (regular accommodation firms) constitutes the majority of the lodging sector in Juiz de Fora, totaling 88% of the mapped companies. Also, in the context of Food, daytime restaurants and day and night bars and restaurants correspond to 50% of the total sample, 25% for each one. Finally, about Events/Ceremonials, we identified that ceremonial companies are the ones with the highest predominance in the city, totalizing 43% of the companies focused on this type of operation.

Next, we present the other variables of analysis: Size and Scope, followed by the Type of Space and Time on the Market (Figure 7).

Note from this figure that the number of companies classified as Small Enterprises (From 10 to 49 employees) corresponds to 31%, and Microenterprises (Up to 9 employees) 35% of the sample. As for coverage, the companies mostly operating at the local level (75%), followed, with 13% at the national level. Although not very expressive, 6% of the companies analyzed operates at the international level.

In this sense, it is important to highlight that, according to the sample data of the companies considered as Microenterprises, 82% of them have operations at the local level, followed by 18% at the national level. On the other hand, for companies considered as 'Small' the result maintains the same perspective, 63% performing at the Local level, 25% at the National level and 12% at the international level. Most of the companies analyzed operate in their own spaces (59%) and 35% of them in rented spaces.

Finally, in reference to the Market Time of tourism companies in Juiz de Fora, most of them are already solidified in the local territory. Thus, 72% of the sample have more than 10 years of existence, followed by 17% with performance between 5 and 10 years. Later, we will make considerations about the research concerning the aspect of market time with the closing moment of the tourist trade in the city, resulting (or not) from the pandemic, in contrast to the correlation with the OET, especially about the Survival indicator.

After presenting some of the institutional aspects, it is important to understand the organizational dynamics of the tourism activity in Juiz de Fora considering now, the relations of the Blocks of Analysis and Scope of the Dimensions/Variables of the Study selected with the listed the categories of analysis (Table 5), focusing on the context of the COVID-19 pandemic, and during the time's horizon of this research.

Table 5. Analysis of categories

Categories	Description	Discussion
Category 1	Trade Closing	Was there a company closure? - Cause for closure?
Category 2	Impacts on the Tourism Sector and Subsector	What is the impact of the Pandemic on Companies? - Impacts on Workers - Impacts on the Wage Bill - Economic Impacts on Sales Volume
Category 3	Type of Customers	-Legal entity -Natural person - Customer Card
Category 4	Suppliers	- Supplier Card - Purchased Products -Relationship

Source: Own elaboration based on the empirical data of research.

Analysis of Categories and according to the Impact of the Pandemic

Category 1: Trade Closing

On the first category of analysis, on the closing of the trade during the pandemic period, the respondents were intended to answer the following questions: "Was there a closing of the Companies? And if there was, what was the reason for the closure? In congruence with the literature (Boto-García & Mayor, 2022; Grimmer, 2022; Mediotte et al., 2021; Ntounis et al., 2022; Robin et al., 2022, among others), several respondents reported that the interruption of tourism was due to the pandemic of COVID-19. Nevertheless, it was asked whether this action was applied in Juiz de Fora, due to such an epidemiological crisis. Using the data collection instrument, of the 66 representatives of the companies analyzed, 85% stated that the companies continued to function. On the other hand, only 15% attest that companies closed during the above-mentioned period. Of these percentages, we highlight that of the companies that maintained their operation, 63% have more than 10 years of experience in the market of Juiz de Fora, 44% of them operating at the local level. On the other hand, of the companies that closed, 100% claim to have been due to the pandemic, which endorses the arguments proposed by the literature.

Category 2: Impacts on the Tourism Sector and Subsector

On the impacts of the pandemic on the Tourism Sector and its Subsectors, we identified that the pandemic did not bring severe impacts for companies, specifically addressing the period of analysis of this research, because we realized that most of these organizations have many years of existence e were established at the local level, which guarantees some reliability and legitimacy in times of crises, reinforcing the OET concerns about the adaptation indicator. Corroborating to this perspective, we emphasize that companies with longer time of existence, as a rule, have fewer problems, in crises, as happened in the pandemic, because they have already been through other tough moments, and already experienced other situations of crises. Moreover, companies with greater financial and asset of resources also seemed to be, in this case, faced the crises with fewer problems.

The impact on workers' life was, first of all, on regime of work itself. Those who do not have official employment ties were the most affected, as liberal, autonomous professionals, individual microentrepreneurs, among others. However, in the empirical case of this work, we verified that of the companies that remained functioning, 68% of the staff belongs to the Labor

Law Consolidation System (CLT), which guarantees, minimally to employees, certain security in situations such as that reported in this study. Another aspect to be highlighted is the place of residence of the employees, an aspect that can be positive in times of crisis. According to the sample of this research, 96% of the workers of the companies analyzed are residents of the city of Juiz de for a and neighboring cities, which facilitates the journey to work, including, to a lesser extent, the burden of companies.

On the salary, we found that 71% of employees receive between 1 and 2 minimum wages, and the closing of the companies could cause negative impacts on the family life of these professionals. Furthermore, for the volume of sales, companies would suffer irreparable damage in case of the total closing of the trade. We identified that most of them would no longer profit from 80% to 100% on the sale of their products and/or services, regardless of seasonality, because the dynamics of the trade occur throughout the year.

Category 3: Type of Customers

Based on the instrument of data collection adopted in this research, we identified that, among the main clients of the companies, individuals and legal entities are concentrated, corresponding to 72% of the customer's portfolio. Within this parameter, 32% companies serve, monthly, in the range of 0 to 200 customers; 18% in the range of 201 to 500 customers; 32% in the range of 501 to 1000 customers; 10% in the range of 1001 to 2000 customers, and 2% in the range above 2000 customers. The evidence suggests the closing of the companies in the period analyzed could correspond to losses about 60% of the services related to non-fixed customers and 40% for companies that have a fixed customer base. Exclusively for legal entities, the data indicate that 27% of the total companies serve this client card. In case of a total suspension of their activities, those organizations would lose 21% of the services directed to non-fixed customers and 79% to companies that have a fixed portfolio of customers.

Category 4: Suppliers

The list of suppliers of the companies of the tourist trade of Juiz de Fora consists of 29% of Small/Medium enterprises located in the city or surroundings, and 22% of the individual service providers. This amount totals 51% of the suppliers for the companies analyzed. It is noteworthy that of the total number of suppliers in the city, most of them are small producers or smaller companies dealing with individual service providers in the city or surroundings. In this sense, if companies stopped functioning, these suppliers would lose up to 50% of the supplies marketed to the contracting companies. Of these, 50% of the main products supplied consists of cleaning and food materials. It is worth mentioning the arguments used by the respondents when they were asked about the advantages of maintaining relationships with suppliers. 43% of them claim that the Quality factor is the most important to keep business with these suppliers, 29% say that the Price factor is the most important, and 28% the Loyalty factor.

In short, we can understand that the pandemic impacted the organizational environment in different ways. In this sense, different levels of selection were seen, since a part of them stopped acting (15%), and a greater part survived (85%). And considering the latter, the OET advocates the analysis of the level of adaptation. Therefore, we demonstrated through the Blocks of Analysis and Scope of the Dimensions/Variables of the Study, what these surviving companies did to maintain themselves during the scenario of Pandemic, especially referring to the temporal horizon of this research. Moreover, this context contributed to identify the operational profile of these companies, which makes it possible to understand empirically some aspects of the organizational reality of the tourist trade of the city of Juiz de for a during this period.

Conclusion, Contributions and Recommendations

This study analyzed the impacts of COVID-19 on the tourism sector in Juiz de Fora (Brazil) influenced by ideas that fundaments the perspective of Organizational Ecology Theory (OET), in particular, evidencing how the pandemic affected the population of companies in the city's tourism sector based on three fundamental categories: (a) through selection, given by the mortality of firms due to the demands and restrictions imposed on the firms' environment by this disruptive event; (b) through adaptation, verified by the measures, practices and strategies adopted by firms due to the pandemic and in that context; and (c) through retention, that is, the maintenance of some of those measures, practices and strategies, making them permanent even after the pandemic's 'strength' diminished.

The main argument developed here is that the pandemic imposed a new condition on all existing businesses in the tourism sector and, in doing so, impacted them inexorably, severing the possibilities for individual exit or exemption. As observed by the results of the study, from the sample surveyed, we verified the mortality of 15% of the companies. This is high considering the short period and especially if we consider the fact that this number may be under-reported as it was not possible to survey all the existing companies and the limitations of the number of responses (39%).

Additionally, regarding the companies that continued operating in the market, it was possible to observe that almost all of them mention having been affected by the pandemic in terms of their management, labor and performance practices. The main measures adopted, also due to legal restrictions, were the reduction of the period of operation and modification in the working hours and work routine of employees; modification of management practices regarding human resources, in particular concerning the reduction of working hours, layoffs and management of the work of online teams; while the strategies adopted, some reactively (such as, for example, having to change their business environments to the virtual mode, even those companies that do not operate in these environments and were forced to do so) or proactively (such as, for example, the creation of new products and the search for new customer niches), were essentially concerned with the gradual and marginal (only the minimum necessary) incrementation, for most companies, of actions that would allow them to keep their businesses running. Some of these actions, especially the simplest and without additional costs (such as the use of 'free' social media, e.g., Facebook, Twitter, etc.) were maintained even with the decline of the pandemic.

In short, there was a selection of companies by the environment through the elimination of the supposedly 'less competitive' companies, the maintenance of those survivors that were able to withstand the extreme and severe shortage of resources for a long time, and then imposing a diverse set of strategies and actions to 'adapt' to the 'new conditions. The results show that 15% of the firms were closed [selection variable] due to the pandemic; all the remaining firms needed to adapt themselves in terms of legal compliance (restrictive laws), managerial practices (human resources and labor routines) and strategies (new technologies and new markets) [adaptation variable] and all of them have kept their business in online mode, even in the current period of pandemic decline [retention variable]. We conclude that an unpredictable and universal disruptive pandemic event determined all companies to reinforce their attention to the environment to a greater or lesser degree, especially in a globalized and unified world.

This study has intrinsic limitations related to the method used, predominantly qualitative, which does not allow the results obtained here to be extrapolated to all the companies in the sector or even to other locations and scales (state or national). The results presented here are valid only for the companies in the study sample. Additionally, it is worth mentioning that only a portion of the companies contacted responded and participated in the survey, which implies that many other non-participating companies may have been equally (or even more drastically) affected by the pandemic, and the mortality rate identified here might be underestimated. Finally, it is worth mentioning that specific characteristics of the studied context may influence the sample and the data obtained, since the predominant profile of the companies in the sector is consisted of micro and small companies, with a low level of professionalization and adoption of sophisticated planning and management techniques (Pimentel et al. 2016). It certainly influences the degree and type of selection, adaptation and retention forms mobilized.

Finally, future studies may explore elements that were beyond the scope of this work, such as, for example, delving deeper into the study of other variables within the theoretical framework of the OET, such as the shape, density, and diversity of all organizations in the sector (which would imply a survey); or studies based on related theories of environmental influence (such as Contingency Theory or Institutional Theory) or a combination of theories, for example, between Organizational Ecology and Contingency Theory. Studies along these lines of research are still scarce and potentially promising especially when related to disruptive environmental events of such magnitude as the COVID-19 pandemic.

References

Aijie, Y. (2011). Niche competitive strategy of hi-tech industrial cluster enterprises based on organization ecological system. In: *Proceedings... of International Conference on E-Business and E-Government (ICEE).* Available at: https://www.infona.pl/resource/bwmeta1.element.ieee-art-000005881547 accessed em 20/07/22.

Aldrich, H. E., Pfeffer, J. (1976). Environments of Organizations. *Annual Review of Sociology,* v.2, p.79-105.

Baum, H. S. (2012). *The organization of hope: Communities planning themselves.* SUNY Press.

Baum, T., & Hai, N. T. T. (2020). Hospitality, tourism, human rights and the impact of COVID-19. *International Journal of Contemporary Hospitality Management, 32*(7), p. 2397-2407. https://doi.org/10.1108/IJCHM-03-2020-0242

Boto-García, D., & Mayor M. (2022). Domestic tourism and the resilience of hotel demand. *Annals of Tourism Research, 93,* 103352. https://doi.org/10.1016/j.annals.2022.103352

Carroll, G. R. Organizational ecology. (1984). *Annual review of Sociology,* v. 10, n. 1, p. 71-93. Available at: https://www.annualreviews.org/doi/abs/10.1146/annurev.so.10.080184.000443, accessed em 12/03/22.

Carroll, G. R., Dobrev, S. D., Swaminathan, A. (2002). Organizational processes of resource partitioning. *Research in organizational behavior,* v. 24, p. 1-40. Available at: https://www.sciencedirect.com/science/article/abs/pii/ S0191308502240022, accessed em 20/07/22.

Chengalur-Smith, S., Sidorova, A. (2003). *Survival of open-source projects: A population ecology perspective.* Available at: https://aisel.aisnet.org/icis2003/66/, accessed em 22/03/22.

Flaxman, S., Mishra, S., Gandy, A., Juliette, H., Unwin, H., Couplan, H. & Bhatt, S. (2020). *Report 13: Estimating the number of infections and the impact of non-pharmaceutical interventions on COVID-19 in 11 European countries.* Imperial College COVID-19 Response Team, p. 1-35. https://doi.org/10.25561/77731. Acesso: 12 fev. 2021.

Freesz, S. & Pimentel, T. D. Ecologia Organizacional: Explorando a Teoria. In: *Proceedings... Encontro Da Associação Nacional De Pós-Graduação E Pesquisa Em Administração*, 46., 2022, on-line. Anais eletrônicos [...]. Maringá: Associação Nacional de Pós-Graduação e Pesquisa em Administração, 2022. Disponível em: http://www.anpad.org.br. Acesso em: 28 out. 2022.

Geroski, P. A. (2001). Exploring the niche overlaps between organizational ecology and industrial economics. *Industrial and corporate change,* v. 10, n. 2, p. 507-540. Available at: https://academic.oup.com/icc/article-abstract/10/2/507/678623, acessed em 08/01/22

Gössling, S., Scott, D., & Hall, C. M. (2020). Pandemics, tourism and global change: a rapid assessment of COVID-19. *Journal of Sustainable Tourism, London, 29*(1), p.1-20. https://doi.org/10.1080/09669582.2020.1758708

Grimmer, L. (2022). Lessons from the COVID19 pandemic: The case of retail and consumer service firms. *Journal of Retailing and Consumer Services, 68,* 103012. https://doi.org/10.1016/j.jretconser.2022.103012

Hannan, M. T., Freeman, J. (1977). The population ecology of organizations. *American journal of sociology,* v. 82, n. 5, p. 929-964. Available at:< https://www.jstor.org/stable/2777807>, acessed em 14/10/21.

Hannan, M. T., Freeman, J. (1984). Structural inertia and organizational change. *American Sociological Review,* 49, 1984, p. 149-164. Available at:< https://www.jstor.org/stable/2095567?&seq=1>, acesso14/10/21.

Hannan, M. T., Freeman, J. (1989). *Organizational ecology.* Harvard university press.

Hannan, M. T., Freeman, J. (2005). Ecologia populacional das organizações. *RAE-Revista de Administração de Empresas,* v. 45, n. 3, p. 70-91. Available at: https://bibliotecadigital.fgv.br/ojs/index.php/rae/article/download/37253/36019, acesso em 01/10/22

Hannan, M. T. (2022). *Rethinking Organizational Ecology in Light of Developments in Cognitive Science and Natural-Language Processing.* Stanford University.

Holzmann, P. F. (2009). *Evolução das franqueadoras de serviços no Brasil: um estudo das variáveis que influenciam a taxa de sobrevivência das empresas sob a ótica da Ecologia Organizacional* [*Evolution of service franchisors in Brazil: a study of the variables that influence the survival rate of companies from the perspective of Organizational Ecology*]. 2009. Dissertação (Mestrado em Administração) – Universidade Presbiteriana Mackenzie, São Paulo. Available at:< http://tede.mackenzie.br/jspui/handle/tede/731>, acesso em 08/01/22.

Hutchinson, G. E. (1978). *An introduction to population ecology.* Yale University Press, New Haven, Connecticut, 1978, USA.

Koller, M. R. T. (2016). Exploring adaptability in organizations: Where adaptive advantage comes from and what it is based upon. *Journal of Organizational Change Management.* Available at: https://www.emerald.com/insight/content/doi/10.1108/JOCM-01-2016-0008/full/html?casa_token=bHyC1fmNIVoAAAAA:BzktzNc0UABZKTUWkC2_4wgSViqQoL8pYMMtN0uFSGzpIreDyI9_ZUocmo01ubHrMg1DAgDmqaLvT8AchntjewXk_H4NrKH_Z8EoqjpIauWbszZz2t0j, accessed em 20/07/22.

Krippendorf, J. (1999). *The Holiday Makers: Understanding the Impact of Leisure and Travel.* London & New York, Routledge, Taylor & Francis.

Lake, D. A (2021). The organizational ecology of global governance. *European Journal of International Relations,* 27(2), p. 345-368.

Liu, M., van Witteloostuijn, A. (2020). Emergence of entrepreneurial populations: a feature dimensionality approach. *Small Business Economics,* 54(4), 971–989, https://doi.org/10.1007/s11187-018-0126-1

Mediotte, E. J., Emmendoerfer, M. L., Santos, Y. T., & Fraga, B. O. Planejamento público e gerenciamento de crises no contexto da pandemia da COVID-19 em destinos turísticos no Brasil: Ações sustentáveis ou reações econômicas? *Dos Algarves: Tourism, Hospitality & Management Journal (DATHMJ), 40.* Special Issue, 1-30, 2021. doi:10.18089/damej.2021.40.1

Morgan, G. (2002). *Imagens da organização: edição executive* [*Organization Pictures: Executive Edition*]. 2ª. ed. São Paulo: Atlas.

Niestadt, M. (2020). *COVID-19 and the tourism sector. European Parliamentary Research Service (EPRS),* 1-2. Disponível em: https://www.europarl.europa.eu/RegData/etudes/ATAG/2020/649368/EPRS_ATA(2020)649368_EN.pdf. Acesso: 12 mar. 2021.

Ntounis, N., Parker, C., Skinner, H., Steadman, C., & Warnaby, G. (2022). Tourism and Hospitality industry resilience during the COVID-19 pandemic: Evidence from England. *Current Issues in Tourism, 25*(1), 46-59. https://doi.org/10.1080/13683500.2021.1883556

Oliveira, R. T. D., Heber, F. (2020). Condicionantes ambientais da avaliação da Pós-Graduação em Administração 2013-2016 [Environmental constraints for the evaluation of the 2013-2016 Graduate Program in Business Administration]. *Revista Pensamento Contemporâneo em Administração,* v. 14, n. 3, p. 98-119. Available at: https://www.redalyc.org/journal/4417/441764512018/movil/, acesso em 07/02/22.

Peli, G., Bruggeman, J., Masuch, M., and O'Nuallain, B. (1994). A Logical Approach to Formalizing Organizational Ecology, *American Sociological Review* (59), pp. 571-593. Available at: https://www.jstor.org/stable/2095932, accessed em 22/08/22.

Petry, J. F., Silva, M. Z., Machado, D. P. N. (2016). Sinal dos tempos: o ambiente da organização que transcende [Sign of the times: the organizational environment that transcends]. *Revista Alcance,* 23(2), p.214-235

Robin, M., Rasel, S., Prayag, G., & Chowdhury, M. (2022). Did Closing Borders to Tourists Save Lives? Tourist Arrival, Self-protective Leadership, and COVID-19 Casualties. *Tourism Review International*, *26*(2), 215-221. https://doi.org/10.3727/154427221X16317419620237

Rocha, C. F. (2015). *Mortalidade empresarial: um estudo sobre a relação entre idade, tamanho e ambiente na indústria de alimentos da Bahia* [*Corporate mortality: a study on the relationship between age, size and environment in the food industry in Bahia*]. Dissertação (Mestrado em Administração) – UNIFACS Universidade Salvador. Available at:< http://teste.tede.unifacs.br:8080/tede/handle/tede/553>, acesso em 10/01/22.

Wholey, D. R., Brittain, J. W. (1986). Organizational ecology: Findings and implications. *Academy of Management Review*, v. 11, n. 3, p. 513-533, 1986. Available at: https://journals.aom.org/doi/abs/10.5465/amr.1986.57140723, acesso em 11/03/22.

World Tourism Organization (UNWTO). (2020). *Tourism is back to 1990 levels as arrivals fall by more than 70%.* Madrid: UNWTO. Disponível em https://www.unwto.org/news/tourism-back-to-1990-levels-as-arrivals-fall-by-more-than-70. Acesso: 15 fev. 2021.

Chapter 7

The Crisis in Tourism Research: A Critical Insight on Bibliometric Studies

Maximiliano E. Korstanje*
University of Palermo, Argentina

Abstract

The culture of metrics as well as the obligations of some researchers to publish in top-tiered journals is gradually devastating the professional applied research. Of course, there are some disciplines such as geography or anthropology which are insensitive to the bibliometric culture, but others like tourism or management are highly determined by these types of pressures. The culture of publishing or perishing is wreaking havoc in the fields of tourism and hospitality. The present piece interrogates furtherly on the problems, advantages and limitations of bibliometric studies in the constellations of tourism research. At the same time, we lay the foundations for understanding the future of the discipline in the years to come.

Keywords: tourism research, indiscipline of tourism, epistemology, culture of metrics, critical insight, tourism research crisis

Introduction

Doubtless, bibliometric studies have gained great recognition and traction over recent years. In the horizons of tourism and hospitality, these studies have been

* Corresponding Author's Email: mkorst@palermo.edu.

In: Tourism in Crisis
Editors: M.E. Korstanje, V. GB Gowreesunkar and S.W. Maingi
ISBN: 979-8-88697-643-4

multiplicated since the turn of the twentieth century (Barrios et al. 2008; Zhao & Ritchie 2007). As an emerging literary genre, the bibliometric analysis provides specialists and policymakers with an updated review not only on the problems that the industry comes across but also on the different academic waves and their respective objects of study. The growth of tourism research has invariably led to a climate of great dispersion where scholars remain unfamiliar with what is being published in other circles (Agapito 2020). Hazard Adams (1988) coins the term *academic tribe* to denote a shared behavior and common academic practices followed by in-group members. These academic practices are mainly based on a specific authority emanated by a group of scholars as well as educational institutions. Of course, needless to say, these groups move not only in specific territories but they keep their concrete frontiers.

In the constellations of tourism, the term is adopted by John Tribe (2010) who refers to the academic tribes as a circle of scholars working in a climate of indiscipline and academic dispersion. Such knowledge fragmentation, which Tribes conceives as a state of indiscipline, depends on the interest gradually captivated other disciplines for the study of tourism. As an object of study, tourism has certainly sparked different academic circles forming disciplines such as sociology, economy, geography, laws, and psychology [only to name a few]. In this vein, Evren & Kozak (2014) understand that the maturation of tourism research coincides exactly with the burgeoning growth of the tourism industry. To wit, Beckendorff & Zehrer (2013) acknowledge that the academic tribes need bibliometric studies to have a snapshot of what is investigated. The agenda of researchers not only is subject to internal and external factors but also is sometimes diffuse or more abstract. Academicians have often the liberty to move in different directions while ignoring the advice of Academia. For that reason, it is vital to develop efficient and accurate engines to understand the evolution of tourism research in the threshold of time. Per these authors, there is a network of scholars who have shed light on the discipline while paving the pre-conditions for the rise of different tribes, that operate in specific territories. The correct identification of the most important authors, as well as the global trends, is very helpful for the consolidation of tourism epistemology but [as authors alert] this should transcend the hegemony of the current bibliometric techniques. The knowledge production [far from being immutable] seems to be subject to countless global forces and trends, bibliometric studies should at the best describe with accuracy. In this vein, relational techniques allow a better fluid understanding of the intersection of impact factors with the emergence of new research techniques and methods.

Bibliometric Studies in Tourism

Today's bibliometric studies focus on the position of authors regarding two important variables: the number of publications that are placed in leading journals and the citation factor. Having said this, the number of citations is often measured through two indexes: the Hirsch index and the I-10 index (Law et al. 2009; Gursoy & Sandstrom, 2016). The H-index signals the maximum value of h given to an author who has published papers that have been cited at least h times. To put this simply, the H-index is centered on an interplay between the number of publications and citations. An author who had published extensively but has received few citations decreases in the H-index, while an author who is widely cited but not much prolific has further possibilities to rank higher. Plausibly, H-index not only explains the correlation between publications and citations but also recreates a hierarchal pyramid of scholars globally (Sheldon, 1991; McKercher 2007). I-10 index, in this discussion, has given further clearer insights on author impact than H-index. I-10 index allows measuring the number of publications with at least 10 citations. Although I-10 index is very simple to calculate and exact regarding the author performance it is not being used by the culture of metrics or the bibliometric studies. This means two important things. On one hand, bibliometric studies are useful but they are limited to standardized forms of measurements. It is important to mention that the utility of bibliometric studies is far from question. It is more than a matter of wording; bibliometric studies help understand how the scholars' networks ultimately operate as well as the trending topics of the discipline. On another, the future of the tourism industry depends on the emergence of new discussions, solutions, and implementations to face global challenges in the years to come (Evren & Kozak 2014). Jafar Jafari's term scientifization of tourism speaks to us of a state of maturation of applied research which is mainly marked not only by the number but also by the credibility of the publication. A mix-balanced insight, escaping any partisan commentary, should characterize the scientific tourism research, as Jafari ultimately adheres (Jafari 2005). Jafari's legacy illuminated the paths of a great gamut of scholars who strongly believed that the impact of tourism research in other disciplines is a clear sign of maturation and evolution (Xiao & Smith, 2006; Wardle & Buckley, 2014; Butler 2015). Therefore, the culture of metrics has strongly gravitated toward the configuration of tourism epistemology from its inception (Beckendorff & Zehrer 2013; Law et al. 2009). This does not prevent some voices develop a critical approach. Some critical works lamented that the bibliometric studies may very well open the doors towards a new obsession for publishing [known as the culture of publishing-or-perishing] (Korstanje 2021; 2023).

Although the bibliometric literature review abounds [most of them located in the national and international contexts or different subsectors of the industry] (Palmer, Sese & Montano, 2005; Leong et al. 2020; Beckendorff 2009; Jiang, Ritchie & Beckendorff 2019; Ye, Li & Law 2013; McKercher 2007), no less true seems to be that few approaches center efforts to discuss its advantages and disadvantages of such technique (Korstanje 2022). At a closer look, one of the pioneering scholars who exerted a radical critique on these studies was Michael C. Hall. Per his viewpoint, the bibliometric assessment over-valorizes the number of publications [even the citation factor] overlooking other hybridized methods. Under normal conditions, private organizations take the lead monopolizing the evaluation protocols over professional fieldworkers and professors. As a result of this, the obsession with productivity and journal impact put the quality factor into a marginal position. What is equally important, bibliometric studies are based on quantitative methods that measure the impact of the paper but not its quality. There is a moment in the discipline where a manuscript published in a highly-ranked journal has more recognition than its real contribution to the specialized literature (Hall 2011). Are contribution and recognition two sides of the same coin?

Answering this vexed question seems to be a complex task to perform. While recognition signals the authors' legacy which is drawn by the stable prestige, the contribution is a specific updating that helps to expand the existing understanding of a certain issue. Whatever the case may be, we give some hints in the next lines. Let us start with the role played by the language in tourism knowledge production. The language [in this case English] occupies a central position in the configuration of current tourism epistemology. Some studies have emphasized the importance of English as an international language. As lingua franca, English not only has been enthralled because its hegemony in business and management issues but also to standardize the applied protocols in tourism research (Oktadiana & Pearce, 2017). Per Douglas Pearce (2014), the internationalization of English has direct and positive consequences on discipline maturation. The adoption of English in non-native communities is explained not only by the expansion of the tourism industry but also by the necessity to convene common practices revolving around tourism research. This poses an interesting dilemma on the tension between internationalization [which leads towards a homogenized sub-culture] and diversity. Contrariwise, Graham Dann (2011) argues convincingly that the Anglophone world has monopolized not only knowledge production but also the review process in the leading journals. For Dann, the use of English as a lingua franca excludes a whole portion of scholars who are not native speakers. In this respect, reviewers serve as real gatekeepers taking the lead in what can be or is not published. One of the troubling aspects of the lingua franca, as Dann observes, remains in the impossibility to reverse mechanical thinking [most of them originated in the Global North]. Knowledge production is centered on a set of pre-assumed stereotypes, beliefs, and hypotheses which cannot be validated beyond the Anglophone world. This creates a state of dissociation between policy and theory. Many scholars [living in the global South] are certainly forced to adopt external theoretical frameworks for their research. Dann toys with the belief that this happens simply because researchers are pressed to publish works in a foreign language. John Tribe goes beyond the power of language emphasizing what he dubbed *the indiscipline of tourism.* As he puts it, the growth of tourism publications in English had unfortunately no direct impact on the consolidation of the discipline. There is a great dispersion in the published material as well as a certain indifference by the side of the Academia to re-organize the academic production (Tribe 1997; 2010). It is not difficult to resist the impression that Tribe lays his fingers on the influence of the economic-based paradigm which evaluates tourism as a source of economic growth and prosperity while overlooking other variables (Airey, et al. 2015).

Strengths and Weaknesses of the Bibliometric Culture

The present piece adopts a more nuanced argumentation. Of course, one must confess that bibliometric analysis has strengths and weaknesses. Among the strengths, we can mention the fast and accurate identification of those themes which are being discussed in academic circles worldwide. This doubtless recreates the condition to bolster a fluid dialogue among the involved stakeholders or simply works as a guideline to resolve the problems that place the industry in jeopardy (Koseoglu, 2016). Nevertheless, the bibliometric studies show some limitations which should be at least discussed.

At first glimpse, the priority for H-index as the only valid key impact factor not only evinces a philosophical quandary but also a dilemma for tourism research. H-index evaluates the impact of a certain author on the literature but rarely it reflects the real contribution to the field [or even says little about the paper quality]. H-index, rather, measures the correlation between the citation factor and the author's productivity. For the sake of clarity, Albert Einstein would get a low H-index with only 4 papers published in his academic life. This reminds me that some of the most recognized or awarded scholars are not the most cited ones. Some scholars have alerted to the inconsistency of the H-index in scientific research. Waltman & Van Eck (2012) argue convincingly that the academic community should re-think the usage of the H-index as the only reliable instrument to measure an author's performance. Originally stimulated to measure the overall scientific impacts of authors, H-index has many inconsistencies and limitations which need to be re-considered. In many ways, H-index is unsystematic at the time of creating the authors' rankings. As the authors go on to write:

> "We argue that to measure the overall scientific impact of a scientist (or some other unit of analysis) the h-index exhibits counterintuitive behavior. More specifically, we assert that the mechanism used by the h-index to aggregate publication and citation statistics into a single number leads to an inconsistent way of ranking scientists. The conclusion that we draw from this is that the h-index cannot be considered an appropriate indicator of the overall scientific impact of a scientist" (Waltman & Van Eck, 2012: 2).

The main problem of the H-index started when epistemologists wonder: who are the most prestigious scholars in a field?

Let's explain this better with an example, two researchers A & B work for the same university for a lapse of 5 years. The premise of the H-index overtly said that if two scientists achieve the same performance improvement also their ranking position will remain untouched. Scientist A published 20 papers nine with twelve citations each and three with four citations each [the rest remains uncited]. In parallel, scientist B produced 12 publications seven with ten citations each and three with five citations each. Applying H-index, scientist B has a higher impact than A. In normal conditions, this assumption restricts the prolificacy of scientist A to the detriment of the number of citations. B scientist who had been less prolific has invariably had a higher impact on the ranking. At the same time, being cited does not mean a genuine contribution to the discipline, so to speak it can be a critical insight. It is argued that some disciplines [such as anthropology, cultural studies, or mobility theories] are less sensitive to citation factors than marketing or management (Korstanje 2016, 2022). The standardized productivity of an ethnographer [since ethnographies take considerable time] goes from one to two papers per year. This leads us to think twice about the impact factor as a social construe that varies by time, language, discipline, and culture. An interesting debate has certainly been put recently into the foreground. There is no clear basis to say that the highly cited papers now will pass the proof of time tomorrow. It is important not to lose sight of the fact that the impact factor [under some conditions] recreates a hierarchy of authors [most of them living in English-speaking countries] who act as real gatekeepers of what can be published or discarded. It is not otiose to admit that authors are often cited fashionably without understanding or reading the entire paper. Some scholars who work in developing countries have no access to published material. As a result of this, their papers lack the necessary bibliographic background or simply are out of focus respecting their object of study. They should limit to reading part of the papers or simply the abstract. There is an interesting point of debate in the global South and North and how access to published material is simply managed. Here an additional problem surfaces; Since the work of reviewers is not paid, some reviewers force authors to cite their papers falling into unethical behavior. Some journals have implemented a new system of reward for reviewers [to solve this problem] but not less true is that the review process puts the author in a situation of dependency. The selection of databases or sampling in the bibliometric studies remains an alternative point of discrepancy for Academia. The sampling process or selection of the material to construct the bibliometric reports is based on top-tiered journals excluding books, doctoral theses, or book chapters. At the same time, there are notable discrepancies with the citations in selected databases like WOS or Scopus, and Google scholar. To wit, even though some books or book chapters are highly cited, they are systematically ignored in these studies. Coming back to Hall's concerns, if we toy with the belief that the number of citations does not suffice to indicate the research quality, why Scimago or WOS are preferably selected in many of these bibliometric works?

Michael Hall (2006) calls on the need to go beyond the Scopus and Web of science datasets in the evaluation of tourism-related journals. This does not authorize to say that scholars should calibrate efforts to find reliable bibliometric tools that successfully combine evaluations [and reviews] based on publication quality. In some cases, citations are incorrectly credited, or engines fail to attribute to the correct authors. For some leading voices, the criterion to mark what is a most cited author or a paper is subject to arbitrary decisions which are unilaterally made or even obscured by unscientific reasoning. As Hall brilliantly notes, impact factors started to be used for purposes that have been not originally imagined. What is more important, estimating the number of citations of an author says little about its prestige or legacy, it rather corresponds with its popularity. In a nutshell, the opportunity of maximizing the value of research is simply given by the community of researchers as well as the possibility to formulate the correct questions.

With the benefits of hindsight, it is tempting to note that Scopus and WOS represent a small portion of the academic tribe. This point merits further debate in scholarship (Hall 2006; Moed, Bar-llan & Halevi 2016). The process of quality evaluation is very complex to perform. It devotes considerable resources, time, and effort to the side of scholarship. Recent studies have widely shown that reviews aimed at evaluating the ranking of publishers or journals obtain different results depending on the used method. Those studies which are based on impact factors or metrics have different outcomes than those centered on the evaluation of experts (Jacso, 2010; Siler & Lariviere, 2022). Just after the 2000s, some critical voices have alerted that the bibliometric studies reaffirm the hegemony of the leading publishers that impose the pay-for-journal logic (Kristensen 2015). It is important to remind that pay-for-journal have restricted access to the published material. This affects particularly those professional researchers in developing economies who have no financial resources to pay for the downloaded manuscripts. Many institutions press their professors to publish in top-tiered journals while they are restricted to the necessary access to update their state of art. The opposite is equally true, far from being original the proposed work is simply rejected by the peer-review process or by editors. Part of these low-skilled academicians falls in the hands of predatory journals that promise faster publications with a pseudo-scientific review. Predatory journals are pseudo-scientific outlets that often violate academic practices with fraudulent practices. In most cases, authors are charged back expensive handling fees while in others the review process is inadequate and poor. Exegetes of predatory journals acknowledge that the handling fee is for ensuring open access. The popularity of predatory journals is explained by two combined factors. On one hand, the exaggerated time the review process takes. Another is the lack of open access for the authors by the side of the most recognized publishers. Universities have devoted considerable financial resources to pay the open access subscription for students but at the same time the professors' wages. This happens because universities are annually evaluated by the number of publications placed by their professors in leading journals. Some professors even are pressed to publish one or two papers in the year to keep their tenure. More ranked the university, more financial resources, and students. This has invariably inspired some academicians to exert a caustic critique on the publishing-or-perish culture as the precondition for the commoditization of higher education (Van Raan 2005). Some of the most important universities have recently called to make a boycott against the leading publishers because of what they considered inappropriate open access policies. Some publishers have come into effect policies to keep open access, but the fees which are charged to authors are very hard to be paid. As stated, bibliometric studies have a direct impact on higher tourism education. Pressed to be more productive, professional fieldworkers leave their courses to less skilled or amateur professors. One of the more concrete effects of this behavior explains the methodological limitations students daily face to end successfully their theses. Additionally, the culture of publishing or perishing put authors in a new dilemma: writing for vocational issues [finding new instruments and topics] or simply writing for the topic of the moment.

Last but not least, another point of discrepancy is associated with *fragmentary coauthors.* Bob McKercher has extensively criticized the fragmentary co-authors as a direct aftermath of the institutional pressure for locating publications in top-tiered journals (McKercher & Tung 2015). This practice consists in submitting a manuscript authored by more than eight authors [some of them having no direct participation in the text] to gain further credits. Although this practice has been [to some extent] accepted, some journals imposed strict protocols to accept manuscripts authored by more than 5 authors. Plagiarism seems to be an added problem of the obsession with metrics and impact factors. Some authors deliver the same paper to more than one journal. Since reviewers are hand-tied to detect plagiarism, journals have concentrated efforts on the adoption of new software. The opposite is equally true, authors claim that they are not paid by journals for their publications. The assigned copyright forms impede the same text, theme or licensee can be republished at a later day. These scholars [though they represent a small portion of the academicians] not only are not in agreement with the current copy-right policies applied by journals because these protocols re-align with the hegemony of larger publishers but also are unwilling to pay the penalties of the missing bus, they submit the same material in various journals. Here, we have discussed the pro and cons of the current metric culture as well as laying the foundations for a new understanding of tourism research for the years to come.

Conclusion

The culture of metrics has imposed some burdens and obligations of some researchers to publish in leading journals seems to be gradually devastating the professional applied research affecting for sure higher tourism education. Some well-versed scholars leave their classrooms to amateur researchers to embrace their professional career. In other cases, professors are certainly pressed to publish in some journals to keep their tenure. Of course, there are some disciplines such as geography or anthropology which are insensitive to the bibliometric culture, but others like tourism or management are highly determined by these types of pressures. The culture of publishing or perishing is wreaking havoc in the fields of tourism and hospitality. The present piece interrogates furtherly on the problems, advantages and limitations of bibliometric studies in the constellations of tourism research. At the same time, we lay the foundations for understanding the discipline in a not so long-distant future.

References

Adams, H. (1988). *The academic tribes*. Chicago, University of Illinois Press.

Agapito, D. (2020). The senses in tourism design: a bibliometric review. *Annals of Tourism Research*, *83*, 102934.

Airey, D., Tribe, J., Benckendorff, P., & Xiao, H. (2015). The managerial gaze: The long tail of tourism education and research. *Journal of Travel Research*, *54*(2), 139-151.

Barrios, M., Borrego, A., Vilaginés, A., Ollé, C., & Somoza, M. (2008). A bibliometric study of psychological research on tourism. *Scientometrics*, *77*(3), 453-467.

Benckendorff, P. (2009). Themes and trends in Australian and New Zealand tourism research: A social network analysis of citations in two leading journals (1994–2007). *Journal of Hospitality and Tourism Management*, *16*(1), 1-15.

Benckendorff, P., & Zehrer, A. (2013). A network analysis of tourism research. *Annals of Tourism Research*, *43*, 121-149.

Butler, R. (2015). The evolution of tourism and tourism research. *Tourism Recreation Research*, *40*(1), 16-27.

Dann, G. M. (2011). Anglophone hegemony in tourism studies today. *Enlightening Tourism. A Pathmaking Journal*, *1*(1), 1-30.

Evren, S., & Kozak, N. (2014). Bibliometric analysis of tourism and hospitality related articles published in Turkey. *Anatolia*, *25*(1), 61-80.

Gursoy, D., & Sandstrom, J. K. (2016). An updated ranking of hospitality and tourism journals. *Journal of Hospitality & Tourism Research*, *40*(1), 3-18.

Hall, C. M. (2006). The impact of tourism knowledge: Google scholar, citations and the opening up of academic space. *EReview of Tourism Research*, *4*(3), 119-36.

Hall, C. M. (2011). Publish and perish? Bibliometric analysis, journal ranking and the assessment of research quality in tourism. *Tourism Management*, *32*(1), 16-27.

Jacsò, P. (2010). Pragmatic issues in calculating and comparing the quantity and quality of research through rating and ranking of researchers based on peer reviews and bibliometric indicators from Web of Science, Scopus and Google Scholar. *Online information review*. 34(6): 972-982.

Jiang, Y., Ritchie, B. W., & Benckendorff, P. (2019). Bibliometric visualisation: An application in tourism crisis and disaster management research. *Current Issues in Tourism*, *22*(16), 1925-1957.

Korstanje, M. E. (2016). Why citation impact is so important for tourism researchers?. *Advances in Hospitality and Tourism Research (AHTR)*, *4*(1), 26-31.

Korstanje, M. E. (2021). The decline of book reviews in tourism. *Published online: 15 February 2021 Free full-text access available at: www. jthsm. gr*, 76.

Korstanje, M. E. (2022). Tourism imagination: a new epistemological debate. *Current Issues in Tourism*, ahead of print. 1-13.

Kristensen, P. M. (2015). Revisiting the "American social science"—Mapping the geography of international relations. *International studies perspectives*, *16*(3), 246-269.

Koseoglu, M. A., Rahimi, R., Okumus, F., & Liu, J. (2016). Bibliometric studies in tourism. *Annals of tourism research*, *61*, 180-198.

McKercher, B. (2007). A study of prolific authors in 25 tourism and hospitality journals. *Journal of Hospitality & Tourism Education*, *19*(2), 23-30.

McKercher, B., & Tung, V. (2015). Publishing in tourism and hospitality journals: Is the past a prelude to the future?. *Tourism Management*, *50*, 306-315.

Law, R., Ye, Q., Chen, W., & Leung, R. (2009). An analysis of the most influential articles published in tourism journals from 2000 to 2007: A Google Scholar approach. *Journal of Travel & Tourism Marketing*, *26*(7), 735-746.

Leong, L. Y., Hew, T. S., Tan, G. W. H., Ooi, K. B., & Lee, V. H. (2020). Tourism research progress–a bibliometric analysis of tourism review publications. *Tourism Review*, *76*(1), 1-26.

Oktadiana, H., & Pearce, P. L. (2017). The "bule" paradox in Indonesian tourism research: issues and prospects. *Asia Pacific Journal of Tourism Research*, *22*(11), 1099-1109.

Palmer, A. L., Sese, A., & Montano, J. J. (2005). Tourism and statistics: Bibliometric study 1998–2002. *Annals of Tourism Research*, *32*(1), 167-178.

Pearce, D. G. (2014). The internationalization of tourism research. *Journal of Travel Research*, *53*(3), 267-280.

Sheldon, P. J. (1991). An authorship analysis of tourism research. *Annals of Tourism Research*, *18*(3), 473-484.

Siler, K., & Larivière, V. (2022). Who games metrics and rankings? Institutional niches and journal impact factor inflation. *Research Policy*, *51*(10), 104608.

Tribe, J. (1997). The indiscipline of tourism. *Annals of tourism research*, *24*(3), 638-657.

Tribe, J. (2010). Tribes, territories and networks in the tourism academy. *Annals of tourism research*, *37*(1), 7-33.

Van Raan, A. F. (2005). Fatal attraction: Conceptual and methodological problems in the ranking of universities by bibliometric methods. *Scientometrics*, *62*(1), 133-143.

Waltman, L., & Van Eck, N. J. (2012). The inconsistency of the h-index. *Journal of the American Society for Information Science and Technology*, *63*(2), 406-415.

Wardle, C., & Buckley, R. (2014). Tourism citations in other disciplines. *Annals of Tourism Research*, *46*(3), 163-184.

Xiao, H., & Smith, S. L. (2006). The making of tourism research: Insights from a social sciences journal. *Annals of Tourism Research*, *33*(2), 490-507.

Ye, Q., Li, T., & Law, R. (2013). A coauthorship network analysis of tourism and hospitality research collaboration. *Journal of Hospitality & Tourism Research*, *37*(1), 51-76.

Zhao, W., & Ritchie, J. B. (2007). An investigation of academic leadership in tourism research: 1985–2004. *Tourism management*, *28*(2), 476-490.

Chapter 8

Responsible Management Practices as Strategic Tools to Avert Crisis Situations in Tourism: The Case of Wellness Centres in Kerala, India

K. P. Anju[1,*]
V. T. Bindu[1,†]
and Babu George[2,‡]
[1]Avinashilingam Institute for Home Science and Higher Education for Women, Coimbatore, Tamil Nadu, India
[2]Alcorn State University, Lorman, MS, USA

Abstract

Responsible Tourism (RT) is a strategy for sustainable destination development. One central promise of sustainability is avoiding disasters, calamities, and crises. In this book chapter, the authors highlight how responsible wellness tourism contributes to sustainability. In doing so, it highlights the crisis dimension. Policy implications are also presented. This study also evaluates wellness providers' economic, socio-cultural, and environmental responsibilities and how these practices avert tourism crises. The case study of a wellness tourism center shows how responsibility principles are implemented there and contribute to preserving the destination's culture and legacy. Responsible tourism practices also result in economic growth, product differentiation, job creation, landscape preservation, and environmental protection. These outcomes forestall crisis situations in allied sectors as well.

* Author's Email: 20phtof001@avinuty.ac.in.
† Author's Email: bindu_tm@avinuty.ac.in.
‡ Corresponding Author's Email: bgeorge@alcorn.edu.

In: Tourism in Crisis
Editors: M.E. Korstanje, V. GB Gowreesunkar and S.W. Maingi
ISBN: 979-8-88697-643-4

Keywords: wellness tourism, responsible tourism, economic responsibility, environment responsibility, socio-cultural responsibility, crisis management

Introduction

Due to abundant recreational opportunities and suitable accessibility, tourism has steadily grown over the last two decades, significantly boosting the local economy (Wang et al., 2020). The development of the tourism sector also benefits the enhancement of work opportunities, thereby raising household incomes, and presrving cultural heritage (Mohamadi et al., 2022). However, if wrongly managed, tourism can create numerous crises for the tourism industry stakeholders, the broader economy, and society (George, 2020; Korstanje & George, 2020). Wellness is associated with prevention and health, whereas well-being is associated with happiness (Thal, Smith, & George, 2021). Wellness tourism must entail much more than a trip to a spa facility. It has to do with creating a holistic healing experience for tourists, both physically and spiritually. It is about giving genuine experiences that allow people to recharge their batteries and return home as healthier and more active people (Dillette et al., 2020; Santhi & Nithya, 2011). Wellness tourism is a specialized segment of the tourism industry that has just undergone rapid growth and is expected to continue (Csirmaz & Pető, 2015). Indeed, the growth rate of wellness tourism continues to outpace global tourism (Nel-lo Andreu et al., 2021). As a result of this expansion, resorts, hotels, wellness retreat amenities, and unique travel packages are increasingly offering health and wellness services through various activities (George & Henthorne, 2009; Koncul, 2012). Accepting these mechanisms enables wellness tourism operators to improve develop, and implement programs that significantly impact tourists, stakeholders, and the local community, in addition to after their vacation is over. Technology and telemedicine are enablers of newer forms of wellness tourism (George, Bucatariu, & Henthorne, 2020).

The idea of responsible tourism has recently drawn scholars' interest. The interaction between tourism and the environment has led to the scholar-practitioner community developing the concept of sustainable tourism. Responsible tourism is concerned with travelling in a manner that has the least amount of negative impacts and damage (Mihalic, 2016). It has been on the rise recently due to a growing desire of travelers to be environmentally conscious inside and outside their homes. As a result, both forms of tourism can be combined to create a more sustainable tourism model that benefits travelers, the environment, the host community, and stakeholders. For the benefit of future generations, a high-quality environment and service sector must be established. It is also essential to pursue sustainable growth by utilizing current commercial trends. To achieve this goal, the tourism and hospitality sector chose responsible tourism as a strategy under community social responsibility. The mode of reliable tourism operations is influenced by the destination's economic, social, and environmental characteristics. (Markose & Tazhathethil, 2022). With the three sustainability pillars of environment, local community, and economy, the word "RT" refers to all stakeholders' activities and understanding of sustainable travel. The RT is considered a means of attaining Sustainable Development Goals and has proven to be a powerful unifier among tourism stakeholders.

As the previous backdrop, Kerala is known for its scenic beauty, cultural attractions, and thriving wellness tourism industry (Nair, 2019). Kerala has established itself as a global healthcare destination, which can be enhanced by cooperating with other sectors, particularly in the tourist industry. (Pordié, 2013), More people are combining their vacations with health travel to revitalize bodies and minds. Experts in the wellness business believe this might pave the way for creating a new type of tourism that is both beneficial to travelers and friendly to the environment and local community: responsible tourism. Many responsible tourism levels have been established in India, Southeast Asia, and Africa. Kerala state aims to embrace RT practices in various locations, including Kovalam, Kumarakom, Thekkady, and Wayanad (Ranjith, 2021).

Background

Wellness Tourism

The Global Wellness Institute defines wellness as the proactive pursuit of behaviors, decisions, and lifestyles that lead to overall healing. Significant problems have arisen as a result of the influx of wellness tourists. The topic of wellness tourism was controversial among locals who opposed its demonization. However, they were worried about the negative impacts of wellness travel. Residents purposefully removed themselves from wellness tourist sites to manage and prevent spatial stigma (Wang et al., 2020). A wellness tourism experience (apart from the entertainment component) can inspire tourists, leading to increased tourist involvement (He et al., 2021). Communities and the national economy are influenced by wellness spa tourism. By enabling the development of wellness practices based on typical elements of local cultural heritage, natural landscapes may also support efforts at product differentiation. Kerala, primarily a rural region with abundant natural resources, can form the core element of this type of strategic approach by combining traditional Ayurvedic practices with other local resources to create a competitive "augmented product" deeply ingrained in local resources and communities. However, implementing such a strategy for the development of wellness tourism requires careful coordination among numerous parties (Page et al., 2017). Wellness travel is a fast-expanding industry that provides outstanding business opportunities through products that enhance or preserve health (Kelly, 2012). People rely on entrenched private sector solutions to Globalization due to several factors, including the aging of the world's population, rising general understanding of health issues, and financial difficulties at traditional medical institutions (Voigt & Pforr, 2013). Wellness has grown into a more comprehensive idea. Wellness tourism increasingly encompasses activities like camping, retreat centers, and rural or environmental tourism (Nawijn, 2010; Brooker & Joppe, 2014). It has been demonstrated that wellness tourism lowers poverty by providing funding for the preservation and conservation of local history and the revival of traditional skills. Its international temples and centers for meditation and yoga draw a lot of wellness tourists (Choe & Seputra, 2020). The authors added that a specific approach must be established for a sustainable expansion of wellness tourism (about developmental policy and plan concerns, entrepreneurial management issues, financial restrictions issues, advertisement/promotion issues, and time-scheduling issues). It might positively affect the area's economy (Hundric et al., 2020). By adhering to sustainable tourism principles and helping to preserve a nation's culture and history, wellness tourism brings about several benefits, including productivity expansion, product diversification, employment generation, landscape conservation, and environmental protection (Smith& Puczko, 2009; Hartwell, 2014).

Responsible Tourism

Responsible tourism encompasses all tourist activities that respect the host country's natural and cultural ecosystems and the needs of all parties involved (Burrai et al., 2019). It can also mean enhancing local populations' quality of life through more significant socioeconomic benefits and better natural resource management (Spenceley et al., 2002). The authors strongly connect responsible tourism and taking steps to make tourism more sustainable. It says that embracing responsibility leads to clear-cut acts, subsequently called sustainable activities. On the other hand, responsible tourism is not synonymous with sustainable tourism (Wall, 2013). According to the definition, responsible tourism is "a behavioral attribute founded on the basic principles of respect for others and their environment," and it also assumes that "Being responsible in one's conduct, as well as in the actions of others'" business administration and management." Responsible tourism attempts to reduce the negative impacts of tourism on people, the environment, and communities by offering travel that enhances working conditions, includes the local community, preserves cultural heritage, and is ecologically friendly (Mondal & Samaddar, 2021). Responsible tourism aims to increase positive social, economic, cultural, and environmental impacts (Eyisi et al., 2021).

Responsible Tourism Initiatives in Kerala

Kerala began its Responsible Tourism initiative in February 2007 with the 'Better Together' state-level consultative gathering. Responsible Tourism (RT), a ground-breaking and far-reaching concept in Kerala tourism, was piloted in four destinations: Kovalam, Kumarakom, Thekkady, and Wayanad, with Kumarakom emerging as a model. A stakeholder workshop was organized on May 6, 2007, to begin the district's responsible tourism activities. All regional stakeholders – people's representatives, government officials, local governments, the tourism sector, civil society organizations, academics, and the media – were invited to participate in the activities. Later, the operations picked up speed, and in January 2008, the Responsible Tourism projects began. The activities primarily concentrated on three dimensions of tourism: social, economic, and environmental.

According to industry experts, both wellness and responsible tourism can be combined to produce more sustainable tourism that helps the traveler and the environment, even though this distinguishes each of these industries. The common aspect that binds them together is the cause of their existence. As a result, wellness and responsible tourism are driven by a desire to eliminate pollution, economic inequities, and overcrowding, among other things. The success of RT initiatives in various tourism industry segments has yet to be determined. To fill this gap in the literature, this study shows how much responsible tourism initiatives contribute to a local community's economic, sociocultural, and environmental development through the activities of wellness tourism stakeholders and to find out the methods of promoting RT through activities of wellness providers.

The COVID-19 Crisis

The COVID-19 pandemic is a global threat that has impacted all aspects of human life. The tourism and hospitality businesses have been particularly hard hit by travel prohibitions, health regulations, and the second and third waves of the pandemic (Jangra & Gupta, 2021). The lockdown/Quarantine resulted in ongoing physical, material, and mental health challenges, resulting in widespread dissatisfaction among ordinary people and an array of severe emotional consequences, including a mix of great anxiety, bewilderment, and explosive emotions, as well as trust and anticipation. The impact was intense for those countries that rely mainly on tourism (Dileep & Nair, 2021). Push-pull factors are predicted to change inadvertently after COVID. Tourism and travel activities have long been considered stress relievers, energizing people. Push incentives following COVID include the urge to de-stress, rest, and rejuvenate. Visiting tranquil and natural locations to soothe and relax the protracted unsettled state of mind after months of anxiety is predicted to be a significant driving element. Travel motives would steer travelers toward real tourism experiences. In the current context, remoteness and inaccessibility would be viewed as advantages. As a result, people would be willing to explore unexplored areas. The remoteness of a destination may emerge as a crucial 'pull' factor post-COVID, as unknown, distant destinations are often thought to be pollution-free (Chugh, 2021). UK surveys show that the demand for wellness activities accelerated by Covid 19, understanding the need for rest and mental health. Healthier food options for the public still adjusting to the lifestyle changes forced by Covid 19 allow a business to serve their customers better and help to make up for lost revenue earned by the stakeholders (Mtapuri & Giampiccoli, 2021) and host the community during the pandemic (Monk, 2020). The planned immplimentation of new strategies enables the tourism industryto thrive post pandemic (Chugh, 2021).

Research Problem

This study has been carried out to answer the following questions:

1) What are the methods to promote responsible tourism through wellness tourism practices?
2) How might responsible tourism practices at wellness centers help minimize the tourism crisis and contribute to sustainable development?

Research Method

The current study is a case analysis of 'Ayurveda Yoga Villa, Holistic Research Centre' in Wayanad, Kerala, to gather information about responsible tourism initiatives at the wellness center. The researcher conducted interviews with practitioners of the Ayurveda yoga villa. This study also makes use of data obtained from the Internet. Internet-based research is becoming more common, particularly in tourism (Janta et al., 2011). Secondary data were gathered from the websites of numerous wellness centers and the Kerala tourism organization's Responsible tourism website, as well as from various journals, periodicals, and newspapers, and by reviewing multiple research papers on the topic. This examination leads to the resolution of the research problems.

Study Area

Wayanad district is one of Kerala's hill stations, with altitudes ranging from 700 to 2100 meters (Rajeevan et al., 2019). Four destinations in Kerala were picked for responsible tourism initiatives, with Wayanad being one of them (Thimm & Karlaganis, 2020). The government initiated considerable efforts to ensure the region's tourism industry's long-term viability, implementing various programs through Responsible Tourism initiatives. The initiatives taken here make Wayanad a better place to live and explore.

Results and Discussion

Analysis of qualitative interviews interspersed with an extensive review of literature helped the researchers identify certain specific themes related to wellness tourism practices and how this helps avert crises.

Promoting Local Products

Supporting local or natural products is one way that wellness resorts can aid in the promotion of responsible tourism. For example, providing visitors with natural bath soaps purchased from local craftspeople can have a significant environmental impact both within and outside the destination. Consumption of certified high-quality regional products can contribute significantly to the economic development of the region in which they are produced (Frisvoll et al., n.d.). It is still widely assumed that wellness tourism consists solely of visits to spas. It encompasses a far more extensive range of activities. Quality local food, a rich cultural offer, authentic local experiences, excellent lodging, mild adventure activities, and mind or body classes are likely to appeal to wellness travelers (Kurniawan, 2018). From a crisis management perspective, they sustain local economic vitality and reduce poverty in the destination areas. There are numerous beneficial multipliers to this as well.

Purchasing Foods That Are Supplied Locally

Wellness resorts are cautious about the cuisine provided to visitors, ensuring that only the freshest and healthiest ingredients are used in their dishes. They may preach and practice responsible tourism by choosing fresh foods from local farms and markets. The food sourced locally to reduce carbon emissions while maintaining health and flavor. People believe that eating functional foods and utilizing herbs as ingredients to replenish the body and mind could improve their health. As a result, it is a must-have for a healthy lifestyle. Wellness tourist operators deliver healthy and proper diets using local products and services. Herbs help the body work better. Some hotels have teamed up with organic farmers in the area. Farms, herbalists, and chefs create and serve functional and healthful cuisines suitable for both the body and the mind (Chen et al., 2013). From a crisis management perspective, this means economic opportunities for the local farming community and minimizing the chances for the agricultural sector to fail. In many mass tourism destinations, there is a crisis in the agriculture sector because of the massive drift of resources, workers, and management attention to tourism. Win-win growth of complementary sectors of the economy is a significant positive step in averting crisis.

Recycling Initiatives Should Be Supported

In addition to onsite recycling services, wellness locations can assist guests in having a more ecologically conscious vacation. These recycling programs help these places substantially reduce waste and assist tourists in being more conscientious of keeping their surroundings clean and recycling objects rather than discarding them. Recycling classes can be held in wellness locations to raise awareness about the need for recycling for interested visitors; this allows visitors to take these habits home with them. Switching to energy-efficient appliances and water systems are just a few additional steps wellness locations may take to promote responsible tourism. From a crisis management perspective, this means minimizing wastage and even trash. This helps maintain the destination neat and clean.

Travelers Are Left with Subliminal Messages

At its best, wellness tourism can give customers subtle pointers about having a more responsible and environmentally friendly wellness vacation. Hotels and resorts that offer wellness tourism vacations, for example, might place messages in the rooms instructing guests not to waste paper or wash towels to help save the environment. Previous studies show that such messages can help avoid the destructive conduct of travelers, thus avoiding crises.

Eradicate Poverty throughout the World in All Its Form

Poverty is a global crisis. Well-being tourism can be generated by wellness, particularly in places where local cultural traditions promote wellness, such as meditation, good cuisine, a diverse range of local employment, and entrepreneurial prospects. The wellness tourism service provides various direct and indirect job opportunities for the workforce's kids, women, and the disabled. Wellness tourism not only contributes to promoting guest well-being, but it may also serve as a model of well-being and generate local revenue.

Ensure That All People of All Ages Have Healthy Lives and Are Well-Adjusted

Illness is a crisis, and programs that support health and well-being, thus, contribute to crisis management efforts. Health and well-being are essential at all stages of life, beginning with childhood. This addresses all main health goals, including reproductive, maternal, neonatal, child, and adolescent health; communicable and no communicable diseases; universal health care; and provision of safe, effective, high-quality, and reasonable medications and vaccinations for all.

Continuing Education That Is Inclusive and Equitable

Lack of inclusivity leads to numerous consequences, including social distrust and unrest. These crises could be overcome by planned Diversity, Equity, and Inclusion (DEI) efforts. Wellness tourism activities frequently incorporate educational components, which provide opportunities for visitors to learn about local culture and customs and for locals to learn about and get more active in this rapidly increasing market.

Ayurveda Yoga Villa Holistic Research Centre: A Mini Case Study

The Ayurveda Yoga Villa Holistic Research Centre and Hospital is a green leaf-certified Wellness Centre located on the Kabani River's shores and bordered by the Nilgiri Biosphere Reserve's evergreen forest, which is the principal source of medicinal herbs. Individualized remedies are delivered after a comprehensive assessment by Ayurvedic doctors with years of experience. Ayurveda therapies, Yoga practices based on yogavaivartha sidhi, Marma treatments, Kalari practices, and Kalari treatments are all included in the treatment process.

Ayurvedic diets, Agnihotrams, and daily routines combine cleansing and balancing an individual's physical, mental, and spiritual health. Ganapathi temple, Ayurvedic herbal manufacturing unit, Gosala, and organic garden are all on campus. Food and dairy products and medicine are produced on their own organically maintained farms to boost the efficacy of Ayurvedic treatments. This research center also works to save indigenous cattle breeds that provide dairy. Medications for Ayurveda therapies are prepared within the research center. Ayurveda therapies are supplemented with spiritual activities and an enlightened atmosphere to purify an individual's physical, mental, and spiritual dimensions while also boosting immunity. Activities of the Centre in the areas of environmental, economic, and social responsibility are presented below:

Environmental Responsibilities

Wellness centers have taken appropriate steps to conserve and safeguard the environment, indirectly and directly. This research center aims to preserve indigenous cattle breeds, which supply dairy and plants for herb collecting. Food cultivated in the retreat center's organic garden is used to prepare food for the guest. Organic fertilizer is is primarily used in agriculture. Environmental efforts have been made. The center's infrastructure is entirely environmentally friendly, as it is created in a lush green location without hurting the entire flora and Fauna.

Economic Responsibilities

Various Responsible activities have been initiated to bring the local community forefront, fulfilling the economic responsibility. When choosing employees equally for men and women, preference is given to the local people. Yoga villa receives foreign people from around the world for various treatments. While acquiring foreign customers, the exchange earnings automatically increase in the district. They bought local products to prepare medicine and empower communities to help grow the local economy. The wellness tourist is also attracted to the various products produced within the district during their wellness trip, like woodcraft, tea powder, honey, ethnic food items, and paper bags.

Socio-Cultural Responsibility

The Ayurveda Yoga Villa administration places a high value on social responsibility. They ensure that the local community is involved in all of their activities. The Ayurveda herbal manufacturing unit, Gosala, Organic farm,

Events, and Ganapathi temple are all maintained by locals. Tribal communities are offered the opportunity to participate in cultural events and traditional rituals. Furthermore, the wellness center provides free treatments to locals as a support form. In the ayurvedic manufacturing unit, an Ayurvedic drug for immunity building during the pandemic was prepared and supplied to inhabitants. They maintain the local tradition by prohibiting cross-massages and other activities. Educate worldwide wellness visitors and locals unfamiliar with Vedic culture, which has ancient roots. Food, dairy products, and medicine are produced on their own organically managed farms to increase the efficacy of Ayurvedic therapies. Traditional clothing is used as treatment uniform.

Table 1 summarizes the various responsible wellness tourism practices at the Centre.

Table 1. Responsible wellness tourism practices in the wellness centre

SI No	Responsible wellness tourism activities	Indicators
1	Environmental Responsibility	• Protection of flora and fauna • Recycling • Use of organic fertilizers in farming • Eradicate waste and emission • The retreat center serves meals grown on organic farms inside the campus.
2	Economic Responsibility	• Employment opportunities for local people equally for males and females • Foreign exchange earnings to the district • Buying local products and empowering communities to help to grow the local economy.
3	Socio-cultural Responsibility	• Offering free treatments to the residents • Building and sustaining decent work for the poor. • Reduced inequality • Serving ethnic food Freshly collected indigenous cow's urine in the morning from the Gosala situated inside the campus. • Performing various traditional rituals inside the Centre • Tradition protection (Example: Restricting Cross massages) • Educate international wellness tourists and locals who are unfamiliar with Vedic tradition. • Food and dairy products and medicine are produced on their own organically • Traditional costume as a uniform to perform the treatment.

Conclusion

Responsible tourism is a globally opted strategy for sustainable destination development and lights up for new policymaking (Markose, Vazhakkatte Tazhathethil, & George, 2022; Okech, Haghiri, & George, 2015). In this study, we have analyzed wellness centers' economic, social, cultural, and environmental responsibilities and Methods for promoting responsible tourism through wellness tourism Activities. Wayanad district is marked as the responsible tourism destination in Kerala, and the activities were initiated in Wayanad in 2007 in Vythiri village and Ambalavayal in 2012. It is among the place where responsible tourism practices are implemented strategically. The destinations' envisaged execution of the measures for RT would aid in the growth of the tourism industry. Wayanad's responsible tourism program seeks to lessen tourism's harmful effects while respecting the local environment. A single segment, like the wellness industry, tried its best to help and obey the RT initiatives of the district. From the study, it is evident that responsible tourism activities of wellness centers are advantageous for tourism in all ways. Suppose more effort is put into making the destination economically and culturally sustained. In that case, responsible tourism may be a helpful strategy for sustainable visitor development in and around the wellness center and for safeguarding the environment.

This study contributes to the potential of the best responsible wellness tourism practices and strategies. The service providers' responsible practices have added multiple dimensions to the policymakers. The outcomes of this study should not be applied to all wellness centers in other growing areas for several reasons, such as differences in geographical locations, policy, and employers. If the government is serious about developing the industry, the initiatives are vital to supporting RT. As a result, empowerment, funding, increased security, and the implementation of tourism rules are necessary for RT to occur in every wellness center in every region. The findings of this article are critical for promoting responsible travel in areas where tourism is still in its early stages after a pandemic. The suggested strategies aid in the development of a resident-tourist-friendly destination in Kerala. The success of RT is within the hands of stakeholders, and tourism stakeholders need to consider these results so that getting resident support and attaining responsible tourism may be easier. This study has certain limitations. First, the data are collected only from one authorized organization, and the findings cannot be generalized. Hence future research suggests conducting an empirical study to determine the impact of responsible tourism initiatives in the wellness center during the post-COVID-19 pandemic.

References

Burrai, E., Buda, D. M., & Stanford, D. (2019). Rethinking the ideology of responsible tourism. *Journal of Sustainable Tourism, 27*(7), 992–1007. https://doi.org/10.1080/09669582.2019.1578365.

Chen, K. H., Chang, F. H., & Kenny, C. W. (2013). Investigating the wellness tourism factors in hot spring hotel customer service. *International Journal of Contemporary Hospitality Management, 25*(7), 1092–1114. https://doi.org/10.1108/IJCHM-06-2012-0086.

Chugh, S. R. (2021). Changing Travel Preferences Post-COVID: The New Normal? *International Journal of Hospitality and Tourism Systems, 14*(C), 15–22.

Csirmaz, É., & Pető, K. (2015). International Trends in Recreational and Wellness Tourism. *Procedia Economics and Finance, 32*(15), 755–762. https://doi.org/10.1016/s2212-5671(15)01458-6.

Dileep, M. R., & Nair, B. B. (2021). COVID-19 and the Future of Tourism: Back to Normal or Reformation? *International Journal of Hospitality and Tourism Systems, 14*(C), 10–14.

Dillette, A. K., Douglas, A. C., Andrzejewski, C., Dillette, A. K., Douglas, A. C., & Dimensions, C. A. (2020). Current Issues in Tourism Dimensions of holistic wellness as a result of international wellness tourism experiences. *Current Issues in Tourism, 0*(0), 1–17. https://doi.org/10.1080/13683500.2020.1746247.

Eyisi, A., Lee, D., & Trees, K. (2021). Developing responsible tourism in emerging economies: the case of Nigeria. *Journal of Tourism and Cultural Change, 0*(0), 1–16. https://doi.org/10.1080/14766825.2021.2019262.

Frisvoll, S., Forbord, M., & Blekesaune, A. (n.d.). *Scandinavian Journal of Hospitality and An Empirical Investigation of Tourists ' Consumption of Local Food in Rural Tourism. July 2015.* https://doi.org/10.1080/15022250.2015.1066918.

George, B. (2020). *International Case Studies in the Management of Disasters: Natural-Manmade Calamities and Pandemics*. Emerald Group Publishing.

George, B. P., & George, B. P. (2004). Past visits and the intention to revisit a destination: Place attachment as the mediator and novelty seeking as the moderator. *Journal of Tourism Studies, 15*(2), 51-66.

George, B. P., & Henthorne, T. L. (2009). The incorporation of telemedicine with medical tourism: A study of consequences. *Journal of Hospitality Marketing & Management, 18*(5), 512-522.

George, B., Bucatariu, L., & Henthorne, T. L. (2020). Technology in medicine: COVID-19 and the "coming of age" of telehealth. In *International Case Studies in the Management of Disasters*. Emerald Publishing Limited.

He, M., Liu, B., & Li, Y. (2021). Tourist Inspiration: How the Wellness Tourism Experience Inspires Tourist Engagement. *Journal of Hospitality and Tourism Research*, 1–21. https://doi.org/10.1177/10963480211026376.

Henthorne, T. L., & George, B. P. (2009). Transformation of Tourism Business in the Communist Cuba: A Critical Analysis. *International journal of business insights & transformation*, *3*(1), 18-29.

Jangra, P., & Gupta, M. (2021). Internet of Medical Things (IoMT) Based Framework for Smart Healthcare Tourism Sector. *International Journal of Hospitality and Tourism Systems*, *14*(C), 173–178.

Janta, H., Ladkin, A., Brown, L., & Lugosi, P. (2011). Employment experiences of Polish migrant workers in the UK hospitality sector. *Tourism Management*, *32*(5), 1006-1019.

Kelly, C. (2012). Wellness tourism: Retreat visitor motivations and experiences. *Tourism Recreation Research*, *37*(3), 205–213. https://doi.org/10.1080/02508281.2012.11081709.

Koncul, N. (2012). Wellness: A new mode of tourism. *Ekonomska Istrazivanja*, *25*(2), 525–534. https://doi.org/10.1080/1331677X.2012.11517521.

Korstanje, M. E., & George, B. P. (2020). Education as a strategy to tackle over tourism for overtourism and inclusive sustainability in the twenty-first century. In *Overtourism* (pp. 341-359). Palgrave Macmillan, Cham.

Kurniawan, L. (2018). Promoting Indonesia as a Wellness Tourism Destination. *KnE Social Sciences*, *3*(10), 250–260. https://doi.org/10.18502/kss.v3i10.3378.

Markose, N., Vazhakkatte Tazhathethil, B., & George, B. (2022). Sustainability Initiatives for Green Tourism Development: The Case of Wayanad, India. *Journal of Risk and Financial Management*, *15*(2), 52-67.

Mihalic, T. (2016). Sustainable-responsible tourism discourse - Towards "responsustable" tourism. *Journal of Cleaner Production*, *111*, 461–470. https://doi.org/10.1016/j.jclepro.2014.12.062.

Mohamadi, S., Abbasi, A., Ranaei Kordshouli, H. A., & Askarifar, K. (2022). Conceptualizing sustainable–responsible tourism indicators: an interpretive structural modeling approach. *Environment, Development and Sustainability*, *24*(1), 399–425. https://doi.org/10.1007/s10668-021-01442-9.

Mondal, S., & Samaddar, K. (2021). Responsible tourism towards sustainable development: literature review and research agenda. *Asia Pacific Business Review*, *27*(2), 229–266. https://doi.org/10.1080/13602381.2021.1857963.

Mtapuri, O., & Giampiccoli, A. (2021). Beyond COVID-19: An Opportunity for a New Tourism Sector. *International Journal of Hospitality and Tourism Systems*, *14*(C), 23–33.

Nair, B. B. (2019). Emerging trends in Wellness Tourism in Kerala. *Global Developments in Healthcare and Medical Tourism*, *February*, 220–235. https://doi.org/10.4018/978-1-5225-9787-2.ch012.

Nel-lo Andreu, M. G., Font-Barnet, A., & Espasa Roca, M. (2021). Wellness tourism-new challenges and opportunities for tourism in Salou. *Sustainability (Switzerland)*, *13*(15), 1–13. https://doi.org/10.3390/su13158246.

Okech, R., Haghiri, M., & George, B. P. (2015). Rural tourism as a sustainable development alternative: An analysis with special reference to Luanda, Kenya. *CULTUR-Revista de Cultura e Turismo*, *6*(3), 36-54.

Page, S. J., Hartwell, H., Johns, N., Fyall, A., Ladkin, A., & Hemingway, A. (2017). Case study: Wellness, tourism and small business development in a UK coastal resort: Public engagement in practice. *Tourism Management*, *60*(September), 466–477. https://doi.org/10.1016/j.tourman.2016.12.014.

Pordié, L. (2013). Spaces of connectivity, shifting temporality. Enquiries in transnational health. *European Journal of Transnational Studies*, *5*(1), 6–26.

Rajeevan, S., Kunnath, S. M., Varghese, T., & Kandambeth, P. P. (2019). Spider Diversity (Arachnida: Araneae) in Different Ecosystems of the Western Ghats, Wayanad Region, India. *South Asian Journal of Life Sciences*, *7*(2). https://doi.org/10.17582/journal.sajls/2019/7.2.29.39.

Spenceley, a., Relly, P., Keyser, H., Warmeant, P., McKenzie, M., Mataboge, a., Norton, P., Mahlangu, S., & Seif, J. (2002). Responsible Tourism Manual for South Africa, Department for Environmental Affairs and Tourism, July 2002. *Responsible Tourism Manual for South Africa*, *2*(July), 3. http://citeseerx.ist.psu.edu/viewdoc/download?doi=10.1.1.114.1494&rep=rep1&type=pdf.

Thal, K. I., Smith, S. L., & George, B. (2021). Wellness tourism competences for curriculum development: a Delphi study. *Journal of Teaching in Travel & Tourism*, *21*(3), 205-220.

Thimm, T., & Karlaganis, C. (2020). A conceptual framework for indigenous ecotourism projects–a case study in Wayanad, Kerala, India. *Journal of Heritage Tourism*, *15*(3), 294–311. https://doi.org/10.1080/1743873X.2020.1746793.

Wall, G. (2013). Taking responsibility for tourism: Responsible tourism management. *International Journal of Contemporary Hospitality Management*, *25*(2), 299–300. https://doi.org/10.1108/09596111311301658.

Wang, J., Huang, X., Gong, Z., & Cao, K. (2020). Dynamic assessment of tourism carrying capacity and its impacts on tourism economic growth in urban tourism destinations in China. *Journal of Destination Marketing and Management*, *15*(December 2019), 100383. https://doi.org/10.1016/j.jdmm.2019.100383.

Wang, K., Xu, H., & Huang, L. (2020). Wellness tourism and spatial stigma: A case study of Bama, China. *Tourism Management*, *78*(January 2019), 104039. https://doi.org/10.1016/j.tourman.2019.104039.

Chapter 9

The Use of Reflexive Thematic Analysis in Tourism Research: The Case of Responsible Pet Lovers

Bintang Handayani*

Independent Researcher

Abstract

This chapter highlights the knowledge production of pets on vacation. Pet on vacation introduces the pet as a nonhuman tourist and responsible pet lover by influencers on Instagram, demonstrating the existence of crisis-resistant travellers during the pandemic and highlighting the inclusion of pets as members of families and the importance of vacation for quality of life. Further, sharing of visual content on Instagram socializes the politics of the tourism future which raise the right to travel for nonhuman tourists (pets) and highlights the notion of responsible pet lovers. The uses of the reflexive thematic analysis approach with constructive theoretical perspectives of Braun and Clarke (2019) as methods for the case study. This research advances the idea of reclaiming the political dimension of the epistemic endeavour and presents a paradigm of promoting the multiple pieces of knowledge to build the alternative platforms of knowledge production that is encouraged by Ana Maria Munar in her seminal work on the house of tourism studies (2016). The use of the reflexive thematic analysis approach within this study context is proposed as making a theoretical contribution because it was found to provide unique insights into these theoretical perspectives.

---

* Corresponding Author's Email: bintang.hrphandayani@gmail.com.

In: Tourism in Crisis
Editors: M.E. Korstanje, V. GB Gowreesunkar and S.W. Maingi
ISBN: 979-8-88697-643-4

Keywords: pets, nonhuman tourists, responsible pet lover, Instagram, reflexive thematic analysis

Introduction

Although tourism studies as a branch of social sciences have highlighted the importance of a non-single perspective for its knowledge production, the uses of (reflexive) thematic analysis in tourism research seem to be limited. It has been noted that knowledge production is not only embedded with the research paradigms but also importantly, it urges cutting-edge approaches, e.g., the researcher's creativity and knowledge based on less-explored issues (Braun & Clarke (2022). To date, cutting-edge strategies of tourism studies are associated with the advancement of Information Communication Technology (ICT) and global trends such as the Covid19 pandemic. These trends urge the inclusion of discourses that are embedded with multi-discipline intra-discipline, inter-discipline, or even indiscipline perspectives (Tribe, 1997). Further, tourism studies standpoints such as tourism politics are noted to build the house of tourism studies (Munar, 2016). In the house of tourism studies, Ana Maria Munar recommends more different investigations of knowledge production, that is, to advance tourism scholarship by promoting multiple pieces of knowledge and building alternative platforms of knowledge production, cooperation, and dissemination. The purpose of this book chapter is to locate the emerging trend of nonhuman tourists and their responsible pet lovers in the field of tourism studies. The use of reflexive thematic analysis is applied to support the claims.

Background and Research Objective

To date, the record of tourism research literature concerning the building of the house of tourism studies seems to be in slow progress (Munar, 2016; Walters, 2016). This is partly due to the occurrence of tourism politics. Tourism politics, for instance, the resistance from the stakeholders and pressure groups about specific issues embedded with the new topic such as inanimate tourists, make it hard to be researched (Winter, 2020). This resistance goes along with some of the schools of thought that are reluctant to open the discourses for knowledge production. Further, tourism scholars seem to be too idle to wake up from the lullaby given by quantitative paradigms, which are testing theories, not theory development. For example, Braun and Clarke (2022) propose using reflexive thematic analysis approaches that allow researcher subjectivity to be used as a research resource. However, some of the ongoing research that is about the inclusion of sustainable tourism includes but is not limited to responsible tourists, and tourism stakeholders have received positive attention (Winter, 2020; Hoarau-Heemstra & Kline, 2022). The most popular tourism research to date has been exploring the responsible prosumption in hospitality, e.g., food waste, responsible guests in the hotel and resort, and smart tourism for sustainable tourism and the hospitality industry (Dolnicar & Grun, 2020; Gretzel, Murphy, Pesonen, & Blanton, 2019). On the contrary, tourism politics of inanimate tourists, e.g., the animals on vacation and their responsible pet lovers, received less attention (Carr & Cohen, 2009).

Research about animals in tourism, i.e., as a tourist attraction and animal-related leisure activities is documented in the literature (Rickly, 2018; Carr, 2017; Markwell, 2015; Fennell, 2012; Carr, 2005). Research also suggests inanimate tourists or nonhuman tourists as a trend in tourism, and have been recorded in the tourism futures studies (Kogan, Hazel, & Oxley, 2019; Ivanov, 2018; Carr, 2017; Gretzel & Hardy, 2015; Carr & Cohen, 2009; Carr, 2005). Not only are inanimate tourists might be less-explored, which makes these issues less popular, but also, it is alleged that some of these emergent trends in tourism are considered problematic e.g., the notion of nonhuman tourists (Ivanov, 2018). Although interesting the question of non-human tourism has been remained as unexplored in the literature. As a rational behavior, tourism is culturally limited to humans whilst non-humans are systematically debarred from any leisure activity [at least in the Western social imaginary] (Korstanje & Seraphin 2022). Fortunately, the manifestation of hashtags such as likes, shares, and re-posts on Instagram could popularize inanimate tourists and their responsible pet lovers (Tang, Ying, & Ye, 2022). As a result, Instagram can be regarded as a medium of tourism politics that shapes tourism futures, such as the cute economy, particularly for nonhuman tourists (pets), and the concept of responsible pet lovers (Maddox, 2020).

Tourism politics raise the right to travel for nonhuman tourists (pets) and highlights the notion of responsible pet lovers. As noted, the sharing of visual content on Instagram may enhance, validate, promote, entertain, personalize, negotiate, and socialize the politics of tourism of the tourism future (Ge & Gretzel, 2018; Tang, Ying, & Ye, 2022). The literature also documents how influencers use content such as pictures of vacationing pets in the age of social media and crisis. It is noted as a method for engaging audiences, brands, and health authorities, in addition to demonstrating the existence of crisis-resistant travellers during the pandemic #quarantine @staycation and highlighting the significance of vacations for improving quality of life and pets as integral members of families (Femenia-Serra, Gretzel, & Alzua-Sorzabal, 2022; Hajibaba, Gretzel, Leisch, & Dolnicar, 2015; Dolnicar, Yanamandram, & Cliff, 2012).

In terms of methodology in the house of tourism studies, the use of constructivism and thematic analysis seems to be limited. Studies about inanimate tourists from other disciplines have implicitly noted the animal tourism futures, e.g., the research about pet insurance and pet health information (e.g., Abrahams et al., 2009; Kogan, Hazel, & Oxley, 2019), the inclusion of pet as a family member in quality-of-life studies, e.g., the research of Albert & Bulcroft (1988); pet and pet owners in social media (Kogan, Hazel, & Oxley, 2019). These are the shreds of evidence for giving voice to the notion of a pet and their responsible pet lovers on vacation (Tang, Ying, & Ye, 2022; Hoarau-Heemstra & Kline, 2022). With this in mind, themes generated from the research into pets and their responsible pet lovers on vacation may enrich the studies of tourism politics of pets on vacation and inanimate tourists in general.

Along with positivism, presumably, houses of tourism studies and the notion of pets and responsible pet lovers on vacation can be developed from the critical paradigm derived from post-positivism, i.e., qualitative approaches and post-positivism such as netnography and reflexive thematic analysis. The nonhuman tourist occurrence in social media as non-influencers and the notion of pets accompanying their humans, i.e., pets as a member of the family explicate the tourism trends in relation to the ICT and sustainable tourism (Albert & Bulcroft, 1988; Abrahams et al., 2009; Kogan, Hazel, & Oxley, 2019). Therefore, the notion of nonhuman tourists e.g., pets as a tourist and their responsible pet lovers are proposed to be added to the house of tourism studies.

Research Philosophy

The reflexive thematic analysis approach, especially the constructive theoretical perspectives of Braun and Clarke (2019), highlights the importance of deep reflection and the role of researcher subjectivity in the qualitative paradigm. The reflexive thematic analysis approach in knowledge production requires active participation, such as reading between the lines of the phenomenon. The reflexive thematic analysis reflects the values of a qualitative paradigm, centring researcher subjectivity but not atheoretical (Braun & Clarke, 2019). Researcher subjectivity includes analysis based on organic and recursive coding processes, and the importance of deep reflection on, and engagement with, data (Braun & Clarke, 2006; Braun & Clarke, 2019). In line with this, a coder's subjectivity includes theoretical sensitivities, interests, and experiences, which act as filters in thematic analysis. The importance of theme conceptualization and whether themes are viewed as (a) summaries of topics or categories, or (b) encapsulating a central idea or meaning and providing an interpretive narrative are both emphasised by Braun and Clarke (2022). Thematic analysis findings are considered ongoing revisions rather than being finished (McAllum, Fox, Simpson, and Unson, 2019).

Thematic analysis explicitly indicates the steps taken by the researcher, which acts as a filter for familiarization of the text (which in this research context includes pictures), coding, and revision-to themes generated from the analysis. Within the tourism studies, thematic analysis was used to explain written and visual texts about luxury in the spectrum of a second home in New Zealand, and the use of thematic analysis is encouraged for future research (Walters, 2016). In this sense, social media posts about pets and pet lovers on vacations can be useful subjects to map the position of the pet as nonhuman tourism and responsible pet lovers. In doing so, potential posts were examined from their underlying meaning-based concept and shared meaning. The use of a deductive approach indicates the basis for employing a deductive approach and is aimed to generate the themes for a pet on vacation movement. Consequently, past studies that revolved around pets as family members, nonhuman tourists when accompanying their families on vacations, and the importance of vacation for family health and quality of life are the basis for the deductive approach (Dolnicar, Yanamandram, & Cliff, 2012).

Empirical Material

A purposive sample derived from the trending topics about responsible pet lovers on Instagram's postings that have led to specific hashtags including #petlover #petinfluencer; were selected and classified into Instagram posts solely about pet(s) on vacation or posts concerning pets and pet lover(s). To examine the effect of postings of these hashtags to the Instagram viewers (active and passive), and what those meanings of the hashtags constructed by responsible pet lovers represent.

The hashtags reflect the inclusion of pet lovers' social behaviour and are considered themes generated for responsible pet lovers. Responsible pet lover behaviour is depicted in travel and vacation experience that includes situations, attributes, choices, actions, and issues on Instagram posts. The themes of tourism politics advocate the nonhuman tourist and the responsible pet lover. They are exposed by the Instagram posts of travel-related and vacation related-experiences by maximizing the value-content production, e.g., giving voices to their pet by translating the behaviour of their pet as a member of the family on vacation. Likes, shares and re-posts on Instagram postings bridge the notion of the right to travel for human pet lovers and nonhuman tourists (pets). The value-content production includes the type of leisure and experience activities, outfits, mode of transportation, accommodations, and facilities which are visualised. Posts frequently use filters to perfect images, which seems to highlight the importance of the structure of the message meaning of the postings. The posts are used as the central (social) meanings, i.e., the use of Instagram as a medium for the pet as a nonhuman tourist movement and responsible pet lovers, and the new age of family vacation, family health, and quality of life.

Concluding Remarks

The results of this study suggested two themes as topic summaries of responsible pet lovers leading tourism politics. The desire of obedient pet owners to bring their household pets along on vacation with them as members of the family, as well as the promotion of animals as nonhuman influencers, are two of the issues at hand. Contrarily, it is discovered that empowering veganism for animals serves as a central theme unifying the meaning of interpretative stories. This study backs up previous research that found pets play an important role in both family life and family vacations, suggesting that the tourism industry considers this business opportunity.

References

Abrahams, A. S., Becker, A. B., Sabido, D., D'Souza, R., Makriyiannis, G., & Krasnodebski, M. (2009). Inducing a marketing strategy for a new pet insurance company using decision trees. *Expert Systems with Applications*, *36*(2), 1914-1921. doi:10.1016/j.eswa.2007.12.032.

Albert, A., & Bulcroft, K. (1988). Pets, families, and the life course. *Journal of Marriage and the Family*, *50*(2), 543. doi:10.2307/352019.

Braun, V., & Clarke, V. (2006). Using thematic analysis in psychology. *Qualitative Research in Psychology*, *3*(2), 77-101. doi:10.1191/1478088706qp063oa.

Braun, V., & Clarke, V. (2019). Reflecting on reflexive thematic analysis. *Qualitative Research in Sport, Exercise and Health*, *11*(4), 589-597. doi:10.1080/2159676x.2019.1628806.

Braun, V., & Clarke, V. (2022). Toward good practice in thematic analysis: Avoiding common problems and be(com)ing a *knowing* researcher. *International Journal of Transgender Health*, 1-6. doi:10.1080/26895269.2022.2129597.

Carr, N. (2017). Recognising the position of the pet dog in tourism. *Annals of Tourism Research*, *62*, 112-113. doi:10.1016/j.annals.2016.10.011.

Carr, N., & Cohen, S. (2009). Holidaying with the family pet: No dogs allowed! *Tourism and Hospitality Research*, *9*(4), 290-304. doi:10.1057/thr.2009.10.

Carr, N. (2005): Holidaying with the family pet: no dogs allowed! In T. Delamere, C. Randall and D. Robinson (eds) *Abstracts of Papers Presented at the Eleventh Canadian Congress on Leisure Research*. Nanaimo, B.C.: Malaspina University-College.

Dolnicar, S., Yanamandram, V., & Cliff, K. (2012). The contribution of vacations to quality of life. *Annals of Tourism Research*, *39*(1), 59-83. doi:10.1016/j.annals.2011.04.015.

Femenia-Serra, F., Gretzel, U., & Alzua-Sorzabal, A. (2022). Instagram travel influencers in #quarantine: Communicative practices and roles during COVID-19. *Tourism Management*, *89*, 104454. doi:10.1016/j.tourman.2021.104454.

Fennell, D. A. (2012). *Tourism and animal ethics*. London: Routledge.

Fennell, D. A. (2013). Tourism and animal welfare. *Tourism Recreation Research*, *38*(3), 325-340, DOI: 10.1080/02508281.2013.11081757.

Ge, J., & Gretzel, U. (2018). A taxonomy of value Co-creation on Weibo – a communication perspective. *International Journal of Contemporary Hospitality Management*, *30*(4), 2075-2092. doi:10.1108/ijchm-09-2016-0557.

Gretzel, U., & Hardy, A. (2015). Pooches on Wheels: Overcoming Pet-related Travel Constraints Through RVing. In Markwell, K. (Ed.). (2015). *Animals and tourism: Understanding diverse relationships* (Vol. 67) (pp. 274-287) Channel View Publications.

Gretzel, U., Murphy, J., Pesonen, J. & Blanton, C. (2019). Food waste in tourist households: A perspective article. *Tourism Review*, https://doi.org/10.1108/TR-05-2019-0170.

Hajibaba, H., Gretzel, U., Leisch, F., & Dolnicar, S. (2015). Crisis-resistant tourists. *Annals of Tourism Research*, *53*, 46-60. doi:10.1016/j.annals.2015.04.001.

Hoarau-Heemstra, H., & Kline, C. (2022). Making Kin and making sense of human-animal relations in tourism. *Ecological Economics*, *196*, 107396. doi:10.1016/j.ecolecon.2022.107396.

Ivanov, S. (2018). Tourism beyond humans – robots, pets, and Teddy bears. Paper presented at the International Scientific Conference "Tourism and Innovations," 14-15th September 2018, College of Tourism – Varna, Varna, Bulgaria.

Kogan, L. R., Hazel, S. J., & Oxley, J. A. (2019). A pilot study of Australian pet owners who engage in social media and their use, experience and views of online pet health information. *Australian veterinary journal*, *97*(11), 433-439.

Korstanje M. E & Seraphin H (2022) "A problem called Alterity: the position of the Other in HBO Saga Westworld". In *Tourism Through troubled times: challenges and opportunities of the tourism industry in 21st century.* Korstanje M. Seraphin H & Maingi S (eds). [7-20]. Bingley, Emerald Publishing.

Maddox, J. (2020). The secret life of pet Instagram accounts: Joy, resistance, and commodification in the internet's cute economy. *New Media & Society*, *23*(11), 3332-3348. doi:10.1177/1461444820956345.

Markwell, K. (2015). *Animals and tourism: Understanding diverse relationships.* Channel View Publications.

McAllum, K., Fox, S., Simpson, M., & Unson, C. (2019). A comparative tale of two methods: how thematic and narrative analyses author the data story differently, Communication Research and Practice, DOI: 10.1080/22041451.2019.1677068.

Munar, A. M. (2016). The House of Tourism Studies and the Systemic Paradigm. In A. M. Munar, & T. Jamal (Eds.), *Tourism Research Paradigms: Critical and Emergent Knowledges.* (pp. 131–153). Chapter 8. Bingley: Emerald Group Publishing Limited. (Tourism Social Science Series, Vol. 22). doi: 10.1108/S1571-50432015 0000022014.

Rickly, J. M. (2018). Considering service animals in tourism. *Annals of Tourism Research*, *71*, 57-58. doi:10.1016/j.annals.2017.12.012.

Tang, J., Ying, T., & Ye, S. (2022). Chinese pet owners traveling with pets: Motivation-based segmentation. *Journal of Hospitality and Tourism Management*, *50*, 31-43. doi:10.1016/j.jhtm.2021.12.006.

Tribe, J. (1997). The indiscipline of tourism. *Annals of Tourism Research*, *24*(3), 638-657. doi:10.1016/s0160-7383(97)00020-0.

Walters, T. (2016). Using thematic analysis in tourism research. *Tourism Analysis*, *21*(1), 107-116. doi:10.3727/108354216x14537459509017.

Winter, C. (2020). A review of research into animal ethics in tourism: Launching the annals of tourism research curated collection on animal ethics in tourism. *Annals of Tourism Research*, *84*, 102989. doi:10.1016/j.annals.2020.102989.

Conclusion

In the introductory section, we have mentioned that tourism researchers and epistemologists have no few problems taking the concept of crisis in their respective scopes of study, or at the best as a valid object of study (Ritchie & Jiang 2019). For some reason, an apologetic discourse focuses on tourism as a formidable instrument that potentiates economic growth, prosperity and political instability in established democracies (Somnez, Apostolopoulos & Tarlow 1999). To some extent, the classic literature recognizes that there are some glitches or caveats which often threaten the future of tourism research. These problems are not seen as part of the system but as anomalies that should be rapidly found and eradicated (Hall, 2010). The socio-economic negative effects involuntarily generated by the tourism industry include the acceleration of climate change and environmental pollution, real-estate speculation, inflation, acculturation process, economic unemployment, and inter-ethnic conflict if not warfare (only to name a few) (Smeral 2009; Blake & Sinclair, 2003). No less true seems to be that the concept of crisis has occupied a central position in social science but in tourism, the term remains uncovered (Papatheodorou, Rossello & Xiao 2010). The limitations of applied research to reverse the negative consequences of tourism are given by two combined factors. On one hand, the precautionary doctrine, which is understood as an academic paradigm based on the importance to locate and eradicate risks that threaten the service sectors, failed to give firm answers to the challenges posed just after the turn of the century. The radicalization of political violence adjoined to the impossibility of governments stopping greenhouse gas emissions has created a chaotic and unpredictable climate. As a result of this, some voices say overtly that post-disaster theory has been adopted as the main leading paradigm to recycle devastated destinations while optimizing resources to fasten the recovery facet (Tucker, Shelton & Bae 2017). On another, experts are systematically trained to believe the tourism industry is a multiplying factor which triggers economic growth. Needless to say, it is part but not the full story. Its negative impacts on the community very well can be imagined as collateral damage that planning can resolve. This invariably behoves us to overlook those variables that probe the industry situates as a real obstacle towards sustainability (Richards & Hall, 2002; Gossling, Hall & Weaver, 2009). At first glimpse, scholars have been oath to adopt crisis as a part of the tourist system over years. To put things bluntly, the figure of crisis connoted serious failures and miscalculations in the planning process (Singh 2004).

Let´s clarify for readers first that the term crisis suggests a period or a moment that not only happens abruptly but also put society or community in jeopardy. Some voices equate the concept of crisis to emergency or disaster. What is important to say is that any crisis escapes to the natural forms of control of society. Like disasters, crises interrogate furtherly the status quo and the dominant institutions (Cohen 2012). Some studies have alerted on the fact that crises resulted from unperceived or exaggerated risks, or serious errors in the decision-making process (Ritchie 2004; Pappas 2018). Whatever the case may be, crises frequently open the doors to new stages and situations mainly marked by evolutionary growth. To set an example, the modern tourism industry resulted from the crisis precipitated by the two World Wars. Accompanied by the globalization process, the technological breakthrough in the 90s decade paved the way for the expansion of the tourism industry worldwide. At the same time, the attacks perpetrated in WTC, the acceleration of climate change as well as the economic downturn and the latest COVID-19 pandemic mainly marked a new state of crisis for the industry (Korstanje & George 2021; 2022). To what extent COVID-19 indicates the end of tourism or simply the mutation towards new forms is a complex answer this book tries to answer. Citing Norbert Elias, the civilizing process derives not only from the discipline orchestrated to regulate life but also from how successful crises are managed (Elias 1969).

As the previous argument is given, Lash & Urry (1993) speak to us of the decentralization of tourism in their seminal book Economies of signs and space. Per their viewpoint, the globalization process ignites a new stage of capitalism characterized by an aesthetic reflexibility. This process leads to a system where cultures, peoples and merchandise are mutually exchanged and commoditized. Gazing at others, outstanding landscapes or looking for authentic experience is a way of possessing the "Other". In this context, capitalism is gradually mutating towards a decentralized form of production and consumption culturally enrooted in the power of the sign. Experts shape the border of global geography in two main grids: safe and unsafe destinations. It is noteworthy that in Lash and Urry´s conceptualization, experts keep the monopoly in the understanding of risk. Their legacy shed the light on the way tourism is constantly changing to new forms and shapes.

With the benefits of hindsight, we have been educated to think of tourism as an all-encompassing and immutable institution. At a closer look, tourism has been historically subject to countless shifts and moments of political instability. Here we present a conceptual model which distinguishes three clear-cut moments or historical stages: a) classic tourism, b) sustainable tourism c) new forms of morbid tourism. Each stage is based on a foundational event that changed the economic means of production and travel behavior. The first stage, dubbed classic tourism, ranges from 1920 (or the interwar period) and 1970. The economic paradigm ruling modern society is the economy of scale. Per this model, products are fabricated in a standardized way. While optimizing resources, the economy of scale recreates mechanical means (and forms) of production while consumerists are not moving with specific preferences. Of course, tourism was not an exception. For this period, the tourist destinations, which are simply cloned, follow the sun-sand-and-beach archetype. Based on the bubble model, these products have been designed to avoid host-guest interaction. At the same time, the top-down planning process appears to be insensitive to the negative effects of tourism on the hosting community.

In 1972, a disrupting event changes this form of production putting the industry upside down. The Arab-Israeli war resulted in an important Oil Embargo by the side of the Arab League that led Western capitalism into a gridlock. A new economic crisis known as stagflation places West between the wall and the deep blue sea. Economists, policymakers and experts agree that Western capitalism should alter the basis and means of production simply because the Oil resources are plausibly compromised. It is not difficult to resist the impression that centralized planning and economy set the pace for a decentralized form of production/consumption. Experts introduce the notion of segmentation while consumers are seen as liberal agents dotted with different (countless) preferences. There is a strong empathy with the locals as well as concerns revolving around the negative effects of tourism on the environment. It is the time for the emergence of Sustainable tourism which crystallises in the Brundtland Report in 1979. From that moment onwards, the problem of resource regeneration as well as sustainability occupies a central position in academic discourses. This period oscillates from 1972 to the 2000s decade. Unlike classic tourism which is closed to the local demands, sustainable tourism not only devotes resources to reverse the negative effects produced by the industry but also revitalizes the host-guest relations. Tourists are in quest of unique and outstanding experiences based on the "understanding of culture and the Other´s lifestyle". Last but not least, the attacks perpetrated by Al-Qaeda on the US in 2001 starts a new epoch where all certainties simply withered away. This epoch is marked by a state of alarmism, high anxiety and uncertainness. Since risks cannot be regulated or eradicated (originally as they have been planned), adaptancy emerges as a leading paradigm. New forms of morbid tourism, include dark tourism, thana tourism, grief tourism, war tourism, slum tourism, and surfaces. These novel forms of consumption confront directly the apollonian sense of beautiness. Although these forms of tourism vary in psychological motivations, there is a clear common component oriented to the consumption of the "Other´s pain" (Korstanje & George 2022). As discussed, tourism is mutating into new shapes and evolving to unknown dynamics all the time. For that, the present book, which invited well-versed and global scholars specialized in the study of the tourism crisis, gives a snapshot of the past, present and future of tourism in a post-COVID-19 context. To put things simply, the current tourism crisis is not limited to the economic downturn, or ostensibly to the effects of COVID-19, it encompasses broader aspects that affect higher-tourism education, the economy, society and even the epistemological issues -without mentioning tourism research. One of the priorities of researchers consists in setting new objects of study in a world traversed by geopolitical tensions, ethnic cleavages, travel bans and regulations, that take in essence part of a much deep re-feudalization process. The end of tourism and hospitality (at least as we know them) is a focal point of entry in this debate which needs to be continued in the next layouts.

References

Blake, A., & Sinclair, M. T. (2003). Tourism crisis management: US response to September 11. Annals of tourism research, 30(4), 813-832.

Cohen, E. (2012). Globalization, global crises and tourism. Tourism recreation research, 37(2), 103-111.

Elias, N. (1969). The civilizing process: Sociogenetic and psychogenetic investigations. New York, Willey Blackwell.

Gössling, S., Hall, C. M., & Weaver, D. B. (2009). Sustainable tourism futures: Perspectives on systems, restructuring and innovations. In Sustainable tourism futures (pp. 21-36). Abingdon, Routledge.

Hall, C. M. (2010). Crisis events in tourism: Subjects of crisis in tourism. Current issues in Tourism, 13(5), 401-417.

Korstanje, M. E., & George, B. (2021). Mobility and globalization in the aftermath of COVID-19: Emerging new geographies in a locked world. Basingstoke, UK: Palgrave Macmillan.

Korstanje, M. E., & George, B. (2022). The Nature and Future of Tourism: A Post-COVID-19 Context. London, CRC Press.

Lash, S. M.,& Urry, J. (1993). Economies of signs and space (Vol. 26). London, Sage.

Papatheodorou, A., Rosselló, J., & Xiao, H. (2010). Global economic crisis and tourism: Consequences and perspectives. Journal of Travel Research, 49(1), 39-45.

Pappas, N. (2018). Hotel decision-making during multiple crises: A chaordic perspective. Tourism Management, 68, 450-464.

Richards, G., & Hall, D. (2002). The community: a sustainable concept in tourism development?. In Tourism and sustainable community development (pp. 19-32). Abingdon, Routledge.

Ritchie, B. W. (2004). Chaos, crises and disasters: a strategic approach to crisis management in the tourism industry. Tourism management, 25(6), 669-683.

Ritchie, B. W., & Jiang, Y. (2019). A review of research on tourism risk, crisis and disaster management: Launching the annals of tourism research curated collection on tourism risk, crisis and disaster management. Annals of Tourism Research, 79, 102812.

Singh, S. (2004). India's domestic tourism: Chaos/crisis/challenge?. Tourism Recreation Research, 29(2), 35-46.

Smeral, E. (2009). The impact of the financial and economic crisis on European tourism. Journal of Travel Research, 48(1), 3-13.

Sönmez, S. F., Apostolopoulos, Y., & Tarlow, P. (1999). Tourism in crisis: Managing the effects of terrorism. Journal of travel research, 38(1), 13-18.

Tucker, H., Shelton, E. J., & Bae, H. (2017). Post-disaster tourism: Towards a tourism of transition. Tourist studies, 17(3), 306-327.

Index

Q

R

S

T

V

W

About the Editors

Maximiliano E. Korstanje (Editor/Chapter Author) is Editor in Chief of *International Journal of Safety and Security in Tourism* (UP Argentina) and Editor in Chief Emeritus of *International Journal of Cyber Warfare and Terrorism* (IGI-Global US). Besides being Senior Researchers in the Department of Economics at University of Palermo, Argentina, he serves in different global institutions. Korstanje was nominated to 5 honorary doctorates for his contribution in the study of the effects of terrorism in tourism. In 2015 he was awarded as Visiting Research Fellow at School of Sociology and Social Policy, University of Leeds, UK and the University of La Habana Cuba. In 2017 is elected as Foreign Faculty Member of AMIT, Mexican Academy in the study of Tourism, which is the most prominent institutions dedicated to tourism research in Mexico. He had a vast experience in editorial projects working as advisory member of Elsevier, Routledge, Springer, IGI global and Cambridge Scholar publishing. Korstanje had visited and given seminars in many important universities worldwide. He has also recently been selected to take part of the 2018 Albert Nelson Marquis Lifetime Achievement Award. a great distinction given by Marquis Who´s Who in the world.

Vanessa Gowreesunkar is Associate Professor in Cultural Tourism at Anant National University in Ahmedabad, India. She has served as Head of Department for the Hospitality and Tourism at the University of Africa.

Shem Wambugu Maingi, PhD (Editor/Chapter Author), is a Lecturer, School of Business, Economics and Tourism, Kenyatta University. He has been a Tourism lecturer and researcher from Kenyatta University for the last twelve (12) years. Dr Shem Maingi has widely published in Scopus indexed journals and books internationally, one of which received a joint award as article of the year 2011. He has edited and authored books on the future and resilience of tourism, notably "Tourism Destination Management in a Post-Pandemic Context: Global Issues and Destination Management Solutions" and "Tourism through troubled times: Challenges and Opportunities of the Tourism Industry in 21st Century" published by Emerald Group Publishing (UK) as well as "Management of Tourism Ecosystem Services in a Post Pandemic Context: Global Perspectives" published by Routledge (UK). He also jointly developed an international policy brief entitled, "Rebuilding tourism post pandemic – Policy recommendations from global case studies" published by Emerald Open Research (UK). He is an expert member of the African Union Economic, Social and Cultural Council (AU-ECOSOCC) Tourism and Infrastructure Cluster. He is also an expert member of the International Scientific Committee on Cultural Tourism of ICOMOS (ICTC) as well as the IUCN WCPA Tourism and Protected Areas Specialist Group TAPAS.

About the Contributors

K. P. Anju is a Research Scholar in the Department of Tourism Management, Avinashilingam Institute for Home Science and Higher Education for Women, Coimbatore, Tamil Nadu, India. Responsible tourism development is one of her areas of research.

V. T. Bindu is an Assistant Professor, Department of Tourism Management, Avinashilingam Institute for Home Science and Higher Education for Women, Coimbatore, Tamil Nadu, India. She holds a PhD in tourism. She has published extensively on various dimensions of tourism and hospitality management.

Mariana Pereira Chaves Pimentel, PhD in Social Sciences - Federal University of Juiz de Fora/UFJF (2016). Master's Degree in Administration - Federal University of Minas Gerais/ UFMG (2011). Bachelor in Tourism / UFMG (2006). Professor and researcher at UFJF, of the undergraduate degrees in Tourism and Human Sciences. Deputy leader of the Social and Economic Observatory of Tourism / OEST and member of the Latin American Center of Tourismology / CELAT. Federal University of Juiz de Fora, Institute of Human Sciences, Department of Tourism. R. José Lourenço Kelmer, Campus Universitário, CEP: 36036-330, Juiz de Fora/MG, Brazil.

Marcela Bifano Costa de Oliveira is a PhD Candidate in Sciences for Development, Sustainability and Tourism, at the University of Guadalajara - Centro Universitario de la Costa, Mexico. Master in Economic and Social Sciences at the Universidad Autónoma de Sinaloa, Mexico (2016). Bachelor's Degree in Tourism at the Universidade Federal de Juiz de Fora, Brazil (2013). Member of the Latin American Center of Excellence in Tourismology

(CELAT); of the Economic and Social Observatory of Tourism (OEST), and Critical Realism, Collective Action and Work (REACT) - Federal University of Juiz de Fora. She works in the areas of Tourism and Sociology, with emphasis on: Public Policies; Social Participation; Development and Collective Action.

Stella Freesz is a Master's student in the Administration Course at PPGA-UFJF. Specialist in Planning and Event Management at Estácio de Sá College. Graduated in Tourism at the Federal University of Juiz de Fora (2014) and in Interdisciplinary Bachelor of Humanities at the Federal University of Juiz de Fora (2012). Has experience in Tourism, with emphasis in Hospitality, acting mainly in the following topics: Events, Management Processes, Destination Management, Human Resource Management, Food and Beverage, Tourist Routes.

Babu George is Professor and Dean in the School of Business, Alcorn State University, MS, USA. His research interests include sustainable tourism and green economic development.

Bintang Handayani is a Senior Lecturer and an animal lover who also works as an academic. She received her BA and Master in Communication Science before pursuing her MBA and PhD in Tourism Management. Handayani is co-author of two books, *Special Interest Tourism in Southeast Asia: Emerging Research and Opportunities* (2019) and *Gazing at Death: Dark Tourism as an Emergent Horizon of Research* (2017). She has expertise in special interest and dark tourism studies and has published extensively in the field.

Lim Kuang Long is currently a Senior Lecturer with Tunku Abdul Rahman University College, Perak Branch Campus, Malaysia. He is also holding the administrative position of Associate Dean for Quality Assurance. He has been serving the institution since 2001. Lim can be reached by email at limkl@tarc.edu.my or limgkuanglong@gmail.com. He possesses a PhD from University Malaya, MSc from University of Nottingham, and BTMgt (Hons) from Universiti Utara Malaysia. He is also a senior assessor for Malaysian Qualification Agency since 2014. His field of expertise is hospitality, tourism, event management, and international business.

Elias Mediotte is a Doctoral student and Master in Administration (concentration in the area of Public Administration) from the Federal University of Viçosa (UFV-MG). He has an MBA/Specialization in Strategic Management of People from the Fundação Mineira de Educação e Cultura University (FUMEC) (2013). Technological Bachelor's Degree in Human Resources Management from Promove Infórium Technology College (MG) (2010). Awarded the Outstanding Professional in Administration 2022, from Minas Gerais, Brazil. Associate Member of the Brazilian Society of Public Administration (SBAP). Member of Research Group/CNPq on Management and Development of Creative Territories (GDTeC) at the Federal University of Viçosa (UFV-MG). Member of the UNESCO Chair in Creative Economy and Public Policies and Coordinator of the World Forum for Creative Cities, Districts and Territories. ORCID ID: https://orcid.org/0000-0003-0370-08064

Keziah Odemba, PhD National Director Ministry of Tourism Kenya. She is experienced in Sustainable tourism development, formulation of policies, plans and strategies, mobilization of tourism stakeholders and a history of organizing events. Skilled in Tourism, Investment, Customer Service, Marketing Strategy, Bilateral Agreement making, Conflict resolution and Climate change adaptation practices Education includes MA Leadership studies; MBA in Marketing; Doctorate in Leadership and experience in mentorship and working with communities.

Thiago Duarte Pimentel has a post-doctorate in Sociology (Social Theory and Critical Realism) from the Federal University of Rio de Janeiro (UFRJ). PhD in Social Sciences from the Federal University of Juiz de Fora (UFJF). Master in Administration from the Federal University of Minas Gerais (UFMG). Graduation in Tourism from UFMG. Full-time professor and researcher at UFJF, in graduate courses (masters and doctorate) in Social Sciences and in Administration (public and business management) and in undergraduate courses: Human Sciences and Tourism. Member of the Board of Directors of the International Sociological Association (ISA) - RC 17 (Sociology of Organizations) and of the International Association of Scientific Experts in Tourism (AIEST). Visiting Professor at universities in the USA, Canada, Mexico, Cuba and Ecuador. Leader of the Research Group Critical Realism, Collective Action and Work (REACT). Director of the Latin American Center of Excellence in Tourism (CELAT) and of the Social and

Economic Observatory of Tourism (OEST). Editor-in-chief of the journal *Anais Brasileiros de Estudos Turísticos (ABET)* and of the *Latin American Journal of Tourismology (RLAT)*. CV: http://lattes.cnpq.br/9841188234449467. Orcid Id: https://orcid.org/0000-0003-1889-069X.

Paulo Rodrigues Cerqueira earned his Bachelor's degree in Social Communication from PUCMinas, with emphasis in Advertising. Master's in Administration from the Federal University of Espírito Santo, with emphasis in Organizational Management. PhD in Administration from the Federal University of Rio Grande do Sul, with emphasis on Organizational Studies. Professional experience as Substitute Professor at the School of Administration of the Federal University of Rio Grande do Sul. Currently, in post-doctoral training in the Graduate Program in Administration at FACC at the Federal University of Juiz de Fora. CV: http://lattes.cnpq.br/7331686290298356

Mrs. H Sandhya is pursuing PhD in Tourism Management from Christ University Bangalore. She successfully completed her MPhil and Masters in Tourism Administration from Christ University Bangalore by securing the first rank. She has industry experience of one year having worked with one of the leading multinational tour operations companies, Kuoni SOTC, Bangalore and teaching experience of over 6 years having associated with some of the prestigious academic institutions and colleges in Kerala. She has worked as Research Associate of the Major Research Project on the Strategic intervention of Destination Management Organizations to enhance competitiveness of tourism destinations. She is a very passionate and keen researcher and her research interests include Destination Management, Destination Branding and Smart Tourism. She is currently working as Academic Auditor and Deputy Academic Coordinator at Kairos Institute, Cochin, Kerala.

Cyril Peter is passionate about hospitality and creating nourishing experiences for guests. While this explains his love for preparing and serving his natural Sri Lankan food to others; it also crosses over to the desire to provide security to those in his care. With a history in the hospitality industry (and qualifications to match) it has become an enduring desire to ensure the industry is as prepared as possible in the face of the rising acts of terrorism. His Masters explored this initially and subsequent research articles and conference papers have continued the same theme in more depth and with more specialities. Cyril's current foci are related (but not limited) to food security, sport and event terrorism, cruise safety, crisis management and business continuity. His PhD was centered around New Zealand's hospitality industry's security readiness.

Terrin George Thomas, currently working as a Credit Assessment Officer at ANZ Bank, Bangalore. His work is evaluating clients' financial information and calculating risk ratios. He has completed B.Com in travel & tourism management and also MBA in tourism & Travel Management. He also has 3 years' experience in Aviation Industry with Indigo Airlines, played a major role as Ramp Co-coordinator, Load Master and Local flight documents dispatcher. He also had worked as an intern with Vivanta by Taj, Madikeri as Front Desk and with Pacific World Travel Company, Bengaluru.

Dr. Bindi Varghese is an Associate Professor in the tourism department at Christ University. As an academician and tourism professional, she has over 20 years of academic experience. She has served as a national and international expert, for over a decade among the educational institutions of India. Currently, she is the president of Kerala Development Society (KDS), New Delhi and is also an issue editor for *ATNA- Journal of Tourism Studies* - UGC care listed journal, published by Christ University, Bangalore. She has authored a book and edited a book in the tourism domain and has completed a Major Research Project on the Strategic intervention of Destination Management Organizations to enhance competitiveness of tourism destinations. She has published over 25 articles in journals and has contributed over 15 chapters in the edited volumes in tourism. The active researches undertaken by her; include; impact assessment studies, medical tourism, destination management organization and ecological studies.